The German Shepherd Handbook

BY

LINDA WHITWAM

ISBN: 979-8627765228

Copyright

Acknowledgements

My sincere thanks to the dedicated breeders, owners and canine experts for sharing their extensive knowledge and enthusiasm for the incomparable German Shepherd. This book, the 16th in The Canine Handbook series, would not have been possible without them.

Specialist Contributors

CHERYL SPURR

JACQUELINE LEVY

MARIE DONAHUE

Other Major Contributors

Stefanie Millington

Larry and Diane Yates

Bobbi King, RVT

Tammey Tilton

Teresa and Tony Mapp

Wendy Sharp

Donna Bonney

Carolyn Day

Dr Sara Skiwski

(Full details appear at the back of the book)

Table of Contents

Author's Note: The German Shepherd Handbook uses **British English**, except where Americans have been quoted, when the original US English has been preserved.

Cover photo: Harro and Lexi, of Reinglen German Shepherds, Wakefield, West Yorkshire, UK
Photographer: Rob Spurr

1. Meet the German Shepherd

The German Shepherd, which used to be known as the Alsatian, has long been one of the most popular breeds on the planet; number two in the US, Canada and New Zealand, and consistently in the top 10 in the UK and most other European countries.

No other dog has such an instinct to serve and, once trained, no other breed can come close to the number and variety of roles German Shepherds fulfil alongside their beloved humans.

....

Service, military, therapy, search and rescue, protection, herding, finding drugs, mines, people, explosives and even illegal hard drives with his phenomenal sense of smell; the GSD can do the lot.

Affectionate with their family and naturally wary of strangers, German Shepherds are highly intelligent and love a challenge. As a working breed, these dogs are happiest when they have something to do. Whether that is training, games, a sport, service work or being involved in family activities, GSDs excel when provided with physical and mental stimulation.

Adults can weigh up to 90lb and reach five feet tall when standing on their hind legs. Such powerful, active machines need lots of socialising and training to grow into relaxed, well-mannered adults.

They are fiercely loyal and their intelligence, coupled with their great desire to please their owners, means they are extremely receptive to positive training techniques and can be trained to a level as high as any canine.

This powerful, athletic dog also excels in obedience and sports events, yet can be the gentlest of creatures with children. Well-trained Shepherds make family companions and protectors second to none. In short, the German Shepherd is, to quote my father: "A proper dog!"

The AKC agrees! They say: "There are many reasons why German Shepherds stand in the front rank of canine royalty, but experts say their defining attribute is character: loyalty, courage, confidence, the ability to learn commands for many tasks, and the willingness to put their life on the line in defense of loved ones.

"German Shepherds will be gentle family pets and steadfast guardians, but, the breed standard says, there's a "certain aloofness that does not lend itself to immediate and indiscriminate friendships."

"Generally considered dogkind's finest all-purpose worker, the German Shepherd Dog is a large, agile, muscular dog of noble character and high intelligence. Loyal, confident, courageous, and steady, the German Shepherd is truly a dog lover's delight."

 Unfortunately, there's just one little drawback with this fantastic breed - the German Shepherd does NOT arrive as the finished article! Good breeders start socialisation and training, but it is ESSENTIAL for owners to devote lots of time to continuing the process to develop the well-rounded adult GSD.

German Shepherds do not give their love and devotion freely. But spend time to train and bond with yours and you will end up with the most loyal companion you could ever wish for, and a beautiful, well-behaved member of the family that is a joy to live with and take anywhere. An owner or handler with a well-trained Shepherd is the envy of dog lovers everywhere.

Is a GSD Right for Me?

German Shepherds are incredible dogs. But, make no mistake, this breed is not for the faint-hearted. Getting a German Shepherd means a daily time commitment for, hopefully, a decade or more. If you haven't already taken the plunge, ask yourself some questions:

- Are you prepared to research GSD breeders to find one that produces puppies from health-tested parents with good temperaments?

- Have you got the space - indoors and outdoors - for a big, active dog?

- Are you an active person or family?

- Are you prepared to give your dog a minimum of an hour or two of your time every day?

- Are you prepared to spend a part of every day training your Shepherd?

- Can you assert your authority through positive training techniques?

- If the dog develops behaviour problems, will you spend the time (and possibly money if you seek professional help) to work through the issues?

- Will you take the dog out whatever the weather – snow, ice, wind and rain are no deterrents for the hardy GSD!

- Can you afford the expense of a big dog?

- Do you like grooming? German Shepherds have a double coat and can shed for America - or Europe!

- Do all your family members like German Shepherds?

If the answers to all of the above are YES, then fantastic! You are just the owner that beautiful little German Shepherd puppy is looking for!

Breed Standard

The **Breed Standard** is what makes a Great Dane a Great Dane and a Chihuahua a Chihuahua. It is a blueprint not only for the appearance of each breed, but also for character and temperament, how the dog moves and what colours are acceptable. In other words, it ensures that a German Shepherd looks and acts like a German Shepherd.

The Breed Standard is laid down by the breed societies. In the UK it's the Kennel Club, and in the US it's the AKC, American Kennel Club, that keeps the register of pedigree (purebred) dogs. The Germans follow the FCI (Fédération Cynologique Internationale) Breed Standard.

Dogs entered in conformation shows run under Kennel Club and AKC rules are judged against an ideal list of attributes. Breeders approved by the Kennel Clubs agree to produce puppies in line with the Breed Standard and maintain certain welfare conditions.

Responsible breeders select only the finest dogs for reproduction, based on the health, looks and temperament of the parents and their ancestors. They do not simply take any available male and female and allow them to randomly breed.

An excellent place to source a reputable breeder is the relevant breed club in your region or country. A full list of UK regional and national clubs is on the Kennel Club website. Type *"Kennel Club German Shepherd Clubs"* into an online search engine to see them all. In the US, the AKC national club is the German Shepherd Dog Club of America at: www.gsdca.org

The UK Kennel Club and AKC also have lists of breeders, In the UK, look for an *Assured Breeder* and in the AKC "Find a Puppy" or "Marketplace" section, try and stick to *Breeders of Merit* or *Breeders with H.E.A.R.T.* as the AKC does not carry out checks on the others.

 The fact that a puppy is registered with the Kennel Club or AKC does NOT mean that the parents have been screened for hereditary diseases, or that you have any guarantee of a healthy pup. A Kennel Club or AKC certificate simply means that the puppy's family tree can be traced back several generations. *Always* ask to see health certificates.

Responsible breeders aim to reduce genetic illnesses by screening their dogs and not breeding from the ones with faulty genes.

In the case of German Shepherds, the major health tests cover hips, elbows, eyes and DM, or Degenerative Myelopathy, a serious spinal cord disorder.

In the UK, the German Shepherd is in the *Pastoral Group* and in the US, it's in the *Herding Group.* Both groups are for dogs that were originally bred to gather, herd and protect livestock.

Types of German Shepherd

Compared with other breeds, the Breed Standard for the German Shepherd is extremely detailed. This is because there are several different types. Most working and Service GSDs come from European lines. The five types are:

American Show Lines – originally imported into North America in the early 20th century. These dogs *(like the one pictured on the previous page)* are bred for their looks and movement and are usually black and tan or red and tan in colour. They are often longer, taller and heavier than working dogs, which may have to be carried when on duty with police or military personnel.

Show GSDs also have a narrower head and are regarded as elegant and light on their feet – the classic German Shepherd gait in the show ring is the *"flying trot."* To achieve this, they have more rear angulation – or a sloping back - which has recently caused controversy.

 The original German Shepherds bred in Germany had straight backs. An exaggerated sloping back can cause orthopaedic issues, although it does not necessarily mean that the dog has hip dysplasia. Always ask to see test results – called "hip scores" and check that the puppy or dog moves freely.

GSDs from show lines generally have less *"drive"* (i.e. an instinctive desire for a great deal of mental and physical activity) than working dogs. This means that they are often more suitable as family pets, compared with working lines. However, owners shouldn't forget that ALL types of German Shepherd have high mental and physical exercise needs compared to most other breeds.

Many do well in Obedience, Agility and other canine events. Potential owners should check for hip and other health certificates as AKC and UK Kennel Club registrations are not stringent compared with European dogs, which come under the German SV (Verein für Deutsche Schäferhunde), which requires a working title and health clearances for hips and elbows.

Working lines were bred to do just that – work! They carry out numerous jobs alongside their handlers and excel in most forms of canine competitions, when they have to use their strength, stamina and brains. Most working GSDs are darker than show ones, with black and tan, black, sable and bi-colour being common.

West German Show Lines – these are handsome examples of the breed. Like the American show lines, they have sloping bodies, but are stockier with larger heads. These dogs are high energy, but with the right owners and training can make excellent family pets and protectors.

West German Working Lines - these dogs are closest to the original German Shepherds bred by Captain Max von Stephanitz. The focus is on work ethic, stable temperament and high drive. Again, bred with a sloping back, these dogs excel at sports, protection and work in the Services.

East German DDR Working Lines – these dark, hardy dogs with big heads, deep chests and athletic bodies were originally developed for border patrol and other military work. They are highly intelligent, full of energy and have endless stamina. Less suitable for families, this dog does well with an experienced handler.

Czech Working Lines - originating from Czechoslovakia, these dogs were again mainly bred for border patrol work. Usually black or dark, these powerful, athletic dogs have a very high working drive. These dogs can excel at Obedience, Agility and Schutzhund, but require lots of physical and mental stimulation.

There are also differences in the ideal coat length between Europe and the US. The long coat is now accepted by the UK Kennel Club alongside the short coat, but the AKC prefers a medium-length coat. Both clubs frown upon blue, white or liver-coloured GSDs.

I can't think of another breed with as many variations as the German Shepherd. Not only are there dogs from show lines and working lines, there are even differences between the working lines, as you have just read. Then there are the mixed lines, which take attributes from both lines.

If you haven't chosen your puppy yet, decide what type of German Shepherd would best fit in with your lifestyle. Study your country's Breed Standard to learn how a well-bred GSD should look and behave, then compare it against the parents of any puppy you view.

Type *"German Shepherd Breed Standard"* into Google, followed by the name of your country's Kennel Club to see the Breed Standard. The FCI (Fédération Cynologique Internationale) Breed Standard applies to European working lines.

Breeders on German Shepherds

Ask anyone who has spent time with one and they will all say the same: there is no other dog quite like the German Shepherd. We asked breeders in the US and UK to tell us a bit about their Shepherds, starting in the UK, where all contributors are *Kennel Club Assured Breeders*:

Larry Yates, of Lornstone German Shepherds, Somerset, registered his first litter in 1966 and is passionate about his bloodlines: "The majority of the dogs we have in our kennels all descend from our first imports, Kent vom Adeloga and Dessa vom Holtkamper at least 15 generations ago."

He and his wife, Diane, travel to Germany four or five times a year: "To show our youngsters, but mainly to be able to compare them with the best that Europe has to offer. The majority of our trips are made either to mate one of our females or visit any male we have on our list as a future sire. We also attend regional shows in Britain.

"From our first litter to our last, we have always tried to breed Shepherds that the man in the street can be proud of. We are always here for our pups throughout their lives.

"We have always had the ambition of breeding the perfect GSD. On this, we have failed, but I think we're pretty close! Every German Shepherd is different. What is important is to understand that what you have is a dog and we, as humans, need to see life from their point of view."

Stefanie Millington, CunAnnun German Shepherds, Norfolk: "I grew up around and was dragged up by German Shepherds. My grandfather was owned by, loved, trained and bred them from the early 1950s to the late 1970s in Germany. It has always been my first breed and, as they say: "Once a Shepherd, always a Shepherd.""

"The GSD is loyal and trustworthy, he is attentive, alert and resilient, steady of nerve, courageous and tractable. As a working dog, he is able to act as a guard, herder, tracker, guide and protector. They should never be over-aggressive or shy.

"First and foremost, it's the love for his owner and the anticipation for praise and play that motivates a German Shepherd. They have a great drive and an unrivalled eagerness to please; they thrive with positive training."

"Whenever I see my GSDs interact with children, I am so astounded at how gentle and caring these big dogs are. A perfect example is our boy Otto, (CunAnnun Ennis). We took him to Crufts 2017, along with my friend and her six and nine-year old daughters. We stayed in a hotel and Otto was absolutely besotted right from the word go."

(Library photo)

"On show day, we decided to do some shopping and the National Exhibition Centre was absolutely packed. Little Shannon got separated from us in the crowd. We could see her, but she couldn't see us and panicked, crying her eyes out. Otto must have heard her and he pulled, slipped his lead and barged through the crowd to get to Shannon! It is just like childcare is built into these amazing dogs."

Cheryl Spurr, Reinglen German Shepherds, West Yorkshire: "I have owned German Shepherds for over 30 years. My husband had always wanted to have GSDs, but I was dubious because they had a bad reputation back then. We went to visit a stud dog who had sired a litter, he was brilliant and we decided to visit when the puppies were about five weeks old.

"The owners lived in a pub. We went to the bar, she said to go around the back and up the stairs, let ourselves in and they'd join us in a few minutes. We did that to be met by Mum of the litter running towards us wagging her tail, jumping up and licking us. I said: "This is the litter for us," and have never regretted my decision. There are lots of stories relating to that dog.

"As a rule, Shepherds are brilliant around children. My kids grew up around them, but it would depend on the breeding; it would be irresponsible to sell a high-drive working dog to an inexperienced pet home with small children and no idea how to train it.

"German Shepherds are motivated by you!! They love their families, they love to work, they are happy when they have a job - and that can be any kind of task. Food and toys are great training aids. I always tell new owners to hand-feed the puppy to build a strong bond quickly."

Carolyn Day, Carjaylyn German Shepherds, Kent: "I love their nature and loyalty. German Shepherd puppies should be playful and inquisitive towards new people and toys, and happy to be brushed. They should be well socialised with other dogs, cats and children. Mine has been brought up around children and the children know that unless she sits, she must not be touched, as stroking and patting is her reward for sitting.

"They are always interested in learning new things, so a reward may be a good pat, extra time with a ball, a tug-o-war toy or a dog treat. This confirms that training has finished and the dog has learnt something new."

Teresa and Tony Mapp, Worcestershire: "We have owned GSDs for many years and always found them loyal, intelligent and friendly. We have six dogs and have had five litters in eight years. We are known as *"hobby breeders"* by the Kennel Club, as we do it for the love of the dogs and the experience, rather than as a business.

"We did hear of one breeder whose dog had a brilliant hip score of 1, but the bitch had a bad temperament and was aggressive, and this was passed to the pups. If you are looking at a litter, make sure you like the Mum; the pups will take after her!

"GSDs emit magical fibres of joy - I read that once and had to laugh! I also heard that cleaning the house when you have a German Shepherd is like cleaning your teeth while eating Oreos!"

And now for the US, where all breeders are members of the prestigious *AKC Bred With H.E.A.R.T. (Health, Education, Accountability, Responsibility and Tradition) Program* or *AKC Breeders of Merit. All* carry out extensive health testing on their breeding dogs:

Jacqueline Levy, Cross Keys K9 Inc, New Jersey: "We do place our dogs with Law Enforcement for scent work, patrol work, search and rescue and as service dogs for veterans with Traumatic Brain Injury (TBI) or PTSD, but most of our dogs go to active homes that need an extra layer of protection and/or companionship."

"The German Shepherd is brilliant. We know it is one of the smartest breeds time and time again, but my personal experience is that a GSD is intuitive, biddable, and easy to train if you put the time in to train the dog. Early and proper socialization is mandatory for puppies to become well-adjusted."

Bobbi King, RVT, Redwood Runs, California, has bred GSDs for nearly 30 years: "I expect my puppies to think, be focused and attentive to me. Well-bred puppies are eager and engage playfully with visitors; they are upbeat and curious. I believe that temperament is extremely important; more dogs are euthanized for behavioral issues than all diseases combined. Lack of early socialization is only part of the problem - a well-bred dog is going to develop well!

"Training is an absolute must. The German Shepherd is very intelligent and responds to the owner's consistency and a few minutes of training per day."

Donna Bonney Hirten Bray Hugel, New York State, grew up with German Shepherds: "I have always been attracted to this breed, I was raised around them from the time I was a very young child. They are loyal, protective and loving!! GSDs are the most intelligent, versatile dog there is. They are easy to train as they want to please their handlers, and training is extremely important as they need a "job." If they get bored, they destroy things. I always say: "A tired puppy is a good puppy!""

Tammey Tilton, Tiltonhaus German Shepherds, Washington State: "I have always been attracted to this breed, I was raised around them from the time I was a very young child. I didn't start breeding until about 10 years ago, I wanted to make sure I had the time to take care of the dogs and their litters before I started my breeding program.

"German Shepherds are alert and very aware of the environment around them, which makes me feel a lot safer out on a walk at night when I have one of mine with me! They are very intelligent and willing to please, which makes it fun and easy to train them. They are also very loyal and protective - that is why it is so important to socialize and train them starting at a young age. Very strong and energetic - they need and want a job to do.

"Breeding is a TON of work, but my family and I are having a blast raising, training and breeding the dogs we dearly love."

We asked breeders to sum up German Shepherds in a few words; people who don't know the breed well may be surprised to see how often the word *loving* appears:

- Intelligent, intuitive, highly capable animals
- Loyal, trustworthy, intelligent and loving
- Crazy, loving, loyal friend
- Versatile, loyal, smart - partners for life!
- Loyal, loving, fun, obedient
- Intelligent, loving, loyal guardians
- Loyal, obedient, loving, energetic, intelligent
- Intelligent, loyal, affectionate, spirited
- Beautiful, loyal, protective and, most of all, loving
- God's perfect creation!

Read on to learn how to train and take best care of your King of the Canines for the rest of his or her life, and how to build a unique bond that will become one of the most important things in your life - and certainly his or hers.

2. History of the Breed

The mid-1800s was a time of great canine experimentation in Europe, and particularly in Victorian England, where the new pastime of dog breeding combined a love of both dogs and hobbies.

Early Experimentation

At that time, there were many different types of dog, but they were usually bred for a specific purpose and were referred to in general terms, like sheepdogs, retrievers, setters, spaniels, hounds, bulldogs, terriers, etc.

Keen dog fanciers began to create their own breeds, taking a pinch of this type of dog and adding a little bit of that one to create a specific dog that could be bred to type. They chose their breeding dogs based on certain abilities and physical, colour or temperament traits that they admired.

This new craze of dog breeding spread right across the social classes. Mostly, the Lords and wealthier fanciers concentrated on sporting and larger breeds, while working men experimented with terriers, bulldogs and smaller dogs, often holding competitions in the back rooms of pubs and presenting a trophy for the best dog.

The world's first official dog show was held in the Town Hall at Newcastle upon Tyne, north east England, on June 28th and 29th, 1859, *pictured.* The dogs were an added attraction alongside the cattle show! The only dogs allowed to take part were sporting dogs, mostly setters and pointers, and all the prizes were guns.

The first show to include non-sporting breeds was held in Birmingham later that year and was such a success that, in 1860, the Birmingham Dog Show Society ran the first National Dog Show.

It attracted 267 entries from 30 breeds judged in 42 classes. It was the forerunner to Crufts, the world's largest dog show, which today judges 20,000 dogs from 220 breeds and is attended by over 165,000 dog lovers.

Fourteen years later, in 1873, the Kennel Club was formed by S.E. Shirley and "12 other gentlemen." Their aim was to have a consistent set of rules for governing the popular new activities of dog showing and field trials, and in 1874 they also produced The Kennel Club Stud Book, the first-ever breed register. The AKC (American Kennel Club) was formed 10 years later.

Max von Stephanitz

In Germany, these canine experiments were practised by local shepherds. They bred dogs that were good at herding sheep and protecting the flock; they had intelligence, speed, strength and a keen sense of smell. However, there were big differences in appearance and ability from one region to another.

The **Phylax Society**, the forerunner to modern German Shepherd clubs, was launched in 1891. Its aim was to standardise the German shepherd breed by hand-picking local sheepdogs with superior qualities for breeding. (Phylax is Greek for *"guardsman"*).

It disbanded after only three years following arguments about what traits the society should promote. Some members, including Max von Stephanitz, *pictured,* believed dogs should only be bred for working purposes, while others thought they should also be bred for appearance. Although it didn't last long, the Phylax Society did introduce the idea of standardising the breed.

With the rise of large, industrialised cities in Germany, predators such as wolves declined, and so did the role of the sheepdog.

Max von Stephanitz was an ex-Cavalry captain and former student of the Berlin Veterinary College, where he gained valuable knowledge about biology, anatomy and the science of movement - all of which he later applied to the breeding of dogs.

He was posted all over Germany as a cavalry officer and in those days, rather than staying on military bases, it was usual to board with rural families, and most German farms had at least a few head of sheep and a herding dog or two.

Von Stephanitz became fascinated with these working dogs. He admired their intelligence, strength and ability, but could not find any single type that he regarded as the perfect working dog. He became inspired with the idea that Germany should have a national herding dog that was extremely intelligent, could think for himself and be a working companion to man.

The dog must also be well-co-ordinated, quick on his feet and protective, noble in appearance and bearing, trustworthy in character, physically sound in joint and muscle, and be born with an innate desire to please and obey the shepherd master.

Von Stephanitz started selecting the best herding dogs from across the countryside for his breeding programme. But he wasn't the only person with a passion to develop the perfect German shepherding dog; other ex-Phylax members were also aiming to do the same.

At a dog show in 1899, he was shown four-year-old yellow and grey Hektor von Linksrhein along with littermate, Luch von Sparwasser, bred by Herr Friedrich Sparwasser of Frankfurt.

Hektor was the result of several generations of selective breeding and completely met von Stephanitz's ideals for the working dog. He admired the dog's strength, intelligence, loyalty and beauty and purchased Hektor on the spot.

He then changed the dog's name to Horand von Grafrath, (von Stephanitz's home and kennels were in Grafrath, Bavaria).

Photo: Hektor, later Horand von Grafrath, the foundation sire of the modern breed. (Note the dog's horizontal back).

At that time, dogs were commonly: **"Black, grizzle, reddish brown, either self-coloured or with tan, white or white with large dark patches or brindle, with or without tan markings."**

Three coat types were described at the time:

- 🐾 **Smooth-coated.** Short dense and hard, around the neck the coat is longer and harder

- 🐾 **Long-haired.** Wavy and hard, the hair on the head partially covering the eyes, and with well-marked beard are moustaches and tail well-feathered

- 🐾 **Wire-haired.** Straight, hard and wiry, the hair on the head and legs being especially short and hard with beard and eyebrows well developed

While the long coat is still considered a fault in the US, the UK Kennel Club now accepts the long coat and has recently started holding conformation classes for long-coated German Shepherds. Hektor and Luch's maternal grandfather was the white Greif von Sparwasser, *pictured*. He and several other dogs bred by Friedrich Sparwasser carried the white gene and took part in German dog shows in the 1880s and 1890s.

Von Stephanitz wrote: "...our German sheepdogs have never been bred for colour, the latter being of complete indifference in a working dog."

FACT ▶ Today, white-coated GSDs are not allowed to enter conformation dog shows run under Kennel Club or AKC rules, despite evidence that the white gene or genes occurs naturally.

It is thought Greif also carried the gene for upright ears, which was not always the norm in shepherd dogs at that time. Sparwasser continued his breeding programme and registered his dogs with the SV. He undoubtedly contributed to the development of the modern GSD, although receives little credit for it today.

In his 1923 book *"The German Shepherd in Words and Picture,"* von Stephanitz describes two dog types important in the development of the breed:

- 🐾 **Sheepdogs from the highland Thuringia region**, with erect ears and the general conformation of the modern German Shepherd. Hektor and Luch are noted as having "Thuringian blood"

- 🐾 **Sheepdogs from the Wurttemberg region**, which were heavier and larger-boned with bushy tails

Von Stephanitz wrote: "Horand embodied for the enthusiasts of that time the fulfilment of their fondest dreams. He was big for that period, between 24" and 24½", even for the present day, a good medium size, with powerful frame, beautiful lines, and a nobly-formed head. Clean and sinewy in build, the entire dog was one live wire. His character was on a par with his exterior qualities; marvellous in his obedient fidelity to his master, and above all else, the straightforward nature of a gentleman with a boundless zest for living.

"Although untrained in puppyhood, nevertheless obedient to the slightest nod when at this master's side; but when left to himself, the maddest rascal. The wildest ruffian and incorrigible provoker of strife. Never idle, always on the go; well-disposed to harmless people, but no cringer, mad about children and always in love.

"What could not have been the accomplishments of such a dog if we, at that time, had only had military or police service training? His faults were the failings of his upbringing, never of his stock. He suffered from a superfluity of unemployed energy, for he was in Heaven when someone was occupied with him and was then the most tractable of dog."

This passage could be describing a 21st century German Shepherd from working lines!

The SV or German Shepherd Dog Club

On April 22, 1899, von Stephanitz and his friend Artur Meyer founded the *Verein für Deutsche Schäferhunde (SV)*. Von Stephanitz was a strong and uncompromising leader, appointing himself President, Judge and Breed Inspector. Three sheep masters, two factory owners, an architect, a mayor, an innkeeper and a magistrate joined them as co-founders.

The first entry into the new SV Stud Book (Zuchtbuch für Deutsche Schäferhunde, or SZ) was *"Horand von Grafrath, SZ 1,"* the foundation dog of the German Shepherd breed.

Horand fathered many pups, his most successful being Hektor von Schwaben, SZ 13, *pictured.* Hektor was the product of inbreeding, and was mated with another of Horand's offspring to produce Heinz von Starkenburg, Beowulf and Pilot, who later fathered a total of 84 pups, again mostly through matings with closely-related females.

Hektor von Schwaben, S. Z. No. 13, stockhaariger deutscher Schäferhund, v. Hektor-Linksrhein gen. Horand v. Grafrath a. Mores-Plieningen, Z. Krieger, Schw. Gmünd, B. Minner, Arnstadt i/Th.

It is thought the entire German Shepherd breed can be traced to these three grandsons of Horand.

Crossbreeding with other breeds was considered out of the question by von Stephanitz, who pursued a programme of planned inbreeding from the best dogs. This inbreeding was regarded as essential to *"fix"* the desired traits for the breed. It is why the modern German Shepherd has a relatively narrow gene pool.

 This all took place before the days of genetic testing and experts believe that DM (Degenerative Myelopathy) and some eye issues were present in these foundation dogs.

According to Wikipedia (and I have been unable to verify this), there are four wolf crosses in the original SV studbook, within registrations SZ 41 to SZ 76. Beowulf's progeny also were inbred and it is from these pups that all German Shepherds draw a genetic link. You can check German Shepherd lineage at www.pedigreedatabase.com.

Von Stephanitz promoted the qualities that we see in today's working GSDs. He was interested in muscle, bone, joint, proud look and bearing, intelligence, stamina and work ethic. SV dogs had - and still have — to undergo thorough testing before they are given a rating based on health, physical and mental characteristics.

Those considered fit for breeding are issued with a *Breed Certificate of Authenticity* from the SV. It details each generation back to the dog's great-great-grandparents and lists information about colours, coat types, health, training, show and event results for each ancestor and sibling. SV ratings are extremely highly regarded among breeders and fans of the working German Shepherd, as they contain lots of information about the health, physical condition and capabilities of the dog.

This contrasts with pedigree certificates from the Kennel Clubs, which contain only a family tree with no indication of health or achievements. To date, more than two million German Shepherds have been registered with the SV.

Verein für Deutsche Schäferhunde (SV) e.V.
Aus Respekt zum Hund.

SV is a major influence in the sport of Schutzhund (literally *"protection dog"),* first held in Germany in 1901 to test the German Shepherd's abilities in tracking, obedience and

protection. Today, Schutzhund (now called IGP) is a rigorous canine sport open to all dogs, with some 3,000 to 4,000 participating every year worldwide.

Photo: A competitor and her dog demonstrating free heeling during the Obedience section of Schutzhund (IGP).

The SV has gone on to become the biggest single breed club in the world, with 50,000 members today. In Germany alone, around 250,000 German Shepherds are registered with the SV, with a further 10,000 puppies registered each year. And several hundred thousand dog lovers in 78 countries are members of the German Shepherd Associations of the World Union.

Modern Era

In 1908, a dog named Queen of Switzerland was the first German Shepherd to be registered with the American Kennel Club, a year after the breed had first been exhibited in America. The German Shepherd Dog Club of America was founded in 1913. The Queen of Switzerland's progeny suffered from health defects as the result of poor breeding, causing the breed to decline in popularity during the early 20th century.

When the UK Kennel Club first accepted registrations for the German Shepherd in 1919, just 54 dogs were registered; by 1926 this had grown to over 8,000. The breed gained international recognition towards the end of World War I when returning soldiers told heroic stories of the courageous German Shepherds.

Illustration of Red Cross dogs working during WWI, from "The Book Of Dogs - An Intimate Study Of Mankind's Best Friend," 1919.

The book describes these German Shepherd dogs: "He is a graceful, powerful dog with beautiful lines and curves denoting both strength and speed. It is not necessary to mention the many uses he has been put to in the present war, as Red Cross, No Man's Land patrol, messenger and ration-carrier.

"It is perhaps as well to say here that any such active, restless, vigorous, and intelligent animal as this becomes a grave responsibility to its owner and should be sedulously cared for and kept in control every minute.

"They become very dangerous when neglected or turned adrift or thrown on their own re-sources by being lost, and once they form a habit of chicken or sheep killing, they become inveterate and persistent in their maraudings and ordinarily must be shot.

"One very beautiful dog of this kind was recently shot in the Catskills after repeated ravages which started a rumour of wolves in the region. This impression was very natural, and when the photographs sent to the Conservation Commission were identified as a dog, the rustic sufferers were still only partly convinced. Dog it was, however, and apparently a very fine example of this new and interesting type."

One survivor of the Great War was Rin Tin Tin. In September 1918, US Air Corporal Lee Duncan found a German Shepherd and her scrawny litter of five pups., They were in a ravaged airfield near the border in Lorraine, France, abandoned by retreating Germans. He chose a male and female pup, while members of his group took the mother and the others back to camp.

Rin Tin Tin, or Rinty as he was known, was the only one to survive and make it to America, where he went on to star in 27 films and to help make Warner Brothers the success it is today. Rinty's movie stardom spread worldwide and he played a big part in greatly increasing the popularity of German Shepherds as family pets.

After World War I, it was thought the word *"German"* in the name would harm the breed's popularity, so the breed was officially renamed *"Alsatian Wolf Dog"* in the 1920s by the UK Kennel Club, after Alsace, France. Eventually, "wolf dog" was dropped after numerous campaigns by breeders.

Of all the hundreds of imports coming into the States in the 1920s and 1930s, only a handful had any lasting influence, including 1922 and 1923 Ch. Pfeffer von Bern, US Grand Victor in 1937 and 1938, and Sieger in 1937.

American breeders diverged from von Stephanitz's ideal working dog. Many of the US dogs went into non-farming homes and breeders focussed on appearance for the show ring, rather than working ability. The hind legs went further under the body, bringing the hocks closer to the ground, and the back angled down from front to back. American German Shepherds were, and still are, known for a graceful movement known as the *"flying trot"* in the show ring.

German Shepherds played a darker role in World War II, when they were used by their Nazi masters to control prison camps and the mass movement of millions of people to concentration camps. Their other roles included messenger, gas detection and munition carrier dogs; they were even sacrificed as living bombs by the Nazis.

After World War II, Germany was in ruins, as was the German Shepherd breed; many had been slaughtered and others starved to death. It was generally believed that the best German Shepherds were in North America. However, von Stephanitz's breeding principles were re-applied and the German Shepherd was brought back to strength in Germany.

The name *"Alsatian"* remained until 1977, when successful campaigns by dog enthusiasts pressured the UK Kennel Club to allow the breed to be registered again as the German Shepherd Dog (GSD).

Discussions about the merits of working German Shepherds versus show line German Shepherds continue today as they did over 120 years ago. There are still health issues that need addressing, but the popularity of the breed is in no doubt. Today there are millions of German Shepherds from working, show and mixed lines throughout North America and Europe, as well as in every country around the world.

....

Sources:

"Dogs Of All Nations," 1917, by W. E. Mason
"The Book Of Dogs - An Intimate Study Of Mankind's Best Friend," 1919, by Ernest Harold Baynes, Louis Agassiz Fuertes
"Towards a nuanced understanding of inbreeding and dogs," Scottie Westfall, Retrieverman
History Extra, BBC History Magazine
Wikipedia
Verein für Deutsche Schäferhunde

3. Before You Get Your Puppy

If you haven't got your puppy yet, then read this chapter before you commit to anything; it will help you find a healthy, happy puppy with a good temperament. If you already have yours, skip to the next chapter.

Once you've decided that the German Shepherd is your ideal dog, the best way to select a puppy is with your HEAD - and not with your heart! You'll soon find hundreds of German Shepherd puppies advertised - but it requires a bit more time and research to find a first-rate breeder.

With their beautiful brown eyes, intelligent expressions and playful personalities, there are few more appealing things on this Earth than a litter of German Shepherd puppies. If you go to view a litter, the pups are sure to melt your heart and it is extremely difficult – if not downright impossible - to walk away without choosing one.

 The German Shepherd has more inheritable health issues than many breeds. A main priority should be to buy a puppy from bloodlines free from genetic diseases.

If you haven't yet chosen your pup and take only one sentence from this entire book, it is this:

FIND AN ETHICAL BREEDER WHO PRODUCES GERMAN SHEPHERD PUPPIES FROM HEALTH-TESTED PARENTS WITH GOOD TEMPERAMENTS.

– even if that means paying a bit more. It will be worth it.

Find a breeder who knows German Shepherds inside out and who does not breed lots of different types of dogs.

After all, apart from getting married or having a baby, getting a puppy is one of the most important, demanding, expensive and life-enriching decisions you will ever make.

German Shepherds are extremely loyal and will love you unconditionally - but there is a price to pay. In return for their devotion, you have to fulfil your part of the bargain.

In the beginning, you have to be prepared to devote much of your day to your new puppy. You have to feed her several times a day and housetrain virtually every hour, you have to give her your attention and start to gently introduce the rules of the house. You also have to be prepared to part with hard cash for regular healthcare and pet insurance.

If you are unable to devote the time and money to a new arrival, if you have a very young family, a stressful life or are out at work all day, then now might not be the right time to consider getting a puppy. German Shepherds are highly driven people-loving dogs that thrive on being involved.

If left alone too long, behaviour issues often result. This is a natural reaction and is not the dog's fault; she is simply responding to an environment that is failing to meet her needs.

Pick a healthy pup and he or she should live 10 to 14 years if you're lucky - so this is certainly a long-term commitment. Before taking the plunge, ask yourself some questions:

Have I Got Enough Time?

In the first days after leaving her mother and littermates, your puppy will feel very lonely and probably even a little afraid. Spend time with your new arrival to make her feel safe and sound. Ideally, for the first few days you will be around all of the time to help her settle and to start bonding.

If you work, book time off if you can - although this is more difficult for some of our American readers who get short vacations - but don't just get a puppy and leave her all alone in the house a couple of days later.

Housetraining (potty training) starts the moment your pup arrives home. Then, after the first few days and once she's feeling more settled, make time for short sessions of a few minutes of behaviour training. German Shepherd puppies are very lively, and this energy can become mischievous if not channelled.

You'll also have to find time to slowly start the socialisation process by taking her out of the home to see new places, strangers, other animals, loud noises, busy roads, etc. - but make sure you CARRY her until the vaccinations have taken effect.

 The importance of socialising German Shepherds cannot be over-emphasised. Start socialisation as soon as possible, as that critical window up to four months of age is when she is at her most receptive to all things new.

The more positive experiences she is introduced to at this early stage, the better, and good breeders will already have started the process.

Once she has had the all-clear after vaccinations, get into the habit of taking her for a short walk every day – more as she gets older. While the garden or yard is fine, new surroundings stimulate interest and help to stop puppies becoming bored.

Also, German Shepherds were bred to be protectors and they can become too wary of strangers, so introducing her to different people - without over-facing her- will help her to become more relaxed around people.

Make time right from the beginning to get your pup used to being handled, gently brushed, ears checked, and later having her teeth touched and cleaned.

We recommend you have your pup checked out by a vet within a couple of days of arriving home - but don't put your puppy on the clinic floor where she can pick up germs from other dogs. Factor in time to visit the vet's surgery for annual check-ups as well as vaccinations, although most now last several years – check with your vet.

How Long Can I Leave My Puppy?

This is a question we get asked a lot and one that causes much debate among new owners. All dogs are pack animals; their natural state is to be with others. So being alone is not normal for them - although many have to get used to it.

Another issue is the toilet; German Shepherd puppies have tiny bladders. Forget the emotional side of it, how would you like to be left for eight hours without being able to visit the bathroom? So how many hours can you leave a dog alone?

FACT ❯ In the UK, canine rescue organisations will not allow anybody to adopt if they are intending to leave the dog alone for more than four or five hours a day.

Dogs left alone a lot get bored and, in the case of dogs originally bred to do a job, like the German Shepherd, they can become destructive without enough mental and physical stimulation. A lonely German Shepherd may display signs of unhappiness by barking, chewing, aggression, digging, eliminating, disobedience or just being plain sad and disengaged.

In terms of housetraining, a general rule of thumb is that a puppy can last without urinating for **one hour or so for every month of age, sometimes longer.** So, provided your puppy has learned the basics, a three-month-old puppy should be able to last for three hours or a little longer without needing to go. Of course, until housetraining kicks in, young puppies just pee at will!

Family and Children

German Shepherds are really good with children. Contrary to popular opinion, they are gentle, loving and patient with the youngsters in their family, provided - and this is really important - **you put the time in from the beginning to socialise and train your puppy.**

German Shepherds are naturally playful; they love games and a challenge. With young children around, it's important to teach the puppy the boundaries of play. Young GSDs are boisterous, they don't know their own strength. While a well-trained GSD would never intentionally harm a child, she could cause injury by jumping up or rough-housing. Don't let play sessions get out of hand.

Pictured is Tanner Tilton with a Tiltonhaus puppy, courtesy of Tammey Tilton.

Of course, you have to socialise your German Shepherd AND the kids! Your children will naturally be delighted about your new arrival, but kids and puppy should not be left unsupervised until each has learned to respect the other - no matter how well they get along in the beginning.

Puppies regard children as playmates - just like a child regards a puppy as a playmate; both are playful, both are easily over-excited. A pup may chase, jump and nip a small child – although it can be the other way around; a timid pup may need protecting from the children!

Lively behaviour is not aggression; it is normal play for puppies. With a German Shepherd you have a willing student, so be prepared to put the time in to teach your pup what is acceptable and what is not. See **Chapter 9. Training a German Shepherd** for more detailed information.

Train your pup to be gentle with your children and your children to be gentle with your puppy.

Your dog's early experiences with children should all be positive. If not, a dog may become nervous or mistrustful - and what you want around children is most definitely a relaxed GSD that does not feel threatened by a child's presence.

Tip Discourage the kids from picking up your gorgeous new puppy every few minutes. Better to let them interact together on the puppy's level, i.e. the floor.

Children (or adults!) shouldn't constantly pester the puppy; sleep is very important to puppies, just as it is for babies. Allow your puppy to eat at her own pace uninterrupted; letting youngsters play with the dog while eating is a no-no, it may promote food gulping or aggression.

Jacqueline Levy, of Crosskeys K9, says: "The success of a dog in a home with children is going to be based on the parents of the children. We only place puppies in homes with small children - not older pups or dogs unless they are proven - and spend time with the parents discussing how to integrate the puppy properly into the family. Education of the family is really important in setting the puppy up to be successful. We do not encourage roughhousing with a puppy at all."

You may find puppyhood a challenge, but survive that and adult Shepherds are more than worth the effort. They are extremely loyal and loving; they will become protective and watch over your children. Take things steady in the beginning and your German Shepherd will undoubtedly form a deep, lifelong bond that your children will remember throughout their lives.

One reason that some Shepherds end up in rescue centres is that owners are unable to cope with the demands of small children AND a dog. German Shepherds need a lot of input from their owners – do you have the time?

Single People

Many singles own dogs, but if you live alone, getting a puppy will require a lot of dedication on your part. There is nobody to share the responsibility, so taking on a big dog like the German Shepherd requires a huge commitment and a lot of your time if the dog is to have a decent life.

If you are out of the house all day, a German Shepherd is NOT a good choice. This breed thrives on being involved, and needs plenty of mental stimulation. Being alone all day is not much of a life for a dog as intelligent, active and loyal as the German Shepherd. However, if you can spend considerable time with the pup, then a German Shepherd will definitely become your best friend.

Older People

If you are older or have elderly relatives living with you, a boisterous young German Shepherd could be a bit too much to handle. If you are determined to get a GSD, then an older, calmer dog might be a better choice - and great company. We recommend getting one from show stock, rather than working bloodlines, as the latter generally require more exercise and mental stimulation.

Dogs can be a great tonic for fit, older people. In his mid-80s my father still walked his dog for an hour to 90 minutes every day – even in the rain or snow. He grumbled occasionally, but it was good for him and it was good for the dog - helping to keep them both fit and socialised! They got fresh air, exercise and the chance to communicate with other dogs and their humans. My father's dog passed away, but at 89 he still walks with a friend's dog every day.

You're never alone when you've got a dog. Many older people get a canine companion after losing a loved one; a husband, wife or previous much-loved dog. A pet gives them something to care for and love, as well as a constant companion.

Bear in mind that dog ownership is not cheap, so budget for annual pet insurance, veterinary fees, a quality pet food, etc. The RSPCA in the UK has estimated that owning a dog costs an average of around £1,300 ($1,700) a year!

Other Pets

However friendly your puppy is, if you already have other pets in your household, they may not be too happy at the new arrival. Socialised German Shepherds generally get on well with other animals, but it might not be a good idea to leave your hamster or pet rabbit running loose; most young GSDs have strong play and prey instincts. The pup has first to learn to fit in alongside other pets - if introduced slowly, they may well become best friends!

German Shepherd puppies are naturally curious and playful and will sniff and investigate other pets. They may even chase them in the beginning. Depending on how lively your pup is, you may have to separate them initially, or put the pup into a pen or crate for short periods to allow the cat to investigate without being mauled by a hyperactive pup who thinks the cat is a great playmate.

This will also prevent your puppy from being injured. If the two animals are free and the cat lashes out, your pup's eyes could get scratched. A timid German Shepherd might need protection from a bold cat - or vice versa. A bold cat and a timid German Shepherd will probably settle down together quickest!

If things seem to be going well with no aggression, then let them loose together after one or two supervised sessions. Take the process slowly; if your cat is stressed or frightened, he may decide to leave. Our feline friends are notorious for abandoning home because the board and lodgings are better down the road...

More than One Dog

Most well-socialised German Shepherds have no problem sharing their home with other dogs. Introduce your puppy to other dogs and animals in a positive, non-frightening manner that will give her confidence.

Supervised sessions help everyone to get along and for the other dog or dogs to accept your new pup. If you can, introduce them for the first time outdoors on neutral ground, rather than in the house or in an area that one dog regards as her own. You don't want the established dog to feel he has to protect his territory, nor the puppy to feel she is in an enclosed space and can't get away.

If you are thinking about getting more than one pup, consider waiting until your first puppy is a few months old or an adult before getting a second.

Young German Shepherds require more time and effort than most

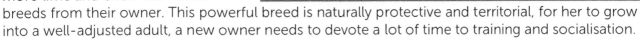

breeds from their owner. This powerful breed is naturally protective and territorial, for her to grow into a well-adjusted adult, a new owner needs to devote a lot of time to training and socialisation.

Waiting to get a second dog means you can give your full attention to one puppy, get housetraining, socialisation and the basics of obedience training out of the way before getting your second. Another benefit is that an older well-trained dog will help teach the new puppy some manners.

 Unless you are extremely experienced with German Shepherds, we don't recommend getting two puppies from the same litter. Apart from all the time involved, your little German Shepherd has to learn to focus on YOU, not her littermate.

In the long term, owning two German Shepherds can be twice as nice — they will be great company for each other - but bear in mind that it's also double the food and vet's bills.

Type, Gender and Colour

Are you looking for a family pet, a guard dog, a dog to do a job, or a dual purpose dog? German Shepherds are perhaps the most versatile of all breeds. Think carefully about EXACTLY what you are expecting of the dog before choosing a breeder.

Some will specialise in show lines, others working, and some in a mixture of the two. Generally, German Shepherds bred from Eastern European and working bloodlines will have a higher *"drive."* They want to work, so you have to keep them mentally and physically stimulated. Puppies from show or mixed lines have lower drives and are a better choice for a family pet — and they still have the same instinct to protect.

Males of all types are heavier than females; they can grow to 90lb (40kg), whereas females are smaller and around 20lb (9kg) lighter on average. Some German Shepherds, particularly males, can be territorial and may *"mark"* their territory by urinating indoors, usually starting at six to 12 months old, during puberty.

FACT Overall, females tend to be less dominant and less suspicious; more friendly towards people. That said, much depends on individual bloodlines, what the dog was bred for, and socialisation. Your main points of reference in terms of size, physical appearance and temperament are the puppy's parents.

Another difference is that females have heat cycles and, unless she is spayed, you will have to restrict a female's activities away from the home when she is in heat every six months or so to stop unwanted attention from males. Gender should be a consideration if you have other dogs. You can't expect an unneutered male to live in a relaxed manner with an unspayed female in heat.

Similarly, two uncastrated males may not always get along; there may simply be too much testosterone and competition.

There are several different colours of German Shepherds - see **Chapter 14. Grooming** for details. If you've set your heart on a particular colour or marking, make sure the health and temperament boxes are ticked as well when you choose your breeder.

FACT ❯ Colours can change dramatically. Black and tan pups are usually born nearly black, sables may lighten or darken, bi-color pups change very little, and only solid blacks stay the same. Look at the parents to get an idea of your dog's colour as an adult.

Plan Ahead

Choosing the right breeder is one of the most important decisions you will make. Like humans, your puppy will be a product of her parents and will inherit many of their characteristics. Natural temperament and how healthy your puppy will be now and throughout her life will depend to some extent on the genes of her parents.

Responsible breeders test their dogs; they check the health records and temperament of the parents and only breed from suitable stock. Sound German Shepherd puppies are not cheap – health screening, socialisation and first-rate care come at a cost.

Expect to pay over $1,000 to $2,500 in the US, depending on type and how much training the breeder has put in, and over £1,000 in the UK for a pedigree pup from health-tested parents. **Jacqueline Levy** adds: "Anything under $1,000 for a puppy is cause for concern, because the price really reflects the amount of money invested in the dogs." See **Chapter 12. German Shepherd Health** to find out what certificates to ask to see.

 BE PATIENT. Start looking months before your planned arrival. There is usually a waiting list for German Shepherd pups from health-tested parents and good breeders, so once you know you can afford a well-bred German Shepherd, get your name on a list.

Phone or email your selected breeder or breeders to find out about future litters and potential dates, but don't commit until you've asked lots of questions. Good breeders will also ask a lot of questions about you, your household and living conditions and how you will take care of and train their much-loved puppy.

A healthy German Shepherd will be your irreplaceable companion for the next decade or more, so why buy one from a pet shop or general ad? Would you buy an old car or a house with potential structural problems just because it looked pretty in a website photo or was cheap? The answer is probably no, because you know you'd have stress and expense at some point in the future.

Visit the breeder personally at least once. With the distances sometimes involved, this is not always possible in the USA, so speak at length on the phone to the breeder and ask lots of questions. Reputable breeders will be happy to answer all your questions - and will have lots for you too. They will provide photos and perhaps even videos and emails of your pup's progress if you can't visit.

In the USA, some may also arrange escorted *"Nanny*

Transport" to safely deliver the pup to your home, or an agreed meeting place. If you are satisfied with the answers to your questions, and have checked the Puppy Contract and Health Guarantee on offer, then go ahead and put your name down on the waiting list.

German Shepherds should be at least eight weeks old before they leave the breeder. Puppies need this time to physically develop and learn the rules of the pack from their mothers and littermates. In some US states it is illegal to sell a puppy younger than eight weeks.

....

Buyer Beware

Good breeders do not sell their dogs on general purpose websites, Gumtree, eBay, Craig's List or Freeads, in car parks or somebody else's house. Puppies in pet shops often come from puppy mills. Two years ago, the UK Government considered banning the sale of puppies in pet shops – sadly, so far, nothing has happened. If you are looking at dogs on Pets4Homes in the UK, follow their guidelines carefully, check the health screening and see the pup with his or her mother.

There is a difference between *a hobby breeder* and a *backyard or backstreet breeder*. Both may breed just one or two litters a year and keep the puppies in their homes, but that's where the similarity ends. In the UK, *hobby breeders* often don't have a website and you will probably find out about them via word of mouth.

Good hobby breeders are usually breed enthusiasts or experts; sometimes they show their pedigree dogs. They carry out health tests and lavish care and love on their dogs. They are not full-time professional dog breeders. NOTE: While it is often a good sign in the UK, the term *"hobby breeder"* can have negative implications in the USA.

Backyard breeders are often breeding family pets. They have less knowledge about the breed, pay little attention to the health and welfare of their dogs and are doing it primarily for extra cash. They may be very nice people, but avoid buying a dog from them.

FACT ⟩ All good breeders - professional or hobby - have in-depth knowledge of the German Shepherd, they take measures to prevent potential health issues being passed on to puppies, and are passionate about the breed.

Here are four reasons for buying from a good breeder:

1. **HEALTH:** German Shepherds have many potentially inheritable health issues. Screening breeding stock and NOT breeding from those that fail the health tests is the best way of preventing genetic disorders from being passed on.

2. **SOCIALISATION:** Scientists and dog experts now realise that the critical socialisation period for dogs is up to the age of four months. An unstimulated puppy is likely to be less well-adjusted and more likely to have fear or behaviour issues as an adult. Good breeders start this process, they don't just leave the puppies in a shed or barn for eight weeks. Socialisation is especially important for German Shepherds, compared with other breeds.

3. **TEMPERAMENT:** Good breeders select their breeding stock based not only on sound structure and health, but also on temperament. They will not breed from an aggressive or overly anxious GSD.

4. **PEACE OF MIND:** Most good breeders give a genetic health guarantee with their puppy, often from a year to two or three years. Some even give a lifetime genetic guarantee. Many also agree to take the dog back at any time in its life if things don't work out - although you may find it too hard to part with your beloved Shepherd by then.

....

How to Spot Bad Breeders

Getting a puppy is such an emotional decision - and one that should have a wonderfully positive impact on you and your family's life for over a decade. Unfortunately, the high price of German Shepherd puppies has resulted in unscrupulous people producing litters for the money.

This section helps you avoid the pitfalls of getting a puppy from a puppy mill, a puppy broker (somebody who makes money from buying and selling puppies), a backyard breeder or even an importer. You can't buy a Rolls Royce or a Lamborghini for a couple of thousand pounds or dollars - you'd immediately suspect that the *"bargain"* on offer wasn't the real thing. No matter how lovely it looked, you'd be right - and the same applies to German Shepherds.

Become Breeder Savvy

❧ Avoid websites where there are no pictures of the owners, home or kennels

❧ If the website shows lots of photos of cute puppies with little information about the family, breeding dogs, health tests and environment, click the X button

❧ Don't buy a website puppy with a shopping cart symbol next to her picture

❧ See the puppies with their mother face-to-face. If this is not possible due to distances, speak at length on the phone with the breeder and ask lots of questions

❧ You hear: "You can't see the parent dogs because......" ALWAYS ask to see the parents and, as a minimum, see the mother and how she looks and behaves with the pups, pictured. If the pups are really hers, she will interact with them.

❧ Good breeders are happy to provide lots of information and at least one reference before you commit

❧ If the breeder is reluctant to answer your questions, look elsewhere

❧ Pressure selling: on the phone, the breeder doesn't ask you many questions and then says: "There are only X many puppies left and I have several other buyers interested." Walk away

❧ You hear "Our German Shepherd puppies are cheaper because...." Walk away

❧ At the breeder's, ask to see where the puppy is living. If the breeding dogs are not housed in the family home, as is often the case with working GSD bloodlines, they should be in large, clean kennels, not too hot or cold, with access to grass and time spent with humans

❧ Ask to see the other puppies from the litter

❧ The mother is not with the puppies, but brought in to meet you

❧ The puppies look small for their stated age

- If the breeder says that the dam and sire are Kennel Club or AKC registered, ask to see the registration papers

- Photographs of so-called "champion ancestors" do not guarantee the health of the puppy

 Look beyond the cute, fluffy exterior. The way to look INSIDE the puppy is to see the parents and, most importantly, check what health tests have been carried out.

"Vet checked" does NOT mean the pup or parents have passed any genetic health tests

- The person you are buying the puppy from did not breed the dog themselves. Deal with the breeder, not an intermediary

- The place you meet the puppy seller is a car park, somebody else's house or place other than the puppies' home

- The seller tells you that the puppy comes from top, caring breeders from your or another country. Good breeders don't sell their puppies through brokers

- Ask to see photos of the puppy from birth to present day

- Be wary of *"rare colours"* or *"rare markings."* Make sure other health and welfare boxes are ticked

- Price – if you are offered a very cheap German Shepherd, he or she almost certainly comes from dubious stock. Anyone selling their puppies at a knock-down price has cut corners - and it's often health screening

- If you get a rescue German Shepherd, make sure it is from a recognised rescue group and not a *"puppy flipper"* who may be posing as a do-gooder, but is in fact getting dogs (including stolen ones) from unscrupulous sources

- NEVER buy a puppy because you feel sorry for it; you are condemning other dogs to a life of misery

- If you have any doubt, go with your gut instinct and **WALK AWAY** - even if this means losing your deposit. It will be worth it in the long run

One UK breeder adds: "Avoid websites that want money straight away to go on their waiting list. Feedback or reviews may not be genuine, so always ask if you can be put in contact with a few of them and ask lots of questions to see if the info adds up. My reviewers are always open for contact.

"If there are a lot of different breeds on the website, then you know they are breeding on a big scale, which means there is no attention to detail or one-to-one rearing. This is why puppies often develop behavioural problems that are hard to reverse – and then you may need to get a professional behaviourist involved.

"Your gut instinct is a good one to follow if something is just not right or adding up when looking through any website."

Jacqueline adds: "Healthy well-bred puppies will have paper, and by this I mean paper that shows that the parents have been tested. My clients get a book that shows all the health testing throughout the lines on both sides.

"Puppies will be clean, curious, bright eyes and obviously well fed. The environment should be clean and conducive to raising puppies as well. Here is where it gets dicey for prospective puppy buyers. The puppy mills often *"stage"* a place that looks appropriate, even staging parents so that buyers will feel comfortable. The reality is the dogs are often bred in mills, treated like livestock or worse, and brought to these staged locations that look picture perfect, but are actually just fronts for the mill dogs."

 Bad breeders do not have two horns coming out of their heads! Most will be friendly when you phone or visit - after all, they want to make the sale. It's only later when problems develop; use this chapter to learn how to spot the signs.

Puppy Mills and Farms

Unscrupulous breeders are everywhere. That's not to say there aren't some excellent German Shepherd breeders out there; there certainly are. You have to do research to find them.

While new owners might think they have bagged a cheap puppy, it often turns out to be false economy in the case of German Shepherds, and emotionally disastrous when the puppy develops health problems due to poor breeding, or behavioural problems due to poor temperament or lack of socialisation. The UK's Kennel Club says as many as one in four puppies bought in the UK may come from puppy farms - and the situation is no better in North America. The KC Press release states: "As the popularity of online pups continues to soar:

- Almost one in five pups bought (unseen) on websites or social media die within six months

- One in three buys online, in pet stores and via newspaper adverts - outlets often used by puppy farmers – this is an increase from one in five in the previous year

- The problem is likely to grow as the younger generation favour mail order pups, and breeders of fashionable breeds flout responsible steps

"We are sleepwalking into a dog welfare and consumer crisis as new research shows that more and more people are buying their pups online or through pet shops, outlets often used by cruel puppy farmers, and are paying the price with their pups requiring long-term veterinary treatment or dying before six months old."

The KC research found that:

- One third of people who bought their puppy online, over social media or in pet shops failed to experience "overall good health"

- Some 12% of puppies bought online or on social media end up with serious health problems that require expensive on-going veterinary treatment from a young age

Caroline Kisko, Kennel Club Secretary, said: "Whilst there is nothing wrong with initially finding a puppy online, it is essential to then see the breeder and ensure that they are doing all of the right things. This research clearly shows that too many people are failing to do this, and the consequences can be seen in the shocking number of puppies that are becoming sick or dying."

Marc Abraham, TV vet and founder of Pup Aid, added: "Sadly, if the *"buy it now"* culture persists, then this horrific situation will only get worse. There is nothing wrong with sourcing a puppy online, but people need to be aware of what they should then expect from the breeder.

"For example, you should not buy a car without getting its service history and seeing it at its registered address, so you certainly shouldn't buy a puppy without the correct paperwork and health certificates and without seeing where it was bred."

Pictured is a UK BVA Eye Certificate.

"However, too many people are opting to buy directly from third parties, such as the internet, pet shops, or from puppy dealers, where you cannot possibly know how or where the puppy was raised.

"Not only are people buying sickly puppies, but many people are being scammed into paying money for puppies that don't exist, as the research showed that 7% of those who buy online were scammed in this way."

The KC has a lot of info on the dos and don'ts of buying a puppy at www.thekennelclub.org.uk/paw

Now you know what to avoid, what should you look out for? Read on to find out:

Top 10 Signs of a Good Breeder

1. His or her breeding dogs are health tested with certificates to prove it.

2. The area where the puppies are kept is clean and the puppies look clean.

3. Their German Shepherds appear happy and healthy. The pups have clean eyes, ears, nose and bum (butt) with no discharge. They are alert, excited to meet new people and don't shy away from visitors.

4. **You see the puppy interact with the mother and other puppies.** The breeder encourages you to spend time with the puppy's parents - or at least the mother - when you visit. He or she is happy for you to visit more than once. If a female dog is brought in to a waiting room, how do you know she is the puppy's real mother?

Photo courtesy of Stefanie Millington, CunAnnun German Shepherds, Norfolk, UK

5. Good breeders are very familiar with German Shepherds, although some may also have one other breed — lots of breeds is a warning sign.

6. They feed their adults and puppies high quality dog food and give you some to take home and guidance on feeding and caring for your puppy. They will also be available for advice afterwards.

7. They provide you with a written *Puppy Contract, Health Guarantee* and *Puppy Pack* or *Going Home Bag* with items to help the pup's transition. They will show you records of the puppy's visits to the vet, vaccinations, worming medication, etc. and explain what other vaccinations your puppy will need.

8. They don't always have pups available, but keep a list of interested people for the next available litter. They don't over-breed, but do limit the number of litters from their dams.

9. They will, if asked, provide references from other people who have bought their puppies; call at least one.

10. And finally ... good German Shepherd breeders want to know their beloved pups are going to good homes and will ask YOU a lot of questions about your suitability as owners.

When visiting puppies, take your time to have a good look around and go inside and outside. Are the breeders happy to show you around everywhere or a bit secretive? You will probably know if it's right or not when you see the surroundings. Walk away promptly if you have any doubts. It's a massive decision, you want to make sure that the puppy you choose will be healthy and happy. If you think it could be a puppy mill, report it to the relevant authorities.

 Take your puppy to a vet to have a thorough check-up within 48 hours of purchase. If your vet is not happy with the pup's condition, return her - no matter how painful it may be. Keeping an unhealthy puppy will only lead to further distress and expense.

Where to Find a Good Breeder

❖ German Shepherd Clubs. The Weltunion der Vereine für Deutsche Schäferhunde (WUSV) has a list of clubs around the world at www.wusv.org/en/countries

❖ The Kennel Club in your country. Look for Assured Breeders in the UK, and an AKC Breeder of Merit in the US - even better is a Bred with H.E.A.R.T. breeder.

❖ Visit dog shows or canine events where German Shepherds are participating and talk to competitors and breeders.

❖ Get a recommendation from somebody who has a German Shepherd that you like - but make sure her dogs are tested.

❖ Ask your vet for details of local, ethical GSD breeders.

❖ Search the internet - there are dozens out there; use the advice in this chapter to find a reputable breeder.

❖ If you are in the UK, visit the German Shepherd stand at Discover Dogs during the annual Crufts dog show in early March.

Questions to Ask a Breeder

Here's a reminder of the questions you should be asking. The Kennel Club also has a three-minute YouTube video entitled *The Dos and Don'ts of Buying a Puppy* at: www.youtube.com/watch?v=1EhTu1TQcEc

1. **Have the parents been health screened?** Ask to see certificates and what guarantees the breeder is offering in terms of genetic illnesses. How long do these guarantees last – 12 weeks, a year, a lifetime? It varies, but reputable breeders will definitely give some form of guarantee, and this should be stated in the Puppy Contract.

2. **What veterinary care have the pups had so far?** Ask to see records of flea treatments, wormings and vaccinations, microchipping.

3. Are you registered with the Kennel Club (UK), AKC (US) or a member of a German Shepherd breed club? Not all good German Shepherd breeders are members, but this is a good place to start.

4. Are your German Shepherds from working, show or dual-purpose bloodlines? Make sure you know what type of GSD you're viewing.

5. **How long have you been breeding German Shepherds?** You are looking for someone who has a track record with the breed.

6. Can you put me in touch with someone who already has one of your puppies?

7. **How many litters has the mother had?** Females should not have litters until they are two years old, and The UK Kennel Club will not register puppies from a dam that has had more than four litters. Check the age of the mother.

8. **What happens to the mother once she has finished breeding?** Are they kept as part of the family, rehomed in loving homes or sent to animal shelters?

9. **Do you breed any other types of dog?** Buy from a specialist, preferably one who does not breed lots of other types of dog - unless you know they have a good reputation.

10. **What is so special about this litter?** You are looking for a breeder who has used good breeding stock and his or her knowledge to produce handsome, healthy dogs with good temperaments.

11. **What do you feed your adults and puppies?** A reputable breeder will feed a top quality dog food and advise that you do the same.

12. **What is the average lifespan of your dogs?** Generally, pups bred from healthy stock tend to live longer.

13. **How socialised and housetrained is the puppy?** Good breeders often start the socialisation and potty training process before they leave.

14. **How would you describe the temperament of the parents?** Temperament is extremely important with German Shepherds. Try to interact with both parents, or at least the mother.

15. **Why aren't you asking me any questions?** A good breeder is committed to making a good match between the new owners and their puppies. If the breeder spends more time discussing money than the welfare of the puppy, draw your own conclusions as to what his or her priorities are — and they probably don't include improving the breed. Walk away.

Choosing a Healthy German Shepherd

Once you've selected your breeder and a litter is available, you then have to decide WHICH puppy to pick, unless the breeder has already earmarked one for you after asking lots of questions. Here are some pointers on puppy health:

1. Your chosen puppy should have **a well-fed appearance.** She should not, however, have a distended abdomen (pot belly) as this can be a sign of worms or other illnesses. The ideal puppy should not be too thin either; you should not be able to see her ribs.

2. **Her nose should be cool, damp and clean** with no discharge.

3. **The pup's eyes should be bright and clear** with no discharge or tear stain. Steer clear of a puppy that blinks a lot, this could be the sign of a problem.

4. **The pup's ears should be clean** with no sign of discharge, soreness or redness and no unpleasant smell.

5. **Check the puppy's rear end** to make sure it is clean and there are no signs of diarrhoea.

6. **The pup's coat should look clean,** feel soft, not matted - and puppies should smell good! The coat should have no signs of ticks or fleas. Red or irritated skin or bald spots could be a sign of infestation or a skin condition. Also, check between the toes of the paws for signs of redness or swelling.

7. **The puppy should be alert,** *like the pup in this picture,* and curious about you and her surroundings, not timid.

8. **Gums should be clean and pink.**

9. **Choose a puppy that moves freely** without any sign of injury or lameness. It should be a fluid movement, not jerky or stiff, which could be a sign of joint problems.

10. When the puppy is distracted, clap or make a noise behind her - not so loud as to frighten her - to **make sure she is not deaf.**

11. Finally, **ask to see veterinary records** to confirm your puppy has been wormed and had her first vaccinations.

Jacqueline says: "Most well-bred puppies with parents of good temperaments will yield puppies that are similar. Sometimes you see a lack of confidence in a puppy that, if not properly addressed early and often, will lead to fear-aggression. We like a happy dog, eager to please, and willing to work without being neurotic, too dependent or too independent."

If you get the puppy home and things don't work out for whatever reason, some breeders will also take the puppy back – either within a limited time frame or for the whole life of the puppy - although if it is more than one year later, you cannot expect the breeder to reimburse you.

Puppy Contracts

Most good breeders provide their puppy parents with an official Puppy Contract. This protects both buyer and seller by providing information on the puppy until he or she leaves the breeder. You should also have a health guarantee for a specified time period. A Puppy Contract will answer such questions as whether the puppy:

- ❧ Is covered by breeder's insurance and can be returned if there is a health issue within a certain period of time
- ❧ Has been micro-chipped and/or vaccinated and details of worming treatments
- ❧ Has been partially or wholly toilet-trained
- ❧ Has been socialised and where he or she was kept
- ❧ What health issues the pup and parents have been screened for
- ❧ What the puppy is currently being fed and if any food is being supplied
- ❧ Was born by Caesarean section
- ❧ And details of the dam and sire

It's not easy for caring breeders to part with their puppies after they have lovingly bred and raised them, and so many supply extensive care notes for new owners, which may include details such as:

- ❧ The puppy's daily routine
- ❧ Feeding schedule
- ❧ Vet and vaccination schedule
- ❧ General puppy care
- ❧ Toilet training
- ❧ Socialisation

The Royal Society for the Prevention of Cruelty to Animals (RSPCA) has a downloadable puppy contract, *pictured,* endorsed by vets and animal welfare organisations; you should be looking for something similar from a breeder.

Type *"RSPCA Puppy Contract"* into Google or read it in full at: https://puppycontract.rspca.org.uk/home

In the US, type *"AKC Preparing a Puppy Contract"* into Google, or visit: www.akc.org/expert-advice/dog-breeding/preparing-a-contract-for-puppy-buyers

4. A Life's Work

Marie Donahue, of Rodina Straze German Shepherds, Maryland, has been involved with working dogs for over 30 years. To say she is passionate about her dogs and their development is an understatement.

She was attracted to the East German Line German Shepherds (Czech Border Patrol Dogs) for their disposition, work ethic, health and athletic build. The goal of her breeding program is to produce dogs with stable temperaments, good health and longevity. Marie raises her puppies utilizing The Puppy Culture program, adding her own training protocols geared specifically towards German Shepherds.

In her own words, Marie gives an insight into some of the incredible work that goes into each litter and why she loves working lines so much. Anyone who has ever wondered if it's worth paying a little extra for a well-bred German Shepherd puppy should read this - they will be left in little doubt.

....

Early Days

My passion in life has always been my animals, my earliest memories are full of dogs and horses. As a child I was not allowed to have either, but dreamed of having my own horse farm one day with dogs at my side.

As a child I spent countless hours reading dog and horse books. Flipping through the photos learning all I could about the different breeds, what they were bred for, their physical traits, and characteristics. I've been told I'm a walking dog encyclopedia! My family couldn't understand my fascination, and I was told it was just a phase. Well, the phase has yet to end, as I have built my life around my animals!

I developed a deep love and appreciation for the working breeds. I grew up watching the Doberman Gang and The Bionic Woman with her German Shepherd named Max.

As a young teenager, I befriended my neighbor's German Shepherd through their fence. This may not sound unusual - but it turned out this was a trained personal protection dog!

Photo: Marie with two of her working German Shepherds and a pair of puppies.

I approached my neighbor and asked if I could walk her dog. She laughed and swore her dog wouldn't let me near him. I told her I'd been petting him through the fence. She didn't believe me, and invited me into the house to see for herself.

The dog's name was Johan. He ran up and greeted me tail wagging. I was then allowed to walk and play with him until his owner passed away and Johan disappeared.

I then approached my Dad's neighbour, who had beautiful Dobermans. I walked right through her gate, past three of them, and knocked on the door to ask if I could walk her dogs. Again, she was shocked I was standing there amongst her dogs and invited me in.

I learned about breeding and conformation showing from her, and bred my first Doberman litter before I was 20. In my mid-20s, I moved to Montana where I began to breed Appaloosa Horses and did so for about 15 years. Having my own ranch fulfilled my childhood dream and allowed me to share my life with many different breeds of dogs.

When my last Doberman passed away, I wanted a working dog that was more suited to handle the cold temperatures of Montana. So, I began to study pedigrees and learn about the differences between the German Shepherd lines. I became captivated by the East German Lines, predominantly the Czech Border Patrol dogs. I was intrigued by the history of these dogs. Just like the Appaloosa Horses I bred, I knew I wanted to preserve a little piece of history that was slowly disappearing.

My foundation dog was a female named Osah of Sapphire Mountain NW1, TD, TKA, ETD. She had a full Czech pedigree and was the pick female of the litter.

She was my greatest love - and greatest frustration! She taught me more than any dog I'd ever had. Her intelligence and independence pushed me to become a better trainer, handler and person. She taught me there are no quick fixes; I had to accept and appreciate her for who she was. She always gave her all in everything she did. Due to unfortunate circumstances, she passed away far too soon. I am so thankful I have a part of her with me always through her progeny.

....

The Puppy Culture and ENS

With breeding, I believe *Every Moment Matters*. My puppies are an extension of our family. I always strive to do the best I can to produce healthy, well adjusted, confident puppies. As a professional dog trainer, I understand how important early socialization is to the future success of each and every dog.

As a dedicated breeder, my goal is to set each puppy up for success, utilizing The Puppy Culture program of puppy raising, training, and socialization. I have also implemented my own training, developed specifically to benefit the German Shepherd Dog and their future family. Puppy Culture is a program developed by professional dog trainer and breeder, Jane Killion. It is a comprehensive, organized program for breeders to follow.

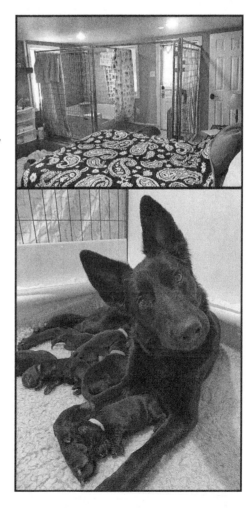

The first 12 weeks of a puppy's life are incredibly important. During this time, a breeder has the power to influence the outcome of a puppy's life by what we choose to teach them. By doing the right things at just the right time, we can give a puppy the best start possible.

Photo: The main puppy whelping room and Adia z Rodina Straze with her litter. Marie's kennel name z Rodina Straze loosely translates to: "of Family Guards" in the Czech language.

My dogs and puppies live in my home and have constant contact with me and my family. From the moment they're born, we spend countless hours sitting in the whelping box just holding them, observing their interactions with one another and doing early ENS (Early Neurological Stimulation). ENS was originally developed by The US Military.

They called it *"Bio Sensor"* - later known to the public as *"Super Dog"* – program. It was designed to improve the performance of dogs used for military purposes, many of which were German Shepherds. Based on years of research, they learned that early neurological stimulation exercises could have important and lasting effects, giving the dog an advantage.

Their studies confirmed that there are specific time periods early in life when ENS has optimum results. The first involves a window that begins on the 3rd day of life and lasts until the 16th.

The Bio Sensor program utilized five exercises designed to stimulate the neurological system, and this has been adopted by The Puppy Culture. Each workout involves handling puppies once each day, one at a time, and each stimulation lasts just three to five seconds. This is what we do:

1. **Tactile Stimulation** - Holding the pup in one hand, the handler gently stimulates (tickles) the pup between the toes on any one foot using a Q-tip. It is not necessary to see that the pup is feeling the tickle.

2. **Head Held Erect** - Using both hands, the pup is held perpendicular to the ground, so that its head is directly above its tail. This is an upwards position.

3. **Head Pointed Down** - Holding the pup firmly with both hands the head is reversed and is pointed downward, so that it is pointing towards the ground.

4. **Supine Position** - Holding the pup so that its back is resting in the palm of both hands with its muzzle facing the ceiling. The pup while on its back is allowed to sleep.

5. **Thermal Stimulation** - Using a damp towel that has been cooled in a refrigerator for at least five minutes, place the pup on the towel, feet down. Do not restrain it from moving.

These exercises produce neurological stimulation that do not naturally occur during this early stage of life - the result being an increased capacity that later results in improved performance.

Specific benefits noted in the Bio Sensor program were:

1. Improved cardiovascular performance.
2. Stronger heart beats.
3. Stronger adrenal glands.
4. More tolerance to stress.
5. Greater resistance to disease.

Puppy Enrichment

Once our puppies turn about four-and-a-half weeks old, we move them into our Puppy Enrichment Building and yard, *pictured on the previous page,* during the day.

Puppies are brought outside first thing in the morning and brought back in once its dark, as they continue to sleep in the house at night. This specially-designed building and yard allows them to have room to run and explore at their own pace on different surfaces and obstacles, inside or out.

I also start individual daily training sessions with the puppies at this age, which continue until they leave us at eight weeks of age. Our training protocols enhance the natural drives in our puppies. They are:

- 🐾 Prey Drive: The desire to chase, obtain and retain
- 🐾 Food Drive: The desire for food, independent of appetite
- 🐾 Pack Drive: The desire to be part of a team
- 🐾 Hunt Drive: The desire to search

Every exercise we do with our puppies is to enhance the natural abilities of this breed.

Photo: "You go first. "..."No, you."... "OK then, wish me luck!!" Marie's five-week-old puppies get used to walking on different surfaces.

When they leave for their new homes, they know about 10 different behaviors, have good engagement and begun walking on a leash. I feel this is very important and provides new owners with a jump start in their relationship with their new puppy.

Spending the amount of time I do with the puppies allows me to really get to know them individually, which aids me in choosing proper placements for them in their new homes.

Through this journey I can't help but think about the whole process of how each puppy finds their home. I believe every dog enters our lives at just the right moment, either to help us, teach us, but always to make us better in the end.

I really feel if you listen to your heart and pay close attention to your puppies, they will let you know when their right person or family comes along.

I had a special puppy named Bee. She was the last one from a litter. She had many opportunities for a good home (and a few questionable ones), but I could tell they just were not right for her, so with me she stayed. I continued to train her and she showed me the areas she was gifted in. Then, another family contacted me, came to visit and when she saw them, she ran up without hesitation - something she hadn't done before, as she was always glued to my side. She never looked back.

It brought tears to my eyes as I watched her play gently with their children and not leave their side. She was so happy, as if she knew this family needed her and had finally found her. Maybe that's why she would just patiently wait beside me when the other families came, trusting I wouldn't send her if it wasn't right for her. She had her life's purpose coming, and she knew that.

Not even a full 24 hours in her new home, this 13-week-old puppy is already fulfilling her purpose and working for her new family.

Photo: The adult dogs relaxing in their outdoor runs.

Versatility of the GSD

There are vast differences within the German Shepherd Breed, depending on lineage and type.

The show line German Shepherd Dogs usually have lower drive than working lines. They have larger bodies, broader heads and more angulation. Typically, they are black and red, or black and tan with classic saddle pattern. They have thicker, longer coats and a pronounced gait that is called a *"flying trot."* They tend to have a more docile temperament, which can make them a more suitable choice as a good family pet. Yet with any German Shepherd, training is still essential.

The working line dogs are valued for their endurance and strong character; beauty is secondary to working ability. Working lines must possess high drive, courage, intelligence, strength, stamina, and solid nerve with a desire to work non-stop.

They have a more athletic and compact structure that is able to stand up to a hard day's work and be easily carried by their handler during duty. They also have shorter, coarser coats, usually sable, bi-color or black. Most significantly, their silhouette is squarer and they lack the flying trot gait favored by show line breeders.

They are much stronger in will and require structure and consistent training in order to make suitable companions. They need an outlet for their energy and drive or they will become a nuisance. Working line dogs do best in experienced homes or with people willing to do the extra amount of work they require.

I have found the German Shepherd to be one of the most versatile dogs I have owned, enjoying and excelling in any task its given. They are extremely intelligent - which does not equate to easy! The smarter the dog, the better handler you must be. They will out think you and take advantage of you if you allow them to. The working line dogs need a firm yet fair handler, take a lot of dedication to raise properly and give them the outlets they need. Training is not optional; it becomes your lifestyle.

There is a reason they are called working dogs. Working German Shepherds must be provided with daily mental stimulation and physical activity or they can become a liability. Just because they are brought into a home as a pet, does not change their genetic make-up, nor working desire.

Their minds must be utilized; it's not just about exercise and playing ball. It's hard to physically wear them out, just give them five minutes and they are ready to go again. You must use their minds, give them some type of a job, and realize they will take up a lot of your time. They are not a dog to just lay on your couch or leave in the back yard.

German Shepherds are such intelligent dogs that love to work; the things you can do with them are limitless. I train and compete my dogs in Obedience, Rally, Tracking, Scent Detection Fast Cat, Tricks, Barn Hunt, Dock Diving, Herding, and a sport called IGP (Schutzund) which was the original Breed Test for the German Shepherd in Germany.

In 2019, I am proud to say that my personal dogs and I earned 46 new titles in these events, with five Rodina Straze dogs hitting the Top 10 GSDs rankings in AKC Fast Cat nationwide. Our breeding program has also produced a Single Purpose Detection Dog, (trained to sniff out one type of odor), Service Dogs and a Gluten Detection Dog.

Photo: Freyja, Belka and Aiko z Rodina Straze proudly displaying their new Scent Work titles.

The long list of events and titles can be confusing! Here are some of the main ones explained:

CD, CDX, UD, UDX are AKC Obedience Titles

RN, RI, RA, RE are Rally Obedience Titles

TD, TDX, TDU are AKC Tracking titles. AKC Tracking is a canine sport that demonstrates a dog's natural ability to recognize and follow a scent, and is the foundation of canine search and rescue work.

CGC - Canine Good Citizen is a 10-skill training program that's open to all dogs - purebred and mixed breed - that focuses on teaching the basics of good manners and obedience.

CGCA - the AKC Community Canine test is the advanced level of AKC's Canine Good Citizen (CGC) program. As with CGC, AKC Community Canine has a 10-step test of skills that dogs must pass to earn the official AKC Community Canine title. The AKC Community Canine program is all about ensuring you have a well-behaved dog while you're out and about in the community.

Whereas CGC happens in a simulated environment, the AKC Community Canine test is conducted in real-life situations, like walking on a busy sidewalk or through a local park. It gives you and your dog the confidence to enjoy every day to the full - no matter what comes your way.

CGCU –The AKC Urban CGC title is another step beyond the basic CGC test, and this tests your CGC skills in an active city or town setting. There are 10-steps to the test that your dog must pass to earn the official AKC Urban CGC title, but it is administered in a place where there are cars, streets to be crossed, noises, and fast-paced distractions.

FAST CAT is a Coursing Ability Test. It's a timed 100-yard dash where dogs run one at a time, chasing a lure.

RATI, RATN, RATO are Barn Hunt titles where your dog hunts for a live rat that is placed in a tube through a maze of straw bales!

Photo: Belka z Rodina Straze resistance training with a parachute to build speed and endurance.

TKN, TKI, TKA, ETD are trick dog titles

TC - German Shepherd Dog Temperament Test, this is given to make sure the dog has a correct temperament for the German Shepherd.

For anyone starting out and wanting to compete with their dog AKC events are welcoming for newcomers; you can find information on the AKC website or your local kennel club. There tends to be numerous events offered, – people are quite friendly and helpful. You tend to see the same people with their dogs at numerous events which leads to gaining friendships and a wonderful support system.

Working Dog Titles – Dog Sport

IGP (Schutzund) Historically was the GSD breed evaluation test. Developed specifically for the German Shepherd Dog, it is a three-part sport which includes Tracking, Obedience and Protection phases – the dog must pass all three phases in the trial.

Schutzhund is intended to demonstrate the dog's intelligence and utility. As a working trial, Schutzhund measures the dog's mental stability, endurance, structural efficiencies, ability to scent, willingness to work, courage, and trainability.

The dog must first pass the **BH** which stands for *Begleithundprüfung*, which translates as *"traffic-sure companion dog test"* - this is the prerequisite temperament and obedience test for IPG. The BH tests basic obedience and sureness around strange people, strange dogs, traffic, and loud noises.

A dog that exhibits excessive fear, distractibility, or aggression cannot pass and go forward to obtain its schutzhund titles. This sport takes a large amount of dedication and time to train your dog to be trial-ready!

NOTE: In the UK, **Working Trials** are very popular with German Shepherd owners. These are held outdoors and have three disciplines: Nose Work, Agility and Control. Tests include heelwork, searching for hidden items, long jump and scaling a wall.

Dogs start at the beginner level, or *"stake,"* which is Companion Dog, and can work all the way up to Patrol Dog. Contact the UK Kennel Club for a list of working trial clubs.

The **Kennel Club Good Citizen Dog Scheme** is the equivalent of the AKC Canine Good Citizen and is the largest dog training program in the UK. There are four levels of courses from Puppy Foundation, to Bronze, Silver and Gold Award.

The Reason Why I Breed

When I had my first GSD litters it was the most amazing and exhausting experience – I had two litters within 12 days. The amount of work involved, endless barking, lack of sleep (which made me not so nice, and extremely forgetful), and worry was finally over. And my husband said: "And you want to do this again?" My answer without hesitation was: "Not two litters, but yes. Definitely!"

The moments of holding that fragile newborn, hearing their little noises when they are content. Watching my crazy dog turn into a gentle, loving, attentive mother, so careful with every move she makes around her puppies. The way she sat and watched them, I never saw her so peaceful and content.

I loved watching the puppies grow and getting to know each one's individual personalities. Pouring more time and love into each puppy to give them the best foundation possible and seeing how capable they are at learning at such young ages.

This handsome Rodina Straze trio are just five-and-a-half months old.

Meeting the wonderful people who found their way to each one of my puppies is absolutely priceless. I feel very fortunate to be a part of the puppies lives that live close to us and watch them grow and flourish in their new homes.

These are a few of the reasons I say yes without hesitation to do all the craziness again.

It fills my heart to know that each puppy has found their perfect family and through this process has allowed me to meet amazing people and gain friendships I would not have otherwise had. I feel truly blessed to be that stepping stone.

....

Written in memory of Osah of Sapphire Mountain. Thank you, my girl, for all you gave me. There's not a day that goes by when you're not in my thoughts. Memories of you still bring tears and my heart still hurts for you every time I have to get my own shoes in the morning. May you rest peacefully till we meet again. 🤍

5. Bringing Puppy Home

Getting a new puppy is so exciting. You can't wait to bring the little fella home. Before that happens, you probably dream of all the things you are going to do together; going for long walks, playing games, snuggling down by the fire, setting off on adventures, or maybe taking part in canine competitions or shows.

Your pup has, of course, no idea of your big plans, and the reality when he or she arrives can be a big shock for some owners!

Puppies are wilful little critters with minds of their own and sharp teeth. They leak at both ends, chew anything in sight, constantly demand your attention, nip the kids or anything else to hand, cry or whine and don't pay a blind bit of notice to your commands... There is a lot of work ahead before the two of you develop that unique bond!

Your pup has to learn what you require from him before he can start to meet some of your expectations - and you have to learn what your pup needs from you.

....

Once your new arrival lands in your home, your time won't be your own, but you can get off to a good start by preparing things before the big day. Here's a list of things to think about getting beforehand - your breeder may supply some of these:

Puppy Checklist

- ✓ A large dog bed or basket
- ✓ Bedding – a Vetbed or Vetfleece would be a good choice, you can buy one online
- ✓ A towel or piece of cloth that has been rubbed on the puppy's mother to put in the bed
- ✓ A puppy gate or pen to initially contain the pup in one area of the house
- ✓ A large crate if you decide to use one
- ✓ A collar or puppy harness with identification tag and leash
- ✓ Food and water bowls, preferably stainless steel
- ✓ Puppy food – find out what the breeder is feeding and stick with that to start with
- ✓ Puppy treats, healthy ones like carrots or apple are best, no rawhide
- ✓ Newspapers, and a bell if you decide to use one, for potty training
- ✓ Poop bags
- ✓ Toys and chews suitable for puppies
- ✓ A puppy coat if you live in a cool climate
- ✓ Old towels for cleaning and drying your puppy and partially covering the crate

AND PLENTY OF TIME!

Later on, you'll also need grooming brushes, flea and worming products and maybe a car grille or travel crate. Many good breeders provide Puppy Packs to take home; they contain some or all of the following items:

- ✓ Registration certificate
- ✓ Pedigree certificate
- ✓ Buyer's Contract
- ✓ Information pack with details of vet's visits, vaccinations and wormings, parents' health certificates, diet, breed clubs, etc.
- ✓ Puppy food
- ✓ ID tag/microchip info
- ✓ Blanket that smells of the mother and litter
- ✓ Soft toy that your puppy has grown up with, possibly a chew toy as well
- ✓ Four or five weeks' free insurance

 **FACT** ❯ In the UK, all puppies have to be microchipped BEFORE they leave the breeder by law - and that must be at eight weeks or older.

Puppy Proofing Your Home

If your German Shepherd is to live indoors, a few adjustments will be needed to make your home safe and suitable. Puppies are small bundles of instinct and energy when they are awake, with little common sense and even less self-control.

Young German Shepherds love to play. They may have bursts of energy before they run out of steam and spend much of the rest of the day sleeping. As one breeder says: *"They have two speeds – ON and OFF!"*

German Shepherds have an incredible sense of smell and puppies love to investigate with their noses and mouths. Check your garden or yard, make sure there are no poisonous or low plants

with sharp leaves or thorns that could cause eye injuries. There are literally dozens of plants harmful to a puppy if ingested, including azalea, daffodil bulbs, lily, foxglove, hyacinth, hydrangea, lupin, rhododendron, sweet pea, tulip and yew.

The Kennel Club has a list of some of the most common ones, type *"Kennel Club poisonous plants"* into Google or visit: http://bit.ly/1nCv1qJ The ASPCA has an extensive list for the US at: http://bit.ly/19xkhoG or Google *"ASPCA poisonous plants."*

Photo courtesy of Donna Bonney, Hirten Bray Hugel, New York State.

Fence off any sharp plants, such as roses, that can injure a dog's eyes. Make sure every little gap has been plugged in any fences. You'd be amazed at the tiny spaces determined puppies can escape through - and your new arrival won't have any road sense.

FACT Dognapping is on the increase. Some 2,000 dogs are now being stolen each year in the UK. The figures are much higher for the US, where the AKC reports increasing dog thefts and warns owners against leaving their dog unattended – including tying them up outside stores.

While most people would not attempt to run off with an adult German Shepherd, a cute little puppy is certainly more of a target.

Puppies are little chew machines and puppy-proofing your home involves moving anything sharp, breakable or chewable - including your shoes. Lift electrical cords, mobile phones and chargers, remote controls, etc. out of reach and block off any off-limits areas of the house, such as upstairs or your bedroom, with a child gate or barrier, especially as he may be shadowing you for the first few days.

Create an area where your puppy is allowed to go, perhaps one or two rooms, preferably with a hard floor that is easy to clean. Keep the rest of the house off-limits, at least until the pair of you have mastered potty training.

This area should be near the door to the garden or yard for toileting. Restricting the puppy's space also helps him to settle in. He probably had a den and small space at the breeder's. Suddenly having the freedom of the whole house can be quite daunting - not to mention messy!

You can buy a purpose-made dog barrier or use a sturdy baby gate, which may be cheaper. Choose one with narrow vertical gaps or mesh, and check that your puppy can't get his head stuck between the bars, or put a covering or mesh over the bottom of the gate initially. You can also make your own barrier, but bear in mind that cardboard, fabric and other soft materials will get chewed.

A puppy's bones are soft, and studies have shown that if pups go up and down stairs regularly, or jump on and off furniture, they can develop joint problems later in life.

Tip Don't underestimate your puppy! Young German Shepherds are lively and determined; they can jump and climb, so choose a barrier higher than you think necessary.

The puppy's designated area or room should not be too hot, cold or damp and free from draughts. Little puppies can be sensitive to temperature fluctuations and don't do well in very hot or very cold conditions. If you live in a hot climate, your new pup may need air conditioning in the summertime, especially if he's long-coated.

Just as you need a home, so your puppy needs a den; a haven where your pup feels safe. Young puppies sleep for 18 hours or more a day at the beginning; this is normal. You have a couple of options; you can get a dog bed or basket, or you can use a crate, which can also speed up potty training. **See Chapter 6. Crate and Housetraining** for getting your German Shepherd used to - and then to enjoy - being in a crate.

It may surprise American readers to learn that common practice in the UK is to contain the puppy in the kitchen or utility room until he's housetrained, and later to allow the dog roam around the house at will. Some owners do not allow their dogs upstairs, but many do.

Some owners prefer to create a safe penned area for their pup, rather than a crate, while others use both a pen and a crate. You can make your own barriers or buy a manufactured heavy duty metal playpen, *pictured.* A fabric pen will not be robust enough for a German Shepherd.

The time any young children spend with the puppy should be limited to a few short sessions a day. Plenty of sleep is *essential* for the normal development of a young dog. You wouldn't wake a baby every hour or so to play, and the same goes for puppies.

Wait a day or two before inviting friends round to see your handsome new puppy. However excited you are, your new arrival needs a few days to get over the stress of leaving mother and siblings and start bonding with you.

While confident, well-socialised puppies may settle in right away, other puppies may feel sad and a little afraid. Make the transition as gentle and unalarming as possible. For young German Shepherds to grow into well-adjusted adult dogs, they have to feel comfortable and relaxed in their new surroundings, and understand their place in the household.

After a few sleep-deprived nights followed by days filled with entertaining your little puppy and dealing with chewed shoes, nipping and a few housetraining "accidents," your nerves might be a tiny bit frayed! Try to remain calm and patient... your German Shepherd puppy WANTS to learn and is doing his best... it just takes a little time for you both to get on the same wavelength.

FACT ⟩ This early period is a very important time for your- how you react and interact with each other during these first few days and weeks will help to shape your relationship and your German Shepherd's character for the rest of his life.

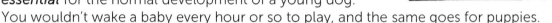

Bones, Chew Treats and Toys

Like babies, puppies like to explore the world with their mouths, so chew treats and toys are a must. There are some things you can't move out of puppy's way, like kitchen cupboards, doors, sofas, fixtures and fittings, so try not to leave your pup unattended for any length of time where he can chew something that is hard to replace.

Tip Avoid giving old socks, shoes or slippers, or your pup will naturally come to think of your footwear as fair game!

You can give a German Shepherd puppy *a raw bone* to gnaw on - NEVER cooked bones as these can splinter. Avoid poultry and pork bones, and ribs - especially pork ribs - are too high in fat. Knuckle bones are a good choice and the bone should be too big for the puppy to swallow. Puppies should be supervised and the bone removed after an hour or so. Don't feed a puppy a bone if there are other dogs around, it could lead to food aggression.

FACT ⟩ Raw bones contain bacteria, and families with babies or very young children shouldn't feed them indoors. Keep any bones in a fridge or freezer and always wash your hands after handling them.

Alternatives to real bones or plastic chew bones are natural *reindeer antler* chew toys *(pictured),* which have the added advantage of calcium, although they are hard and have been known to crack teeth. Natural chews preferred by some breeders include ears, dried rabbit pelt and tripe sticks – all excellent for teething puppies - once you have got over the smell!

Tip Rawhide chews are not recommended as they can get stuck in a dog's throat or stomach, but bully sticks (pictured) are a good alternative.

Made from a bull's penis(!) they can be a good distraction from chewing furniture, etc. and help to promote healthy teeth and gums. Bully sticks are highly digestible, break down easily in the stomach and are generally considered safe for all dogs. They are made from 100% beef, normally contain no additives or preservatives, come in different sizes and dogs love 'em. NOTE: Puppies should be supervised while eating bully sticks or any other treats.

Dental sticks are good for cleaning your dog's teeth, but many contain preservatives and don't last very long with a determined chewer. One that does last is the **Nylabone Dura Chew Wishbone,** made of a type of plastic infused with flavours appealing to dogs. Get the right size and throw it away if it starts to splinter after a few weeks.

Another long-lasting treat option is the **Lickimat (pictured),** which you smear with a favourite food. This inexpensive mat, available online, will keep your puppy occupied for some time – although they can leave a bit of a mess.

Other choices include **Kong toys,** which are pretty indestructible, and you can put treats (frozen or fresh) or smear peanut butter inside to keep your dog occupied while you are out. All of these are widely available online, if not in your local pet store.

As far as toys go, the **Zogoflex Hurley and** the **Goughnut** are both strong and float, so good for swimmers – and you'll get your money back on both if your German Shepherd destroys them! For safety, the Goughnut has a green exterior and red interior, so you can tell if your dog has penetrated the surface - as long as the green is showing, you can let your dog "goughnuts."

A natural hemp or cotton tug rope is another option, as the cotton rope acts like dental floss and helps with teeth cleaning. It is versatile and can be used for fetch games as well as chewing.

One UK breeder says: "Personally, I would only use balls if they are on ropes, A friend's dog died because he got a tennis ball stuck in his throat. At least a ball on a rope has a hole in, so dog can still breathe if it gets stuck. Another benefit of a ball on rope is that you can interact with your dog, rather than throwing it away from you; therefore it helps to build a bond between you."

Jacqueline Levy, of Crosskeys K9, New Jersey, added: "Toys should be age-appropriate and nothing that can compromise your puppy or dog by being swallowed, splintered or cracked.

"We do not recommend any kind of rope toys, toys that have stuffing, tennis balls - the fuzz on the balls abrades the teeth - golf balls (some contain lead) and toys that are cheaply made and easily destroyed. Rope toys or any type of toy containing string can be ingested and get trapped in the intestines.

"Treats should be wholesome, have a current expiration date, and the less processed the better. We absolutely do not recommend rawhide treats of any kind, rather we suggest you rely on animal products such as bully sticks, trachea, tendons and other useful, nutritious chews for your dog. Antlers can be hard enough to crack teeth, so be careful with any chews or toys that are hard enough to adversely affect your dog's teeth.

FACT Puppies' stomachs are sensitive, so be careful what goes in. Even non-poisonous garden plants can cause intestinal blockages and/or vomiting. Like babies, pups can quickly dehydrate, so if your puppy is sick or has watery poop for 48 hours or more, seek medical advice.

The First Few Days

Before you collect your puppy, let the breeder know what time you will arrive and ask her not to feed the pup for a couple of hours beforehand - unless you have a very long journey, in which case the puppy will need to eat something. He will be less likely to be car sick and should be hungry when he lands in his new home. The same applies to an adult dog moving to a new home.

When you arrive, ask for an old towel or toy that has been with the pup's mother — you can leave one on an earlier visit to collect with the pup. Or take one with you and rub the mother with it to collect her scent and put this with the puppy for the first few days. It will help him to settle in. In the US, some puppies are flown to their new homes; but you should still get a Puppy Pack that includes something with the mother's scent and a toy.

Get copies of any health certificates relating to the parents and a Contract of Sale or Puppy Contract that outlines everyone's rights and responsibilities — see **Chapter 3. Before You Get Your Puppy** for details. It should also state that you can return the puppy if there are health issues within a certain time frame — although if you have picked your puppy carefully, it should not come to this. The breeder will also give you details of worming and any vaccinations, as well as an information sheet.

Find out exactly what the breeder is feeding and how much; dog's digestive systems cannot cope with sudden changes in diet - unless the breeder has deliberately been feeding several different foods to her puppies, in which case they will be used to different foods. In the beginning, stick to whatever the pup is used to; good breeders send some food home with the puppy.

The Journey Home

Bringing a new puppy home in a car can be a traumatic experience. Your puppy will be sad at leaving his mother, brothers and sisters and a familiar environment. Everything will be strange and frightening and he may whimper and whine or even bark on the way home.

If you can, take somebody with you on that first journey — some breeders insist on having someone there to hold and cuddle the pup to make the journey less stressful for the pup.

Under no circumstances have the puppy on your lap while driving. It is simply too dangerous - a German Shepherd puppy is extremely cute, wriggly and far too distracting. Have an old towel between your travel companion and the pup as he may quite possibly pee - the puppy, not the passenger!

These six-week-old Tiltonhaus pups will be off to their new homes in two weeks, courtesy of Tammey Tilton.

If you have to travel any distance, take a crate — either a purpose-made travel crate or a wire crate that he will use at home. Travel crates can be soft canvas or hard plastic. A plastic one should have holes in the sides to allow air flow. Cover the bottom of the crate with a waterproof material and then put a comfortable blanket on

top. You can put newspapers in half of the crate if the pup is partly housetrained. Don't forget to allow the pup to relieve himself beforehand, and if your journey is more than a couple of hours, take water to give him en route. He may need the toilet, but don't let him outside on to the ground as he is not yet fully vaccinated.

Arriving Home

As soon as you arrive home, let your puppy into the garden or yard, and when he "performs," praise him for his efforts. These first few days are critical in getting your puppy to feel safe and confident in his new surroundings. Spend time with the latest addition to your family, talk to him often in a reassuring manner. Introduce him to his den and toys, slowly allow him to explore and show him around the house – once you have puppy-proofed it.

German Shepherd puppies are extremely curious - and amusing, you might be surprised at their reactions to everyday objects. Puppies explore by sniffing and mouthing, so don't scold for chewing. Instead, put objects you don't want chewed out of reach and replace them with chew toys. Some puppies can be more "mouthy" than others; if yours is like this, make sure he has safe toys to chew.

Well-socialised German Shepherd owners usually get on well with other animals. However, it is important to introduce them to each other in the right conditions. Do it slowly and in supervised sessions on neutral territory or outdoors where there is space so neither feels threatened - preferably once the pup has got used to his new surroundings, not as soon as you walk through the door. Gentleness and patience are the keys to these first few days, so don't over-face your pup.

 Have a special, gentle puppy voice and use his new name frequently - and in a pleasant, encouraging manner. Never use his name to scold or he will associate it with bad things. The sound of his name should always make him want to pay attention to you as something good is going to happen - praise, food, playtime, and so on.

Resist the urge to keep picking your puppy up – no matter how irresistible he is! Let him explore on his own legs, encouraging a little independence.

One of the most important things at this stage is to ensure that your puppy has enough sleep – **which is nearly all of the time** - no matter how much you want to play with or cuddle him. If you haven't decided what to call your new puppy yet, "Shadow" might be a good suggestion, as he will follow you everywhere!

These eight-week-old Rodina Straze puppies are being leash-trained in preparation for their new homes, courtesy of Marie Donahue.

Our website receives emails from worried new owners. Here are some of the most common concerns:

- My puppy won't stop crying or whining
- My puppy is shivering
- My puppy won't eat
- My puppy is very timid
- My puppy follows me everywhere, he won't let me out of his sight

❖ My puppy sleeps all the time, is this normal?

These behaviours are quite common at the beginning. They are just a young pup's reaction to leaving his mother and littermates and entering into a strange new world. It is normal for puppies to sleep most of the time, just like babies. It is also normal for some puppies to whine during the first couple of days.

 FACT ❭ German Shepherd puppies from breeders who have already started socialisation and training will already have some idea about what is expected of them. They are likely to settle in quicker than those left to their own devices away from the family.

Our photo shows the safe play area where three-week-old puppies gain experience of different objects and surfaces, courtesy of Marie Donahue, Rodina Straze German Shepherds, Maryland, US.

Make your new pup as comfortable as possible, ensuring he has a warm (but not too hot), quiet den away from draughts, where he is not pestered by children or other pets. Handle him gently, while giving him plenty of time to sleep. If you have children teach them how to handle the pup safely.

Tip Some breeders recommend keeping the pup in a crate near your bed for the first couple of nights, so he knows he is not alone.

If he makes sad little whimpering noises or barks, talk softly and gently stroke him. Resist the urge to pick him up or every time or he will learn that crying always gives him the reward of your attention.

A puppy will think of you as his new mother and it is quite normal for him to want to follow you everywhere, but after a few days start to leave your pup for short periods of a few minutes, gradually building up the time. A puppy unused to being left alone at all can grow up to have separation anxiety - see **Chapter 8. Traits and Behaviour** for more information.

If your routine means you are normally out of the house for a few hours during the day, get your puppy on a Friday or Saturday so he has at least a couple of days to adjust to his new surroundings. A far better idea is to book time off work to help your puppy to settle in, if you can, or if you don't work, leave your diary free for the first couple of weeks.

Helping a new pup to settle in is virtually a full-time job. This can be a frightening time for some puppies. Is your puppy shivering with cold or is it nerves? Avoid placing him under stress by making too many demands. If he leaves his food, take it away and try it later. Don't leave it down all of the time or he may get used to turning his nose up at it. If your puppy is crying, it is probably for one of the following reasons:

❖ He is lonely

❖ He is hungry

❖ He wants attention from you

❖ He needs to relieve himself

If it is none of these, then physically check him over to make sure he hasn't picked up an injury. Try not to fuss too much! If he whimpers, reassure with a quiet word. If he cries loudly and tries to get out of his allotted area, he may need to go to the toilet. Even if it is the middle of the night, get up and take him outside. Praise him if he performs.

The strongest bonding period for a puppy is between eight and 12 weeks of age. The most important factors in bonding with your puppy are TIME and PATIENCE, even if he makes a mess in the house or chews something. Spend time with your pup and you will have a loyal friend for life.

FACT German Shepherds are very focused on their human and that emotional attachment may grow to become one of the most important aspects of your life – and certainly his.

Where Should the Puppy Sleep?

Where do you want your new puppy to sleep? In the beginning, you cannot simply allow a pup to wander freely around the house. Ideally, he will be in a contained area, such as a pen or crate, at night. While it is not acceptable to shut a dog in a cage all day, you can keep your puppy in a crate at night until housetrained. Some adult dogs still prefer to sleep in a crate.

You also have to consider whether you want the pup to permanently sleep in your bedroom or elsewhere. If it's the bedroom, don't let him jump on and off beds or couches, or race up and down stairs until he has stopped growing, as this can cause joint damage.

 Some breeders recommend putting the puppy in a crate (or similar) next to your bed for the first two or three nights before moving him to the permanent sleeping place. Knowing you are close and being able to smell you will help overcome initial fears.

He may still cry when you move him further away or out of your bedroom, but that should soon stop - you just have to block your ears for a couple of nights! He will have had those few days to get used to his new surroundings and feeling safe with you.

Eight or nine-week-old puppies can't go through the night without needing to pee (and sometimes poo); their bodies simply aren't up to it. To speed up housetraining, consider getting up in the night from Day One for the first week or so to let your pup outside for a pee. Just pick him up, take him outside with the minimum of fuss, praise the pee and put him back into the crate. After that, set your alarm for an early morning wake-up call.

NOTE: While I and many breeders recommend getting up in the night in the beginning, a few breeders are against it, as they don't believe it speeds up housetraining. Ask your own breeder's advice on this one.

We don't recommend letting a new pup sleep on the bed. He will not be housetrained and also a puppy needs to learn his place in the household and have his own special place. It's up to you whether to let him on the bed or not when he's older, but my advice is: if you value a good night's sleep, don't!

If you do allow your dog to sleep in the bedroom but not on the bed, be aware that it is not unusual for some to snuffle, snore, fart and - if not in a crate - pad around the bedroom in the middle of the night and come up to the bed to check you are still there - or see if you want to play! None of this is conducive to a good night's sleep.

While it is not good to leave a dog alone all day, it is also not healthy to spend 24 hours a day together, as a dog can become too dependent. While this is very flattering for you, it actually means that the dog is nervous and less sure of himself when you are not there. The last thing you want on your hands is an anxious German Shepherd.

A German Shepherd puppy used to being on his own every night is less likely to develop attachment issues, so consider this when deciding where he should sleep.

....

Breeders' Advice for New Owners

We asked a number of German Shepherd breeders what essential advice they would give to new owners and this is what they said, starting in the US with **Marie:** "Don't overload the puppy with new people or places.

"Let the puppy settle in their new environment with their family before introducing new dogs, people or places. Proper socialization is not meeting new dogs or people. It is learning to ignore new dogs and people when in public, and focusing attention on their handler.

"Also, puppies should be kept lean while growing. You should just be able to see their ribs. Carrying excess weight can promote Hip Dysplasia and joint issues. Limit exercise, jumping and stairs while growing to protect their joints.

Jacqueline Levy tells new owners: "We register all of our dogs and litters with the American Kennel Club, and recommend you register your puppy to you with the AKC."

Photo courtesy of Jacqueline.

"The benefits of registration include a month of free pet insurance and a veterinary visit with a doctor that is in the AKC network. The AKC also provides additional services for registered dog owners, club activities and for the welfare of dogs in general. We recommend getting your pet microchipped, and the AKC Reunite program offers registration of that chip for a one-time fee and hassle-free service."

Donna Bonney, of Hirten Bray Hugel, New York State, adds: "Puppies are learning all new things and don't understand everything just yet. They will need to learn boundaries, what is acceptable behaviour, etc. All my pup families get an AKC puppy packet which has a downloadable puppy handbook, list of dangerous household products and much more."

Tammey Tilton, Tiltonhaus German Shepherds, Washington State, says: "Build a bond with your puppy! Spend quality time with your puppy every day. Take your puppy on short walks, but don't jog with your German Shepherd puppy until it is over a year old.

"Play fun games with your puppy and get him or her into a puppy class and start obedience training. You'll be amazed how quickly your puppy will catch on and it will build a stronger bond between you and your puppy. If you love and bond with your puppy he will love and bond with you.

"Socializing your puppy should also be at the very top of the list of goals for your puppy. This will make a happy well-adjusted dog, I would recommend exposing your puppy to as many different experiences as possible, while protecting against traumatic experiences.

"Do your best to make meeting people and other dogs, going to new places, seeing and touching new things all good experiences for your puppy. If you will take the time to socialize your puppy early on I believe you will not regret it. You will up with a dog that is friendly, well-tempered and a joy to be around.

"To help you puppy have a better chance of not developing hip and elbow problems, do not over-feed your puppy. If you allow your puppy to become overweight, it will be at much higher risk of developing hip and elbow problems and, subsequently, arthritis as well.

"Avoid activities that require your puppy to jump or suddenly change direction or stop, and do not do a lot of running with your puppy or really long walks until he or she is a year old, as these are also very hard on a young puppy's joints."

UK breeder Carolyn Day, of Carjaylyn German Shepherds, agrees: "Make sure that the puppy does not over-exercise, jump up or down objects, or climb chairs, so that they have the best possible hip and elbow development for the first year.

"Also, make sure your garden is safely fenced so you can begin toilet training and lead training prior to the completion of vaccinations. And give your puppy enough time and space to settle in."

Cheryl Spurr, Reinglen German Shepherds, West Yorkshire, says: "My first piece of advice is: It's a dog, not a baby! *Photo courtesy of Cheryl.*

"The biggest danger to new puppies is the amount of exercise people want to give them. The recommended amount of exercise for a German Shepherd puppy is five minutes of enforced exercise per month of age twice a day, maximum. That does not include running on their own.

"They will stop doing that when they are tired, but they will keep playing with you or walking with you for as long as you want them to. So, you have to be the sensible one and stop them doing too much. And no jumping on or off high furniture."

Wendy Sharp, Sharphouse's German Shepherds, Kent, says: "Don't exercise too much. Give them plenty of company, but do leave them alone in their crate or bed for short periods, so they have down-time when they need to be alone - even if you are in the next room. And don't change the food on arrival home; the breeder should supply some of the food they have been eating.

Worcestershire breeders **Teresa and Tony Mapp** add: "If you don't want it chewed, don't leave it lying around! Beware of wires. Pups will tend to go around the back of the sofa (or somewhere hidden) for a sleep and when they wake, a trailing wire can be very tempting!

"We always give a list of poisons, including chocolate, raisins and grapes, garlic and onions, Ibuprofen, azaleas, foxgloves and several other plants. There are also some common things that many people don't realise can be fatal to a dog, even in small doses.

"A bad dog is not born it's made - you will get out what you put in. And they are so worth it!"

Vaccinations and Worming

It is a good idea to have your German Shepherd checked out by a vet soon after picking him up. In fact, some Puppy Contracts stipulate that the dog should be examined by a vet once he has settled in and within a few days.

This is to everyone's benefit and, all being well, you are safe in the knowledge that your puppy is healthy, at least at the time of purchase. Keep your pup on your lap away from other dogs in the waiting room as he will not yet be fully protected against canine diseases.

Vaccinations

All puppies need immunisation and currently the most common way of doing this is by vaccination. An unimmunised puppy is at risk every time he meets other dogs as he has no protection against potentially fatal diseases – and it is unlikely a pet insurer will cover an unvaccinated dog.

It should be stressed that vaccinations are generally quite safe and side effects are uncommon. If your German Shepherd is unlucky enough to be one of the *very few* that suffer an adverse reaction, here are some signs to look out for; a pup may exhibit one or more of these:

MILD REACTION - Sleepiness, irritability and not wanting to be touched. Sore or a small lump at the place where he was injected. Nasal discharge or sneezing. Puffy face and ears.

SEVERE REACTION - Anaphylactic shock. A sudden and quick reaction, usually before leaving the vet's, which causes breathing difficulties. Vomiting, diarrhoea, staggering and seizures.

A severe reaction is rare. There is a far greater risk of your German Shepherd either being ill and/or spreading disease if he does not have the injections.

The usual schedule is for the pup to have the first vaccination at eight or nine weeks of age, usually before leaving the breeder. This gives protection from a number of diseases in one shot.

In the UK these are Distemper, Canine Parvovirus (Parvo), Infectious Canine Hepatitis (Adenovirus) and Leptospirosis. Most vets also recommend vaccinating against Kennel Cough (Bordetella). In the US this is known as DHPP. Puppies in the US also need vaccinating separately against Rabies. There are optional vaccinations for Coronavirus and - depending on where you live and if your dog is regularly around woods or forests - Lyme Disease.

A puppy requires a second vaccination two to four weeks later. He is clear to mix with other animals two weeks after the second vaccinations.

- ❖ Boosters for Distemper, Parvo and Canine Hepatitis are every three years
- ❖ Boosters for Leptospirosis are every year

Leptospirosis is a bacterial infection that attacks the body's nervous system and organs. It is spread through infected rat pee and contaminated water, so dogs are at risk if they swim in or drink from stagnant water or canals. Outbreaks can often happen after flooding.

Diseases such as Parvo and Kennel Cough are highly contagious and you should not let your new arrival mix with other dogs - unless they are your own and have already been vaccinated - until two weeks after his last vaccination, otherwise he will not be fully immunised. Parvovirus can also be transmitted by fox faeces.

The vaccination schedule for the US is different, depending on which area you live in and what diseases are present. Full details can be found by typing *"AKC puppy shots"* into Google, which will take you to this page: www.akc.org/content/health/articles/puppy-shots-complete-guide

US breeder **Jacqueline Levy,** of Crosskeys K9, New Jersey, has this advice for her new owners: "Your puppy has been examined by our veterinarian and received routine de-worming bi-weekly, and the first and second set of vaccinations. We recommend the next vaccinations at 16 weeks. Your veterinarian will provide you with a schedule for future deworming (including heartworm), boosters/vaccinations and the rabies shot, which should be given after 16 weeks and/or as mandated by the laws in your state and area."

Avoid take your new puppy to places where unvaccinated dogs might have been, like the local park. This does not mean that your puppy should be isolated - far from it. This is an important time for socialisation. It is OK for the puppy to mix with other dogs that you 100% know are up-to-date with their vaccinations and annual boosters. Perhaps invite a friend's dog round to play in your yard/garden to begin the socialisation process.

Once your puppy is fully immunised, you have a window of a few weeks when it's the best time to introduce him to as many new experiences as possible - dogs, people, traffic, noises, other animals, etc. This critical period before the age of four and a half to five months is when he is at his most receptive to socialisation. It is important that all of the experiences are **positive** at this stage of life; don't frighten or over-face your little puppy. Socialisation should not stop after a few months, but should continue for the rest of your dog's life.

The vet should give you a record card or send you a reminder when a booster is due, but it's also a good idea to keep a note of the date in your diary. Tests have shown that the Parvovirus vaccination gives most animals at least seven years of immunity, while the Distemper jab provides immunity for at least five to seven years. In the US, many vets now recommend that you take your dog for a titer test once he has had his initial puppy vaccinations and one-year booster.

Titres (Titers in the US)

Some breeders and owners feel strongly that constantly vaccinating our dogs is having a detrimental effect on our pets' health. Many vaccinations are now effective for several years, yet some vets still recommend annual "boosters."

One alternative is titres. The thinking behind them is to avoid a dog having to have unnecessary repeat vaccinations for certain diseases as he already has enough antibodies present. Known as a VacciCheck in the UK, they are still relatively new here; they are more widespread in the USA.

To *"titre"* is to take a blood sample from a dog (or cat) to determine whether he has enough antibodies to guarantee immunity against a particular disease, usually Parvovirus, Distemper and Adenovirus (Canine Hepatitis). If so, then an annual injection is not needed. Titering is not recommended for Leptospirosis, Bordetella or Lyme Disease, as these vaccines provide only short-term protection. Many US states also require proof of a Rabies vaccination.

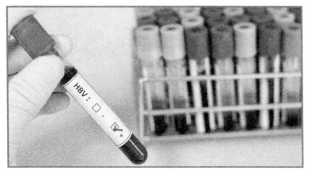

The vet can test the blood at the clinic without sending off the sample, thereby keeping costs down for the owner. A titre for Parvovirus and Distemper currently costs around $100 or less in the US, and a titre test in the UK costs as little as £40.

Titre levels are given as ratios and show how many times blood can be diluted before no antibodies are detected. So, if blood can be diluted 1,000 times and still show antibodies, the ratio would be 1:1000, which is a strong titre, while a titre of 1:2 would be "weak." A ***strong (high) titre*** means that your dog has enough antibodies to fight off that specific disease and is immune from infection. A ***weak titre*** means that you and your vet should discuss revaccination - even then your dog might have some reserve forces known as ***"memory cells"*** that will provide antibodies when needed. If you are going on holiday and taking your dog to kennels, check whether the kennel accepts titre records; many don't as yet.

One UK breeder said: "Most people don't realise that there are tests you can do to ensure that you don't over-vaccinate or over-worm your dog. It is well known that, although very rare, all vaccinations can have potential adverse reactions. These can range from mild problems such as cystitis to a severe autoimmune disease. There are also a lot of discussions going on as to whether the over-vaccination of dogs may be linked to the increased rates of cancers.

"When my puppies go to their new homes, I tell all my owners to follow their vet's advice about worming and vaccinating, as the last thing new owners require is to be at odds with their vets. However, a few owners do express concern about all the chemicals we are introducing into our puppies' lives and if they do, I explain how I try to give my dogs a chemical-free life, if possible, as adult dogs. All dogs must have their puppy vaccinations.

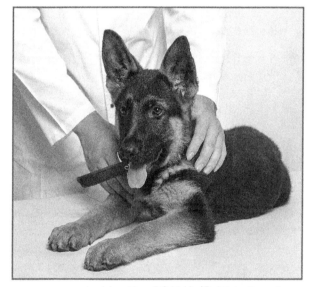

"Instead of giving my adult dogs their core vaccinations for Canine Distemper, Parvovirus and Adenovirus (Hepatitis) every three years, I just take my dogs down to the local vet and ask them to do something called a titre test, also known as a VacciCheck.

"They take a small amount of blood and send it to a lab and the lab checks for antibodies to the diseases. If they have antibodies to the diseases, there is no reason to give dogs a vaccination. If a puppy has its puppy vaccinations, it is now thought that the minimum duration of immunity is between seven and 15 years.

"However, you should note that there is a separate vaccination for Leptospirosis and Canine Parainfluenza, which is given annually. Leptospirosis is recommended by the BSAVA (British Small Animal Veterinary Association). Leptospirosis is more common in tropical areas of the world and not that common in England. In order to make a decision about whether to give this to your dog annually, you need to talk to your vet and do some research yourself so you can make an informed decision. It may be that Leptospirosis is a problem in your area.

"We vaccinate our children up to about the age of 16. However, we don't vaccinate adults every one to three years, as it is deemed that the vaccinations they receive in childhood will cover them for a lifetime. This is what is being steadily proved for dogs and we are so lucky that we can titre test our dogs so we don't have to leave it to chance."

Another breeder added: "I do not vaccinate my dogs beyond the age of four to five years, I now have them titre tested. Every dog I have titre tested aged five to 10 years has been immune to the diseases vaccinated against when younger. I believe many vets over-vaccinate."

The (UK) Kennel Club now includes titre testing information into its Assured Breeder Pack, but has yet to include it under its general information on vaccines on its website. The AKC (American Kennel Club) discusses titering here: www.barkingbulletin.com/great-akc-wellness-plus-benefit or type ***"titer test Embrace Pet Insurance"*** into Google for more info.

Worming

All puppies need worming (technically, deworming). A good breeder will give the puppies their first dose of worming medication at around two weeks old, then probably again at five and eight weeks before they leave the litter – or even more often. Get the details and inform your vet exactly what treatment, if any, your pup has already had.

The main worms affecting puppies are roundworm and tapeworm. In certain areas of the US, the dreaded heartworm can also pose a risk. If you live in an affected area, discuss the right time to start heartworm medication when you visit your vet for puppy vaccinations – it's usually from a few months old.

The pill should be given every month when there is no heavy frost (frost kills mosquitos that carry the disease); giving it all year round gives the best protection. The heartworm pill is by prescription only and deworms the dog monthly for heartworm, round, hook, and whip worm.

Roundworm can be transmitted from a puppy to humans – often children - and can in severe cases cause blindness, or miscarriage in women, so it's important to keep up to date with worming.

 Worms in puppies are quite common, often picked up through their mother's milk. If you have children, get them into the habit of washing their hands after they have been in contact with the puppy – lack of hygiene is the reason why children are susceptible.

Most vets recommend worming a puppy once a month until he is six months old, and then around every two to three months. If your German Shepherd is regularly out and about running through woods and fields, it is important to stick to a regular worming schedule, as he is more likely to pick up worms than one which spends less time in new places.

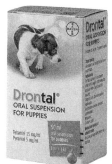 Fleas can pass on tapeworms to dogs, but a puppy would not normally be treated unless it is known for certain he has fleas - and then only with caution. You need to know the weight of your puppy and then speak to your vet about the safest treatment to get rid of the parasites.

It is not usually worth buying a cheap worming or flea treatment from a supermarket, as they are usually far less effective than more expensive vet-recommended preparations, such as Drontal. *NOTE: Buy age-appropriate worming treatments*.

Several people living in the US have contacted our website claiming the parasite treatment **Trifexis** has caused health issues in their dogs. http://www.max-the-schnauzer.com/trifexis-side-effects-in-schnauzers.html

Breeders must worm their puppies as they are all born with worms picked up from the mother's milk. However, there are ways to reduce worming treatments for adult dogs.

Following anecdotal reports of some dogs experiencing side effects with chemical wormers, more owners are looking to use natural wormers on their dogs. If you go down this route, check exactly which worms your chosen herbal preparation deals with – it may not be all of them.

A method of reducing worming medication by testing your dog's stools is becoming more popular. You send a small sample of your dog's poo(p) off in an envelope every two to three months. If the result is positive, your dog needs worming, but if negative, no treatment is necessary.

In the UK this is done by veterinary labs like Wormcount www.wormcount.com and similar options are available in the US – there is even a *"fecal worm test"* available at just over $20 from Amazon.com.

6. Crate and Housetraining

Used correctly, crates can help speed up housetraining (potty training). They also give you and your puppy short breaks from each other and keep the dog safe at night or when you are away from the house. Many adult dogs grow to love their crates. Breeders, trainers, behaviourists, and people who show, compete or train working dogs use them.

Using A Crate

A crate should always be used in a humane manner. Spend time getting your puppy or adult dog used to a crate so he comes to regard it as his own safe haven, and not a punishment cell or prison.

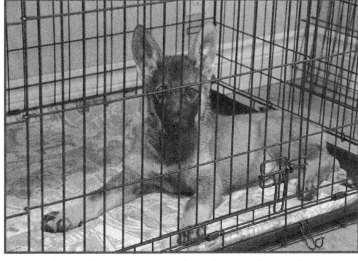

Crates may not be suitable for every dog – or owner. Dogs are social animals; they thrive on interaction. Being caged for long periods is a miserable existence for any dog, but particularly an active and athletic dog like the German Shepherd.

A crate should never be used as a means of confinement while you are out of the house for six, or eight or more hours every day. A larger kennel system is a better option if you regularly have to leave your dog for long periods.

Dogs can't sweat like humans and some German Shepherds have long, thick coats, so they can overheat. When you buy a crate for daily use, we prefer a heavy duty wire one that allows air to pass through, although some breeders like the plastic ones.

Big dogs like the GSD can suffer from joint problems if they are confined in a small space for too long. However, used properly and sparingly, a crate can become a great asset - both for you and the dog - especially when housetraining.

A couple of points to remember:

1. Always remove your dog's collar before leaving him inside when you are not there. Sadly, dogs have been known to die after panicking when their collars got caught.

2. If the door is closed, your dog must have access to water while inside. Non-spill water bowls are available from pet shops and online, as are bowls to attach to the bars.

Crates are ideal for giving you or the puppy some down time. You cannot watch a puppy 24/7 and a crate is a safe place for him while you get on with doing other things. Young puppies need lots and lots of sleep – but they are easily distracted, so a crate is a quiet, safe place where they can get some of that sleep during the day.

You first have to get him used to the crate so he looks forward to going in there - some breeders may have already started the process.

NOTE: An eight-week-old puppy should not be in a crate for longer than two hours at a time.

A crate is also an excellent way of safely confining a puppy at night. Not every owner wishes to use a crate, but used correctly they:

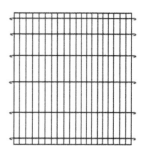

- ❧ Are a useful housetraining tool
- ❧ Create a canine den
- ❧ Give you a break
- ❧ Limit access to the rest of the house until potty trained
- ❧ Are a safe place for the dog to nap or sleep
- ❧ Provide a safe way to transport your dog in a car

Which Crate and Where?

The crate should be large enough to allow your dog to stretch out flat on his side without being cramped, and he should be able to turn around easily and sit up without hitting his head on the top.

While a small female might be fine in a 42" (107cm) crate, many adult German Shepherds need a 48" (122cm) one to be comfortable.

The bigger the crate, the higher the cost, so most owners buy just the one and use crate dividers while the pup is growing. You can buy an inexpensive adjustable crate divider *(pictured, above)*, make one yourself, or put a box inside - preferably metal or hard wood. Blocking part of it off while he's small will help him to feel safe and secure, which he won't do if he's got the whole four-foot crate to roam around in.

 Covering the crate with an old blanket is a good way of creating a den for your new puppy at night. Only cover on three sides - leave the front uncovered - and leave a gap of a few inches at the bottom of all three sides to allow air flow. During the day, many owners cover half of the crate to make it cosier for the pup.

Place the crate in the kitchen or another room where there are people during the day, preferably one with a hard, easy-to-clean floor. German Shepherd puppies are curious and like to see what is going on. If you have children, strike the balance between putting the crate somewhere where the pup won't feel isolated, yet allowing him some peace and quiet from the kids.

Avoid putting the crate in a closed utility room or garage away from everybody, or he will feel lonely and sad. If you are using a room off the kitchen, allow the pup free run of the room and use a pet gate *(pictured)* or baby gate, so he can see what's going on.

The chosen location should be draught-free, not too hot and not in bright sunshine.

If your German Shepherd is to live in the house, some breeders recommend putting the crate right next to the bed for the first night or two – even raised up next to the bed - to help the puppy settle in quicker. A few owners have even been known to sleep on the sofa or an air mattress next to the crate for the first one or two nights!

After that, you might put the crate in a place where the dog can hear or smell you during the night, e.g. the landing, or leave it in the same place downstairs all the time.

You can buy or create a puppy playpen to use as well as - or instead of - a crate.

If you have the space, put a pen around the crate to allow the puppy more freedom, or use a pet gate to block off the room where the puppy is. Put the following items inside the crate:

- ❖ Bedding – Vet Bed or other bedding your puppy won't chew in a few days
- ❖ A towel or similar item that has been rubbed with the mother's scent
- ❖ A non-spill water bowl
- ❖ A healthy chew to stop him gnawing the crate and bedding
- ❖ A toy to keep him occupied

At night, remove the water from the crate. Add an extra blanket if you think he might get cold overnight; he has been used to the warmth of his littermates and mother.

German Shepherd puppies are little chew machines so, at this stage, don't spend a lot of money on a fluffy floor covering for the crate, as it is likely to get destroyed.

The widely available "Vet Bed" is a good choice for bedding. Washable Vet Beds are widely used in vets' clinics to make dogs feel warm and secure. Made from double-strength polyester, they retain extra heat and allow air to flow though. They have drainage properties, so if your pup has an accident, he will stay dry.

Vet Beds are also a good option for older dogs, as the added heat is soothing for aging muscles and joints. You can buy "Vet Bedding" by the roll, which keeps the cost down.

 Consider putting a Snuggle Puppy in the crate with the new puppy. The Snuggle Puppy (pictured) is a safe soft toy with a heartbeat.

One UK breeder adds: "In their new home, the puppies have the heartbeat sound like they had from laying on mum. We've had really good feedback from families about the Snuggle Puppies."

Whining

If your puppy is whining or whimpering in the crate, make sure:

A. **He doesn't need the toilet.**

B. **He is warm.**

C. **He is physically unharmed.**

Then the reason he is whimpering is because he doesn't want to be alone. He has come from the warmth and security of his mother and litter, and the Brave New World can be a very daunting place for a two-month-old puppy all alone in a new home.

He is not crying because he is in a cage. He would cry if he had the freedom of the room - he is crying because he is separated. Dogs are pack animals and being alone is not a natural state for a dog.

However, with patience and the right training, he will get used to being alone and being in the crate. Many adult German Shepherds choose the crate as their favourite resting place. Some owners make the crate their dog's only bed, so he feels comfortable and safe in there. Here are more tips to help your puppy settle in his crate:

- ❧ Leave a ticking clock next to the crate

- ❧ Leave a radio on softly nearby

- ❧ Lightly spray DAP on a cloth or small towel and place in the crate

FACT ❱ DAP, or Dog Appeasing Pheromone, is a synthetic form of the pheromone that nursing German Shepherds (and other breeds) give off after giving birth and then again after weaning to reassure their puppies that everything is fine.

DAP has been found to help reduce fear in young puppies, as well as separation anxiety, phobias and aggression caused by anxiety in adult dogs. According to one French study: "DAP has no toxicities or side effects and is particularly beneficial for sick and geriatric dogs." Google *"Canadian Veterinary Journal Dog Appeasing Pheromone"* for more details of the study.

NOTE: There is also an ADAPTIL collar with slow-release DAP, which is designed to reduce fear in anxious adult dogs. It gets good reports from many, not all, owners.

UK breeder Cheryl Spurr, of Reinglen German Shepherds, West Yorkshire, adds: "I send home Adaptil collars with my puppies, it does help them to settle as long as new owner is also consistent and follows the training I start before they leave."

Whether or not you decide to use a crate, the important thing to remember is that those first few days and weeks are a critical time for your puppy. Make him feel as safe and comfortable as you can. Bond with him, while at the same time gently and gradually giving him positive experiences with new places, humans and other animals.

Travel Crates

Special travel crates are useful for the car, or for taking your dog to the vet's or a show or competition. Choose one with holes or mesh in the side to allow free movement of air rather than a solid one, in which a dog can soon overheat.

Put the crate on the shady side of the interior and make sure it can't move around; put the seatbelt around it. If it's very sunny and the top of the crate is wire mesh, cover part of it so your dog has some shade and put the windows up and the air conditioning on.

Don't leave your German Shepherd unattended in a vehicle for more than a few minutes, especially if it's hot as they can quickly overheat - or be targeted by thieves.

Alternatively, you can buy a metal grille to keep your dogs confined to the back of the car, such as the one in this *photo, courtesy of Cheryl Spurr. Pictured left to right are: Tip, Lexi and Kassi.*

Cheryl adds: "Crate training applies to travel too. Often, people get frustrated if a dog has an accident in the car, but forget to let them out before they set off. I also use a Ventlock on the car boot to keep it open slightly, allowing air to flow, if they have to be in there."

Allowing your dog to roam freely inside the car is not a safe option, particularly if you - like me – are a bit of a "lead foot" on the brake and accelerator! And try to avoid letting your German Shepherd ride with his head out of the window - even if it does look macho! Wind pressure can cause ear infections or bits of dust, insects, etc. to fly into unprotected eyes. A dog will also fly forward if you suddenly hit the brakes.

Getting your Puppy Used to a Crate

Once you've got your crate, you'll need to learn how to use it properly so that it becomes a safe, comfortable den for your dog. Many breeders will have already started the process but, if not, here's a tried-and-tested method of getting your dog firstly to accept a crate, and then to actually want to spend time in there. These are the first steps:

1. Drop a few puppy treats around and then inside the crate.

2. Put your puppy's favourite toy in there.

3. Keep the door open.

4. Feed your puppy's meals inside the crate. Again, keep the door open.

 Place a chew or treat INSIDE the crate and close the door while your puppy is OUTSIDE the crate. He will be desperate to get in there! Open the door, let him in and praise him for going in. Fasten a long-lasting chew inside the crate and leave the door open. Let your puppy wander inside to spend some time eating the chew.

5. **After a while, close the crate door and feed him some treats through the mesh.** At first just do it for a few seconds at a time, then gradually increase the time. If you do it too fast, he may become distressed.

6. **Slowly build up the amount of time he is in the crate.** For the first few days, stay in the room, then gradually leave for a short time, first one minute, then three, then 10, 30 and so on.

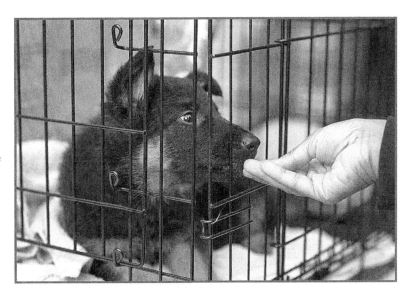

Next Steps

7. Put your dog in his crate at regular intervals during the day - maximum two hours.

8. **If your pup is not yet housetrained, make sure he has relieved himself BEFORE you put him in the crate.** Putting him in when he needs to eliminate will slow down training.

9. **Don't crate only when you are leaving the house.** Place the dog in the crate while you are home as well. Use it as a *"safe zone"* or *"quiet zone."* By using the crate both when you are home and while you are gone, your dog becomes comfortable there and not worried that you won't come back, or that you are leaving him alone. This helps to prevent separation anxiety.

10. If you are leaving your dog unattended, give him a chew and remove his collar, tags and anything else that could become caught in an opening or between the bars.

11. Make it very clear to any children that the crate is NOT a playhouse for them, but a *"special room"* for the dog.

12. Although the crate is your dog's haven and safe place, it must not be off-limits to humans. You should be able to reach inside at any time.

The next points are important:

13. Try and wait until your dog is calm before putting him in the crate. If he is behaving badly and you grab him and shove him in the crate, he will associate the crate with punishment. If you can't calm him down, try NOT to use the crate. A better option is to remove the privilege of your attention by either leaving the room or putting the dog in another room until he calms down.

14. The crate should ALWAYS be associated with a positive experience in your dog's mind.

15. Don't let your dog out of the crate when he is barking or whining, or he'll think that this is the key to opening the door. Wait until it has stopped whining for at least 10 or 20 seconds before letting him out.

 Reminder:

❧ During the day the crate door should not be closed until your pup is happy with being inside

❧ At night-time it is OK to close the door

❧ Consider keeping the pup right next to you for the first one or two nights

❧ If you don't want to use a crate, use a pet gate, section off an area inside one room, or use a puppy pen to confine your pup at night

---

Housetraining

You have four major factors in your favour when it comes to toilet training a German Shepherd:

1. They are one of the most intelligent breeds on the planet.

2. They are highly biddable (willing to learn).

3. They are extremely loyal and want to please their owners.

4. They respond well to rewards - praise, treats or toys.

Another point to remember is that Shepherds are not like companion dogs that want to be with you all the time. They were bred to work and think independently, and once they have got used to a crate, they are generally quite happy to spend some down-time in there.

Puppies naturally want to keep their space clean; it's genetic. From when he can first walk at the age of about three weeks, a pup will move away from his mother and sleeping area to eliminate.

The aim of housetraining it to teach the puppy exactly WHERE this space starts and finishes. When a puppy arrives at your home, he may think that a corner of the crate, the kitchen, or anywhere else in the house is an OK place for him to relieve himself.

Through training and vigilance, you will teach him that the house is part of his and your "space" and therefore it's not OK for him to pee or poop indoors.

Many good breeders will have already started the potty training process, so when you pick up your puppy, all you have to do is ensure that you carry on the good work!

Pictured is devoted mother Rubi with her first litter, at seven days old, courtesy of Teresa and Tony Mapp, Worcestershire, UK.

FACT ⟩ The speed and success of housetraining depends to some degree on the individual dog and how much effort the breeder has already put in. However, the single most important factor in success is undoubtedly the owner.

The more vigilant you are during the early days, the quicker your German Shepherd will be housetrained. It's as simple as that.

How much time and effort are YOU prepared to put in at the beginning to speed up housetraining? Taking the advice in this chapter and being consistent with your routines and repetitions is the quickest way to get results. Clear your schedule for a week or so and make housetraining your No.1 priority - it will be worth it.

I get complaints from some American readers when I say: "Book a week or two off work and housetrain your dog!" I know Americans get much shorter vacation time than almost anybody else, but honestly, if you can take a few days off work to monitor housetraining at the beginning, it will speed the process up no end!

If you're starting from scratch when you bring your puppy home, your new arrival thinks that the whole house is away from his sleeping quarters, and therefore a great place for a pee or a poop! And, if yours is a rescue German Shepherd, he may well have picked up some bad habits before arriving at your home.

In these cases, time, patience and vigilance are essential to teach your dog the new ways.

German Shepherds, like all dogs, are creatures of routine - not only do they like the same things happening at the same times every day, but establishing a regular routine with your dog also helps to speed up obedience and toilet training.

 To keep things simple in a pup's mind, it's a good idea to have a designated area in your garden or yard that the pup can use as a toilet. Dogs are tactile creatures, so they pick a toilet area that feels good under their paws.

Dogs often like to go on grass - but this will do nothing to improve your lawn, so think carefully about what area to encourage your puppy to use. You may want to consider a small patch of crushed gravel in your garden – but don't let the puppy eat it - or a particular corner of the garden or yard away from any attractive plants.

Many breeders advise against using newspapers or puppy pads, as they can slow down potty training. Newspapers can encourage a pup to soil inside the house. Because dogs are tactile, and puppy pads are soft and comfy - dogs like going on them! When you remove the pads, the puppy may be tempted to find a similar surface - like a carpet or rug.

A general rule of thumb is that puppies can last for one hour per month of age without urinating, sometimes a bit longer. So:

- An eight-week pup can last for two hours
- A 12-week-old pup can last for three hours
- A 16-week pup can last for four hours
- A six-month-old can last for six hours

NOTE: This only applies when the puppy is calm and relaxed.

 If a puppy is active or excited, he will urinate more often, and if he is excited to see you, he may urinate at will.

To speed up the process even more, set your alarm clock to get up in the night to let the pup out to relieve himself for the first week. You might hate it, but it will shorten the overall time spent housetraining.

....

Potty Training Tips

Follow these tips to speed up housetraining:

1. **Constant supervision** is essential for the first week or two if you are to housetrain your puppy quickly. If nobody is there, he will learn to pee or poop inside the house.

2. **Take your pup outside at the following times:**

- As soon as he wakes – every time
- Shortly after each feed
- After a drink
- When he gets excited
- After exercise or play
- Last thing at night
- Initially every hour or two - whether or not he looks like he wants to go

Photo of this puppy courtesy of Donna Bonney, Hirten Bray Hugel, New York State.

You may think that the above list is an exaggeration, but it isn't! Housetraining a pup is almost a full-time job in the beginning. If you are serious about toilet training your puppy quickly, then clear your diary for a week or two and keep your eyes firmly glued on your pup...learn to spot that expression or circling motion just before he makes a mess on your floor.

❧ Take your pup to **the same place** every time, you may need to use a lead (leash) in the beginning - or tempt him there with a treat. Some say it is better to only pick him up and dump him there in an emergency, as it is better if he learns to take himself to the chosen toilet spot. Dogs naturally develop a preference for going in the same place or on the same surface. Take or lead him to the same patch every time so he learns this is his toilet area.

3. **No pressure – be patient.** You must allow your distracted little darling time to wander around and have a good sniff before performing his duties – but do not leave him, stay around a short distance away. Unfortunately, puppies are not known for their powers of concentration, so it may take a while for him to select the perfect bathroom spot!

4. **Housetraining is reward-based.** Give praise and/or a treat IMMEDIATELY after he has performed his duties in the chosen spot. German Shepherds like to please you and love praise, and reward-based training is the most successful method for quick results.

5. **Share the responsibility.** It doesn't have to be the same person who takes the dog outside all the time. In fact, it's easier if there are a couple of you, as this is a very time-demanding business. Just make sure you stick to the same principles, command and patch of ground.

6. **Stick to the same routine.** German Shepherds understand and like routine. Sticking to the same times for meals, short exercise sessions, playtime, sleeping and toilet breaks will help to housetrain him quicker, and help him settle into his new home.

7. **Use the same word** or command when telling your puppy to go to the toilet – or while he is in the act. He will gradually associate this phrase or word with toileting and you will even be able to get him to eliminate on command after some weeks.

8. **Use your voice if you catch him in the act indoors.** A short sharp negative sound is best - **ACK! EH!** It doesn't matter, as long as it is loud enough to make him stop. Then either pick him up or run enthusiastically towards your door, calling him to the chosen place and patiently wait until he has finished what he started indoors.

Tip It is no good scolding your dog if you find a puddle or unwanted gift in the house but don't see him do it; he won't know why you are cross. And only use the negative sound if you actually CATCH HIM MID-ACT.

❧ **No punishment.** Accidents will happen at the beginning, do not punish your pup for them. He is a baby with a tiny bladder and bowels and little self-control. Housetraining takes time - it is perfectly natural to have accidents early on. Remain calm and clean up the mess with a strong-smelling cleaner to remove the odour, so he won't be tempted to use that spot again.

FACT ❱ German Shepherds have a sense of smell hundreds of times better than ours. Use a special spray from your vet or a hot solution of washing powder to completely eliminate the odour inside the house.

Smacking or rubbing his nose in it can have the opposite effect - he will become afraid to do his business in your presence and may start going secretly behind the couch or under the bed, rather than outside.

9. **Look for the signs.** These may be:

    a. Whining

    b. Sniffing the floor in a determined manner

    c. Circling and looking for a place to go

    d. Walking uncomfortably - particularly at the rear end!

    Take him outside straight away, and try not to pick him up all the time. He has to learn to walk to the door himself when he needs to go outside.

10. **Use a crate at night-time** and, for the first few nights, consider getting up four hours after you go to bed to take the pup outside, gradually increasing the time. By the age of four or five months a German Shepherd pup should be able to last through a short night – provided you let him out last thing at night and first thing in the morning. Before then, you will have a lot of early mornings!

Don't let one or two little accidents derail your potty training - accidents WILL happen! Here is a list of some possible scenarios and action to take:

❧ **Puppy peed when your back was turned** – Don't let him out of his crate or living space unless you are prepared to watch his every move

❧ **Puppy peed or pooped in the crate** - Make sure the crate isn't too big; it should be just enough for him to stand up and turn around. Also, make sure he is not left in the crate for too long

❧ **Puppy pooped without warning** - Observe what he does immediately beforehand. That way, you'll be able to scoop the pup up and take him outside next time before an accident happens

❧ **Puppy pees on the same indoor spot daily** - Make sure you clean up completely, and don't give your puppy too much indoor freedom too soon

And finally, one British breeder added this piece of advice: "If you are getting a puppy, invest in a good dressing gown and an umbrella!"

Bell Training

Bell Training is a method that works very well with some dogs. There are different types of bells, the simplest are inexpensive and widely available. They consist of a series of adjustable bells that hang on a nylon strap from the door handle *(pictured)*.

Another option is a small metal bell attached to a metal hanger that fixes low down on the wall next to the door with two screws *(pictured, overleaf)*. The technique is quite simple.

As with all puppy training, do it in short bursts of five to 10 minutes or your easily-distracted little student will switch off!

1. Show your dog the bell, either on the floor, before it is fixed anywhere or by holding it up. Point to it and give the command *"Touch," "Ring,"* or whatever word you decide.

2. Every time he touches it with his nose, reward with praise.

3. When he rings the bell with his nose, give him a treat. You can rub on something tasty, like peanut butter, to make it more interesting.

4. Take the bell away between practice sessions.

5. Once he rings the bell every time you show it to him, move on to the next step.

6. Take the bell to the door you use for housetraining. Place a treat just outside the door while he is watching. Then close the door, point to the bell and give the command.

7. When he rings the bell, open the door and let him get the treat outside.

8. When he rings the bell as soon as you place a treat outside, fix the bell to the door or wall.

9. The next time you think he needs to relieve himself, walk to the door, point to the bell and give the command. Give him a treat or praise if he rings it, let him out immediately and reward him again with enthusiastic praise when he performs his duty.

 In between training sessions, ring the bell yourself EVERY time you open the door to let him outside.

Some German Shepherds can get carried away by their own success and will ring the bell any time they want your attention, fancy a wander outdoors or see a squirrel!

Make sure that you ring the bell every time he goes out through the door to potty, but DON'T ring the bell if he is going out to play. And if he starts playing or dawdling around the garden or yard, bring him in!

....

Breeders on Crates and Housetraining

Jacqueline Levy, of CrossKeysK9, New Jersey, says: "It takes two to four weeks to potty train a German Shepherd if the client is consistent with the dog. Consistency among family members with respect to commands and routines will avoid any confusion and prevent your dog from misunderstanding.

"As soon as your puppy wakes up, put him outside. Make sure they pee and poop and then always put them outside after playing, after they wake up from a nap, 15 minutes after they eat, and before bedtime. Patience and giving the dog a ton of praise when they go outside goes a long way."

Photo of Heidi and her puppies, courtesy of Jacqueline.

"Never leave a puppy unsupervised. If the puppy has an accident, it's technically your fault, not his or hers. You cannot correct a dog that has soiled in the house if you have not caught the dog in the act. Otherwise,

the dog is being corrected for something they did and they cannot make that connection, so the correction is useless and the behaviour continues.

"The crate is a lifesaver. Crate training is very helpful at first, and then becomes a refuge for the dog. We always recommend the crate for housetraining, to give the dog its own personal space and den if the dog is overstimulated or needs to quiet down. We recommend a full-sized crate with a divider that can be adjusted as the dog grows. They need just enough room to turn around, and not enough room to sleep on one side and poop or pee in the other."

"Puppies should be crated and let out every two hours until they are housetrained. We always make the crate a happy place and not a punishment. If the dog goes into the crate, we give him a treat. When we want the dogs in their crates, we throw a treat in there and in they go."

Donna Bonney, of Hirten Bray Hugel, New York State, says: "A new puppy is usually housetrained in a few weeks. Consistency is key and NEVER use puppy pads!! I absolutely believe in crate training. My dogs all love their crates, it is their safe space. They put themselves in the crates when they just want some down time to relax. I recommend using the plastic crates, as it is more of a homey feeling, as opposed to the metal ones that remind me of a jail cell."

Marie Donahue, of Rodina Straze German Shepherds, Maryland, says: "Housetraining has a lot to do with the living conditions the puppy came from. If a puppy is raised in a dirty environment, they are harder to housetrain, because it is normal to defecate in their living space.

"Crate training is a must for any dog and will help with housetraining. I crate train all of my dogs. Crate training teaches your dog patience, and it becomes their den and safe space. It reduces stress, and keeps your dog out of trouble when you cannot supervise them. Crating a dog prevents and relieves Separation Anxiety issues, as they learn to relax when being alone."

Pictured is Marie's 2.5-year-old Adia z Rodina Straze TC, TKA, CGCA, CGCU, SPOT, BCAT, RATI, RATN

Tammey Tilton, of Tiltonhaus German Shepherds, Deer Park, Washington: "Housetraining takes anything from a few days to a couple of weeks. It will all depend on your puppy's age, personality, and your training skills. Watch for signals that your puppy may have to eliminate: panting, circling, and sniffing the ground are all possible signs.

"You should take your puppy outside to the same area each time and be patient. Say: "Go potty," when your puppy eliminates praise him and say: "Good potty." Take your puppy out first thing in the morning, 20 minutes after eating, after your puppy wakes up from naps and the last thing before going to bed. If your puppy does have an accident, do not punish him, just pick him up and take him to the place he is supposed to eliminate and say: "Go potty.""

"I believe it's best if you don't give your puppy any food after dinnertime or water an hour or two before bedtime. About half an hour before going to bed, play with your puppy to tire him out, then take him outside to eliminate. If possible, let your puppy sleep in your bedroom and place your puppy's crate close to your bed.

"If your puppy is crate-trained, you should confine him there to sleep. If your puppy is not crate-trained, you should leave his crate open and tether the puppy close to his crate, so he can go into his crate if he wants to. Keep the tether short, because puppies usually won't soil the area where they sleep."

Pictured, courtesy of Tammey, are Otto and Oakley vom Tiltonhaus, at four weeks.

"A ticking clock may help calm your puppy. Ignore any whining, as it usually will stop in 20 minutes. If your puppy continues to whine, stroke him until comforted. Do not give too much attention, as this will only reinforce the behaviour, causing more whining. If your puppy has been quiet for a few hours and suddenly starts whining, he may need to eliminate. Pick your puppy up to take him to the spot for eliminating, as this prevents accidents."

Tammey added: "I use crates. I love them and all my dogs learn to love them too. They like to spend a lot of their time in their crates of their own choosing. I leave the doors open most of the time and often find my German Shepherds relaxing in their crates. Start your puppy in the crate young and use it as a resting place. Start putting them in after they are all tired out from a busy day of play, and make it positive by feeding treats or giving them a bone to chew on. Make the time in the crate very short at first and work your way up to longer periods of time."

UK breeders give similar advice, although dogs are often crated for shorter periods in the UK, compared with the US. **Stefanie Millington,** of CunAnnun German Shepherds, Norfolk, UK, says: "When my puppies leave us, most of them are almost housetrained already. German Shepherds are probably one of the easiest dogs to housetrain, I find.

"My advice would be to take puppy out after sleep, after food, after drink and about every two hours in between. Give lots of fusses and praise once the job is done outside, and ignore and properly clean up any accidents. All my puppies are crate-trained, which is necessary, as mine are not raised in kennels. All of them love their crates as their den; a spot to call their own and to chill out. Crates are open in the daytime with access to the patio for play, toilet etc. They are only locked in their crate at night-time."

Carolyn Day, of Carjaylyn German Shepherds, Kent, says: "Normally a puppy will be housetrained by four months, but this will always depend on the time put in by the owner - getting up to open the door to the outside area where the dog can do its toileting, praising and getting the dog into a routine of walks."

Pictured is Carolyn's Ava, aged nine months.

She adds: "I do use a crate as this is a safe place for my German Shepherd and she can access it at any time. The door is always open, unless I have strangers coming, then she will have a dog biscuit and door will be shut until she has been introduced to them."

Cheryl Spurr, of Reinglen German Shepherds, West Yorkshire, says: "Most of our puppies are housetrained before they leave us at eight or nine weeks. I recommend letting them out often, each time they wake up, each time they have been fed and each time they are playing. Don't make a fuss if they have an accident. Give them a command for the toilet (I say: "Go wee!"), then praise when they have done it by saying: "Good Dog" and give a treat.

"I have crates open for my dogs all the time, so they can go in whenever they want. They usually sleep in them, but that's their choice. My tips are to always make the crate a nice place to be by feeding and having toys in there; never make it a punishment."

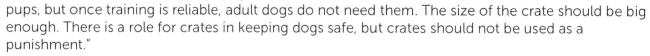

Wendy Sharp, of Sharphouse's German Shepherds, Kent, says: "Some pups have started to housetrain before they leave the breeder. Mine often know to go on newspaper or naturally want to go outside.

"Timing of garden visits are important. Do not play too much on these visits until pup has performed, then gentle play is good as a reward."

Pictured are two of Wendy's pups sheltering from the sun under the old tractor.

She added: "I do like crates for young pups, but once training is reliable, adult dogs do not need them. The size of the crate should be big enough. There is a role for crates in keeping dogs safe, but crates should not be used as a punishment."

And finally, **Teresa Mapp,** of Worcestershire, UK, says: We start housetraining at four weeks, as soon as they are out and about with the other dogs. The majority of our pups only have one or two accidents after they are homed. As soon as they wake, out for a wee; after they eat, out for a wee; after they play, out for a wee; if they have a drink, out for a wee. Persistence pays off!

"This is obviously easier when you have one pup, rather than a litter - and we have spent many hours in the rain, waiting for them all to "perform!""

She added: "When we first heard of crates, it seemed cruel, but they are havens for many dogs. Our old girl still goes in ours when the youngsters get boisterous, and the others will go in there just for a bit of quiet time. If there are children, they should be taught that this is the pup's area, then the puppy has somewhere to go when she needs to sleep. The crate should not be in direct sunlight.

"We feed our new arrival in the crate, just five to 10 minutes at first. The next feed may last 15 minutes inside the crate, then outside for a few minutes, and build up like that. They should have water at all times and a toy. We usually hide a few treats in a puppy raggy mat - that keeps them busy hunting biscuits for a good while!

"A crate can also be useful if you have a bored, destructive dog. They will be very upset if they are told off for chewing a door frame and probably not understand why you are telling them off, as they chewed it hours ago. If they are in a crate, they cannot chew it! I would not leave a dog for more than four to four-and-a-half hours at a time."

 If your breeder has already started the housetraining process, ask if he or she uses a particular phrase, such as "Go toilet!" "Pee pee!" "Wee wee!" or "Go potty!"

7. Feeding a German Shepherd

Providing the right nutritional fuel helps keep your dog's biological machine in excellent working order. And while it is important for all breeds to have a good diet, it is especially important for German Shepherds, because:

1. They are large, athletic dogs.

2. They are a working breed.

3. To develop a healthy skeleton, fast-growing GSD puppies need a well-balanced diet fed in the correct quantities.

4. Good nutrition can delay or lessen the effects of hip dysplasia and arthritis.

5. Some German Shepherds have sensitive stomachs or skin issues. The right food can help reduce or eliminate potential problems.

....

According to the National Center for Biotechnology Information (NCBI): "Rate of growth, feeding methods, feed consumption, specific nutrients, and electrolyte balances within the diet have all been shown to influence hip dysplasia." The NCBI specifically highlights rapid weight gain and too much calcium as risk factors.

The topic of feeding can be a minefield; owners are bombarded with advertisements and numerous choices. There is not one food that gives every single GSD the strongest bones, the most energy, the shiniest coat, the best digestion, the least gas and the longest life.

You could feed a high-quality food to a group of German Shepherds and find that most of them thrive on it, some do not so well, while a few might get an upset stomach or itchy skin. The question is: *"Which food is best for MY German Shepherd?"*

We do not recommend one brand of dog food over another. However, we do have lots of tips to help you choose what to feed, and several breeders share their experiences on nutrition for German Shepherds.

....

Life Stages

All puppies should stay with their mothers and littermates until at least seven or eight weeks old, to give the mother enough time to teach her offspring important rules about life. Initially, pups get all their nutrients from their mother's milk and then are gradually weaned (put on to a different food by the breeder) from three or four weeks of age.

Unless the puppy has had an extremely varied diet at the breeder's, continue feeding the same puppy food and at the same times as the breeder when you bring your puppy home. It is always a good idea to find out what the breeder feeds, as she knows what her bloodlines do well on. Later you may wish to investigate other options. If you switch foods, do so gradually, as dogs' digestive systems cannot handle sudden changes of diet. (By the way, if you stick to the identical brand, you can change flavours in one go). These ratios are recommended by Doctors Foster & Smith Inc:

- Days 1-3 add 25% of the new food
- Days 4-6 add 50%
- Days 7-9 add 75%
- Day 10 feed 100% of the new food

Feed your puppy three or four times a day up to the age of 12-16 weeks. If at any time your puppy starts being sick, has loose stools or is constipated, slow the rate at which you are switching the food. Puppies soon dehydrate, so seek veterinary advice if vomiting or diarrhoea continues for more than a day.

Some German Shepherd breeders purposely feed their pups a wide variety of different foods over the first few weeks of life to reduce the risk of them developing sensitive stomachs or becoming fussy eaters.

 If you live far away from the breeder, fill a large container with water from the breeder's house and mix it with your own water back home. Different types of water, e.g. moving from a soft to a hard water area or vice versa, can upset a sensitive pup's stomach.

The German Shepherd is a large, big-boned breed that can weigh anything from 50 to 90 pounds when fully grown. Puppies grow at an amazing rate, especially in the beginning. However, it is very important that they grow at a **controlled** rate. Giving your puppy more or less food will not affect adult size, it will only affect the rate of growth.

FACT ⟩ **If fed too much or the diet is too rich, German Shepherd puppies can actually grow TOO quickly. While they may look roly poly and very cute, it can actually be dangerous. Their bodies become larger quickly, but their skeletons don't have time to catch up. This can leave them vulnerable in later life to bone, joint, tendon and muscle problems.**

Like other large breeds, German Shepherds reach physical maturity relatively slowly, at 18 months to two years of age - although some Eastern European lines are not fully grown until three years old (and many GSDs behave like giant puppies for a lot longer)! Puppies grow very quickly for six months, followed by slower growth up to 12 months, then slower again for the next year.

There are three **Life Stages** to consider when feeding:

- Puppy
- Adult
- Senior, also called Veteran

Some manufacturers also produce a Junior feed for adolescent dogs. Each represents a different physical stage of life. If you decide on a commercially-prepared food, choose one approved either for **Puppies** or for **All Life Stages**.

While other breeds may stay on a Puppy food for up to 12 months, German Shepherds can be switched over at around six months old. This is also the time to reduce feeds from three to two a day.

An **Adult** feed won't have enough protein, and the balance of calcium and other nutrients will not be right for a pup. Puppy food is very high in calories and nutritional supplements. Some manufacturers offer foods specifically formulated for German Shepherds. They may be worth considering, but read the label first, they may be similar to general adult feeds.

NOTE: Feeding senior German Shepherds is covered in **Chapter 17. Caring for Older Shepherds.**

Photo of Rubi making sure her five-week-old pups clear their bowls, courtesy of UK hobby breeders Teresa and Tony Mapp, of Droitwich, England. They say: "When we have a litter, we feed them a bit of everything so that when owners take them home, they can feed their preference and the pups will have tried most things."

Reading Dog Food Labels

A NASA scientist would have a hard job understanding some manufacturers' labels, so it's no easy task for us lowly dog owners. Here are some things to look out for on the manufacturers' labels:

- **The ingredients are listed by weight and the top one should always be the main content,** such as chicken or lamb. Don't pick one where grain is the first ingredient; it is a poor-quality feed. If your German Shepherd has a food allergy or intolerance to wheat, check whether a food is gluten free; all wheat contains gluten

- **Chicken meal (dehydrated chicken) has more protein than fresh chicken, which is 80% water.** The same goes for beef, fish and lamb. So, if any of these "meals" are No. 1 on the ingredient list, the food should contain enough protein

- Anything labelled *"human-grade"* is higher quality than normal dog food ingredients. E.g. Human-grade chicken includes the breast, thighs and other parts of the chicken suitable for human consumption. Human-grade chicken complies with United States Department of Agriculture (USDA) welfare standards

- A certain amount of flavourings can make a food more appetising for your dog. **Choose a food with a specific flavouring,** like *"beef flavouring"* rather than a general *"meat flavouring,"* where the origins are not so clear

- Find a food suitable for the German Shepherd breed and your dog's age and activity level. Talk to your breeder or vet, or visit an online GSD forum to ask other owners' advice.

- **Natural is best.** Food labelled *'natural'* means that the ingredients have not been chemically altered, according to the FDA in the USA. However, there are no such guidelines governing foods labelled *'holistic'* – so check ingredients and how they have been prepared

- In the USA, dog food that meets American Feed Control Officials' (AAFCO) minimum nutrition requirements has a label that states: *"[food name] is formulated to meet the nutritional levels established by the AAFCO Dog Food Nutrient Profiles for [life stage(s)]"*

 If you live in the USA, we recommend looking for a food "as fed" to real pets in an AAFCO-defined feeding trial. The AAFCO label is the gold standard, and brands that do costly feeding trials indicate so on the package.

Dog food labelled *'supplemental'* isn't complete and balanced. Unless you have a specific, vet-approved need for it, it's not something you want to feed your dog long term.

The *Guaranteed Analysis* listed on a sack or tin legally guarantees:

- Minimum percentages of crude protein and crude fat, and

- Maximum percentages of crude fibre and moisture

While it is a start, don't rely on it too much. One pet food manufacturer made a mock product with a guaranteed analysis of 10% protein, 6.5% fat, 2.4% fibre, and 68% moisture (similar to what's on some canned pet food labels) – the ingredients were old leather boots, used motor oil, crushed coal and water!

- **Protein** – found in meat and poultry, protein should be the first ingredient and is very important. It helps build muscle, repair tissue and contributes to healthy hair and skin

According to the National Research Council, a growing **puppy** requires a diet with about 29% **protein.** An adult German Shepherd requires around 21%-24% protein. German Shepherds are muscular, high energy dogs and not enough will result in underdevelopment. However, protein is packed with calories and too much can lead to weight gain and increased stress on the kidneys and liver

- **Fats** – these are a concentrated form of energy that give your dog more than twice the amount of energy that carbohydrates and proteins do. Common fats include chicken or pork fat, cottonseed oil, vegetable oil, soybean oil, fish oil, safflower oil, and many more. They are highly digestible and are the first nutrients to be used by the body as energy. AAFCO recommends 8% fat for German Shepherd puppies and 5% for adults

- **Fibre** – found in vegetables and grains. It aids digestion and helps prevent anal glands from becoming impacted. The average dry dog food has 2.5%-4.5% crude fibre, but reduced-calorie feeds may be as high as 9%-10%

- **Carbohydrates** typically make up anywhere from 30%-70% of a dry dog food. They come mainly from plants and grains, and provide energy in the form of sugars

- **Vitamins and Minerals** – have a similar effect on dogs as humans. Glucosamine and chondroitin are good for joints

- **Omegas 3 and 6** – fatty acids that helps keep German Shepherds' skin and coat healthy. Also good for inflammation control, arthritic pain, heart and kidneys

Well-formulated dog foods have the right balance of protein, fat, carbohydrates, vitamins, minerals and fatty acids. If you're still not sure what to choose for your German Shepherd, check out these websites: www.dogfoodadvisor.com/best-dog-foods/german-shepherds run by Mike Sagman in the US and www.allaboutdogfood.co.uk run by UK canine nutritionist David Jackson.

How Much Food?

An adult German Shepherd needs anything from 1,300 calories to 2,100 calories a day. The correct amount of food depends on a number of factors:

- Breed
- Gender
- Age
- Natural energy levels
- Metabolism
- Amount of daily exercise
- Health
- Environment
- Number of dogs in the house or kennel
- Quality of the food
- Whether your GSD is working, competing, performing a service or simply a pet

German Shepherds were bred to work and are an active breed. However, within the breed, energy levels vary from one dog to the next, and much also depends on whether the dog is working or living in the home as a pet. Dogs that have been spayed may be more likely to put on weight, and growing puppies and young dogs need more food than senior dogs with a slower lifestyle.

Maintaining a healthy body weight for dogs – and humans – is all about balancing calories taken in with calories burned. If a dog is exercised two or three times a day, working as a service dog, competing in Schutzhund, Tracking, Agility or other events, he will certainly need more calories than a relatively inactive or older German Shepherd.

Certain health conditions, e.g. underactive thyroid, diabetes, arthritis or heart disease, can lead to dogs putting on weight, so their food has to be adjusted accordingly. And just like us, a dog kept in a very cold environment will need more calories to keep warm than a dog in a warm climate, as he burns extra calories in keeping warm.

FACT ❯ A dog kept on his own is more likely to be overweight than a dog kept with other dogs, as he receives all of the food-based attention.

Manufacturers of cheap foods may recommend feeding more than necessary, as a major ingredient is cereal, which is not doing much except bulking up the weight of the food – and possibly triggering allergies. The daily recommended amount listed on dog food sacks or tins can be too high – after all, the more your dog eats, the more they sell!

Tip There is an excellent leaflet that clearly explains each component of a dog's diet and how much to feed your dog based on weight and activity level. It can be found at: http://dels.nas.edu/resources/static-assets/banr/miscellaneous/dog_nutrition_final_fix.pdf or by searching for "Your Dog's Nutritional Needs National Academies" online.

Feeding Options

We are what we eat. The right food is a very important part of a healthy lifestyle for dogs as well as humans. Here are the main options explained:

Dry Dog Food - also called kibble, is a popular and relatively inexpensive way of providing a balanced diet. Millions of dogs thrive on kibble. It comes in a variety of flavours and with differing ingredients to suit the different stages of a dog's life. Cheap kibble is often false economy with German Shepherds.

Canned Food - another popular choice — and it's often very popular with dogs too. They love the taste and it generally comes in a variety of flavours. Some GSD owners feed kibble mixed with some canned food. These days there are hundreds of options, some are high quality, made from natural, organic ingredients with herbs and other beneficial ingredients.

As with dry food, read the label closely. Generally, you get what you pay for and the origins of cheap canned dog food are often somewhat dubious. Some GSDs can suffer from stomach upsets with too much tinned or soft food. Avoid fillers and preservatives, and brands with lots of grain or recalls.

Semi-Moist – this food typically has a water content of around 60%-65%, compared to 10% in dry food, making it easier to digest. It also has more sugar and salt, so is not suitable for some dogs. Semi-moist treats are shaped like pork chops, bacon *(pictured)*, salamis, burgers, etc. They are the least nutritional of all dog foods, full of sugars, artificial flavourings and colourings, so avoid giving them regularly.

Home-Cooked - some owners want the ability to be in complete control of their dog's diet and to know exactly what their dog is eating. Feeding a home-cooked diet to a GSD can be time-consuming and expensive. The difficult thing (as with the raw diet) is sticking to it once you have started out with the best of intentions, but your dog will love it and he won't be eating preservatives or fillers. Some high-end dog food companies now provide boxes of freshly-prepared meals with natural ingredients.

Dehydrated - this lightweight food is only minimally processed. It offers many of the benefits of raw feeding, including lots of nutrients, but with none of the mess or bacteria found in raw meats. Gentle heating slowly cooks proteins and helps start the digestive process, making it easier on the digestive tract of older German Shepherds, or those with sensitive stomachs. Owners just add water and let it stand for a minute or two to reconstitute the meal.

Freeze-Dried – this is usually raw, fresh food that has been freeze-dried by frozen food manufacturers. It's a more convenient, hygienic and less messy option than raw, and handy if you're going on a trip. It contains healthy enzymes but no preservatives. It is highly palatable and keeps for six months to a year. It says *"freeze-dried"* on the packet, but the process bumps up the cost and it is not available from every pet store — although it is widely available online. A good option for owners who can afford it.

The Raw Diet

Opinions are divided on a raw diet. There is anecdotal evidence that some dogs thrive on it, particularly those with food intolerances or allergies, although scientific proof is lagging behind. Claims made by fans of the raw diet include:

- Reduced symptoms of - or less likelihood of - allergies, and less scratching
- Better skin and coats
- Easier weight management
- Improved digestion
- Less doggie odour and flatulence
- Higher energy levels
- Reduced risk of bloat
- Helps fussy eaters
- Fresher breath and improved dental health
- Drier and less smelly stools, more like pellets
- Overall improvement in general health and less disease
- Most dogs love a raw diet

If your Shepherd is not doing well on a dry dog food, or has skin issues, you might consider a raw diet. Some commercial dog foods contain artificial preservatives, grains and excessive protein and fillers – causing a reaction in some dogs. Dry, canned and other styles of processed food were mainly created as a means of convenience – for humans, not dogs!

Some nutritionists believe there are inherent beneficial enzymes, vitamins, minerals and other qualities in meats, fruits, vegetables and grains in their natural, uncooked state.

However, critics of a raw diet say that the risks of nutritional imbalance, intestinal problems and food-borne illnesses caused by handling and feeding raw meat outweigh any benefits.

It is true that owners must pay strict attention to hygiene when preparing a raw diet and it may not be a suitable option if there are children in the household. The dog may also be more likely to ingest bacteria or parasites such as Salmonella, E. Coli and Ecchinococcus - although freeze-dried meals reduce the risk.

 **Raw is not for every dog; it can cause loose stools, upset stomach and even vomiting in some, and there are other dogs that simply don't like the taste.**

There are two main types of raw diet, one involves feeding raw, meaty bones and the other is known as the BARF diet (*Biologically Appropriate Raw Food* or *Bones And Raw Food)*, created by Dr Ian Billinghurst.

Raw Meaty Bones

The diet is:

- Raw meaty bones or carcasses form the bulk of the diet. **Cooked bones should NOT be fed, as they can splinter**
- Table scraps both cooked and raw, such as vegetables

Australian veterinarian Dr Tom Lonsdale is a leading proponent of the raw meaty bones diet. He believes the following foods are suitable:

- Chicken and turkey carcasses, after the meat has been removed for human consumption

- Poultry by-products, including heads, feet, necks and wings
- Whole fish and fish heads
- Sheep, calf, goat, and deer carcasses sawn into large pieces of meat and bone
- Other by-products, e.g. pigs' trotters, pigs' heads, sheep heads, brisket, tail and rib bones
- A certain amount of offal can be included in the diet, e.g. liver, lungs, trachea, hearts, tripe
- Table scraps and some fruit and vegetable peelings, but should not make up more than one-third of the diet

Low-fat game animals, fish and poultry are the best source of food. If you feed meat from farm animals (cattle, sheep and pigs), avoid excessive fat and bones too large to be eaten. It depends on price and what's available locally - start with your local butcher or farm shop.

FACT Dogs are more likely to break their teeth eating large knuckle bones and bones sawn lengthwise than when eating meat and bone together.

You'll also need to think about WHERE and WHEN you are going to feed. A dog takes some time to eat a raw bone and will push it around the floor, so the kitchen may not be the most hygienic place. Outside is one option, but what do you do when it's raining? If you live in a hot climate, evening feeding may be best to avoid flies.

Establishing the right quantity to feed is based on your dog's activity levels, appetite and body condition. A very approximate guide of raw meaty bones for the average dog is:

15%-20% of body weight per week, or 2%-3% a day.

So, if your GSD weighs 75lb (34kg), he requires 11¼lb-15lb (5-6.8kg) of carcasses or raw meaty bones weekly. *These figures are only a rough guide for adult dogs in a domestic environment, NOT working dogs.*

Dr Lonsdale says: "Wherever possible, feed the meat and bone ration in one large piece requiring much ripping, tearing and gnawing. This makes for contented pets with clean teeth." More information is available from www.rawmeatybones.com

NOTES: Pregnant or lactating females and growing puppies need more food. This diet may not be suitable for old dogs used to a processed diet or those with dental issues, or in households with children, due to the risk of bacterial infection from raw meat.

- Monitor your dog whilst eating, especially in the beginning
- Don't feed bones with sharp points, and remove any bone before it becomes small enough to swallow
- Raw meaty bones should be kept separate from human food and any surface the uncooked meat or bones have touched should be thoroughly cleaned afterwards

 Puppies can and do eat diets of raw meaty bones, but consult your breeder or vet before embarking on this diet with a young dog.

The BARF diet - A variation of the raw meaty bones diet is the BARF created by Dr Ian Billinghurst, who owns the registered trademark "Barf Diet."

A typical BARF diet is made up of 60%-75% of raw meaty bones - with about 50% meat, such as chicken neck, back and wings - and 25%-40% of fruit and vegetables, offal, meat, eggs or dairy foods. Bones must not be cooked or they can splinter inside the dog. There is lots of information on the BARF diet on the internet.

Top Tips for Feeding your GSD

1. If you choose a manufactured food, pick one where meat or poultry (or meat or poultry meal) is the first item listed. Most German Shepherds do not do well on foods with lots of cheap cereals or sugar.

2. Getting the right balance of protein, fats and carbohydrates is especially important with German Shepherds. Do some research into the correct balance for your dog's age, size and activity levels.

3. If you decide on a commercial kibble, choose a high quality one specially formulated for large breed dogs.

4. Some GSDs suffer from sensitive skin, 'hot spots' or allergies. A cheap food, often bulked up with grain, will only make this worse. A dry food described as *"hypoallergenic"* on the sack means *"less likely to cause allergies."*

5. Consider feeding a probiotic, such as a spoonful of natural, live yoghurt, to your GSD's meals to help maintain healthy gut bacteria.

6. Feed your adults twice a day, rather than once. Smaller feeds are easier to digest, and reduce the risk of Bloat as well as gas.

7. Establish a feeding regime and stick to it. Dogs like routine. Stick to the same times, morning and tea-time. Feeding too late won't give your dog's body time to process the food before bed. Feeding at the same times also helps your dog establish a toilet regime.

8. Take away uneaten food between meals. Most German Shepherds love their food, but any dog can become fussy if food is constantly available. Remove the bowl after 15-20 minutes – even if there is some left. A healthy, hungry dog will look forward to the next meal and should soon stop leaving food. If he's off his food for a couple of days or more, it could be a sign of illness.

9. Feeding time is a great training opportunity - particularly for the commands **SIT** and **STAY** and the release.

10. Some owners fast their German Shepherds for one day a week - check with your breeder or vet whether this is appropriate for your dog.

11. Use stainless steel or ceramic bowls. Plastic bowls don't last as long and can trigger an allergic reaction around the muzzle in some sensitive dogs. Ceramic bowls are best for keeping water cold, but can crack.

12. Don't feed too many tidbits or treats between meals. It is extremely important that GSDs have the right balance of protein and fat in their diets and treats can throw this out of the

window – and cause obesity. Feed leftovers in the bowl as part of a meal, rather than from the table, as this encourages attention-seeking behaviour, begging and drooling.

13. Use apple or carrot slices, or other healthy alternatives, as training treats for puppies.

14. Don't feed cooked bones, as these can splinter and cause choking or intestinal problems. And avoid rawhide, as a dog can gulp it without chewing, causing an internal blockage.

15. Obesity can lead to health issues, such as joint problems, diabetes, high blood pressure and heart disease, so keep your dog's weight in check. Your German Shepherd's tummy should be higher than his rib cage. If his belly is level or hangs down below it, reduce his food.

16. The following items are poisonous to dogs: grapes, raisins, chocolate, onions, Macadamia nuts, any fruits with seeds or stones, tomatoes, avocadoes, rhubarb, tea, coffee and alcohol.

17. Check your dog's faeces (aka stools, poo or poop)! If the diet is suitable, the food should be easily digested and produce dark brown, firm stools. If your dog is producing soft or light stools, lots of gas or diarrhoea, then the diet may need changing; consult your vet or breeder for advice.

18. And finally, always make sure that your dog has access to clean, fresh water. Change the water and clean the bowl every day or so – it gets slimy!

 If your dog is not responding well to a particular family member, get that person to feed the dog every day. The way to a dog's heart can often be through his stomach!

What the Breeders Feed

We asked a number of breeders what they give their dogs. This is what they said, starting with the UK breeders, who are all Kennel Club Assured Breeders:

Larry and Diane Yates, of Lornstone German Shepherds, Somerset, UK breeders with over 50 years' experience: "Our main diet for the dogs is a quality complete dried food, Dodson and Horrell, the 19% Chicken and Rice for the adults, and the Puppy/Junior 25% protein for the babies. We have used this for nearly 15 years and have tried other brands, but always returned to this one.

"However, we do use a whole variety of different foods, which we either add to or replace their usual daily food. In the majority of cases, we only feed six days per week. *This obviously depends on the condition of each individual dog, i.e. puppies, in-whelp or post-natal females are not fasted.*

"All our dogs get a weekly treat of an oily fish, hard-boiled eggs complete with shells (we keep chickens), raw chicken wings, necks or feet. All dogs get marrow bones - never roast bones! At least once a week we make and feed a stew using vegetable waste, potato peelings, greens etc. and add rice, pasta, barley.

"We honestly believe that this wide variety of foods has meant that we have never had a dog with any food intolerances, which we see on a regular basis with animals in our boarding kennel."

Stefanie Millington, of CunAnnun German Shepherds, Norfolk, UK, has more than 40 years' experience with the breed. She says: "There is a lot happening with allergies - not only in dogs, but also in humans. I believe it's down to increased "artificial" nutrition and living. Artificial, processed food that humans feed themselves and their animals cannot be healthy on a long-term basis. I suffer from Crohn's disease, which I have kept under control for over 30 years by eating healthy and fresh foods.

"My dogs are fed natural, mainly BARF; a lot of bones, carcasses, fruit, veg - all preferably raw - a bit of dairy, yoghurt, cheese, goat's milk. Once a week, I supplement this with a steamed/dried high meat content semi-moist kibble, Platinum Dog Food, which I also use as weaning food for my puppies to start them off. For training treats I use home-dried offal, lungs, heart, liver and kidneys, sliced thinly and dried for approximately five hours at around 90°centigrade in the oven. I use lots of fresh bones of mixed variety as toothbrushes. I also supplement with cod liver oil and kelp.

"I have never had a dog suffer from any allergies or stomach issues. Having said that, mine are out and about all day, running in the yard, garden and around the property, and some of them in the night as well, with access to their beds inside.

"In general, there are a lot of stomach issues within the breed and I know of some large show kennels where dogs suffer a lot of stomach issues: colitis, bloat, etc. I believe this is due to being locked up in kennels 23 hours out of 24 and fed on cheap grain-rich diets without proper nutrition."

Wendy Sharp has bred Sharphouse's German Shepherds, in Kent, for 15 years and says: "I feed a muesli-type food and the dogs thrive on it. It is a mix of biscuit and flakes of grain... it is not strictly a kibble food, it's less boring than kibble, and more for working dogs.

"It has no pretty different-coloured biscuits, it's just plain and simple. I add a little warm water to it with perhaps a little tinned dog meat mixed in. They eat it well and it doesn't cost a fortune. I have always used Puppy Royal Canin for litters up till they are a year old, as I think that it is good for fast-growing large breeds. This is just my way of feeding. My dogs have lots of energy, good coats and are full of beans. They're very happy, thriving bright-eyed dogs.

"Janet *(pictured, right, with Quinn)* has passed her test to be a PAT (therapy) dog and one of the stipulations is that they are not fed raw food.

"A lot of people try to make me change to raw food to feed a more natural diet, but I think the complete dog foods are made to suit the dietary requirements of dogs through years of development and research. So why do we think that giving them a bowl of raw food we've made up ourselves is as balanced a diet as the complete food made up by expert nutritionists?

"There are a lot of strong opinions on raw feeding and I think you have to do what suits your dog and lifestyle. Like anything, you have to decide for yourself and not go with the fashion."

Hobby breeders Teresa and Tony Map, of Worcestershire, UK, have bred five litters in their home over the last eight years. Teresa says: "We feed our dogs two meals a day; JWB complete with a little tinned food mixed in for variety. The food is all balanced and easy. We did try BARF and a couple of the dogs found this too rich - it upset their tummies.

"To be balanced nutritionally, they should have fresh raw vegetables and prepping this and the meat is much more time-consuming. Dogs who eat BARF should be wormed more regularly."

Carolyn Day, of Carjaylyn German Shepherds, Kent, has bred Tibetan Terriers for 20 years and German Shepherds for three. She says: "My German Shepherd is fed dry food and working dog chicken and vegetable. At times, she has had a raw diet or cooked dog food, but she regurgitated food and her poop was very loose on raw.

"I find the dry food nutritious, she has firm poop, and a healthy coat and teeth. Also, because the food is dry, it can be left down so she can graze. There are less flies, so worming is effective."

Cheryl Spurr, of Reinglen German Shepherds, West Yorkshire, has owned German Shepherds for 30 years and bred them for seven. She says: "All my dogs are raw-fed, apart from one. Feeding a more natural diet is something I have always been interested in. I prefer the raw diet; my dogs look amazing on it. I do have a utility room where I feed, but before that it was just in the kitchen, unless they were having something messy, when they would be fed outside.

"They are fed on chicken carcass, rabbit, lamb bones, beef bones, fish, mince (chicken, beef, duck, lamb, boar), beef heart, lungs, other offal, green tripe, eggs, veg. I have a separate freezer for the dogs' food and a separate fridge where I defrost it. It is much cheaper than kibble and cheaper than complete raw food, as I do it myself. I think as long as you keep the bowls and feeding area clean, there should be no problems - the biggest problem is the smell of the tripe!"

Here are comments from American breeders, starting with **Jacqueline Levy, of Cross Keys K9, New Jersey:** "Our philosophy is **kibble plus.** We feed kibble as the mainstay of the diet and supplement with fresh-cooked chicken or beef, turkey, eggs, oatmeal, pumpkin, and canned fish like sardines. We do not follow a raw diet or BARF diet. Our dogs donate blood and they can't do it if they are on a raw diet.

"Some of our dogs are on a raw diet in their new homes and, according to our clients, they are often leaner and shed less because of it. My husband and I had cancer, so we have compromised immune systems, and safe handling of food is a must. Raw food would increase our susceptibility, so we don't bother with it. However, I do like raw freeze-dried food like Ziwipeak. It has all the benefits of raw food without the issues of safe handling and raw food problems like listeria, E. coli, etc."

Jacqueline also has this advice for her new puppy owners: "Your puppy should eat at least two times a day, preferably a food that does not contain artificial preservatives, animal by-products, artificial colors and nutrient-poor fillers. For this reason, we do not recommend most mass-market commercial dog foods. We recommend Honest Kitchen and Diamond Naturals Chicken and Rice (the one we use the most), or another premium quality dog food.

"Beware of giving your German Shepherd puppy too much calcium while he grows up, as too much calcium can contribute to bone and joint problems. The calcium to phosphorus ratio is one of the key factors to maintaining an even, steady growth of your dog and should be 1:1."

Marie Donahue, of Rodina Straze German Shepherds, Maryland, breeds DDR and Czech working dogs using the Puppy Culture Programme and says: "I feed a dry, balanced kibble called Inukshuk, it's from a family-owned company in Canada. My dogs do very well on it and it is easy to bring while traveling and competing. I also supplement with K9 Cravings raw and Nuvet supplements."

Donna Bonney, of Hirten Bray Hugel, New York State: "I am currently feeding Taste of the Wild Ancient Grains with Lamb. It's just about the only dog food without chicken that wasn't going to break the bank – and it's had no recalls either. I would love to feed raw, however, it is very expensive here and I do not have the time."

Tammey Tilton, of Tiltonhaus German Shepherds, Washington State, has been surrounded by German Shepherds all her life and bred them for 10.

She says: "For my adult dogs I switch between Victor Nutra Pro and Victor Hi-Pro Plus; it has never had a recall. I also feed Olewo Beets and Carrots for healthy skin and coat. It helps to prevent allergies, is a natural dewormer, aids immune system health, it's a quick cure for diarrhea - and much more. It comes from Germany, the website is www.olewousa.com "

"I also feed one teaspoon of organic coconut oil for skin and coat health - it must be virgin cold press - and we buy it at Costco. One teaspoon of Life Line Wild Alaskan Salmon Oil, which is Nature's perfect source of DHA for brain, eye and heart health. It also reduces excessive shedding by replenishing moisture in an animal's skin to prevent flaking.

"One teaspoon of Life Line Certified 100% Organic Icelandic Ocean Kelp, which promotes dental, skin and coat health, increases circulation, helps with arthritis pain and reduces joint inflammation, supports the immune system to fight off disease and allergies, helps maintain their thyroid to keep them at a healthy weight, increases their stamina and endurance and much more!"

Pictured enjoying a dip is Tammey's seven-month-old Annie from Ursi CGS, Spot-On.

"Also, one tablespoon of organic food grade Diatomaceous Earth. This supports their immune system and is an organic alternative for fleas, ticks and parasite control and natural de-wormer. You can buy at Northwest Seed and Pet. We mix this all together and give to our adult dogs every morning!

"These are some of the toppers I add to my dog food (I change it each day): raw turkey neck chopped into five pieces, raw hamburger, raw beef heart, chicken and beef liver, raw chicken, beef tripe, chicken gizzards, canned mackerel, organic bone broth, Greek plain yogurt, goat milk, raw eggs raw apple cider, blueberries, cottage cheese, sea meal and raw honey are just a few of the things.

"I buy bully sticks and give to my dogs once a week, or I give them a raw beef marrow bone. For treats, I mix all these together and put in treat bag: Earthborn Holistic Large Breed Dog Food (the pieces are bigger than Victor dog food, so they work good for treats), Happy Howie's Gourmet Meat Rolls, carrots, string cheese, cooked chicken (all cut into bite-size pieces). I also cut back on their dog food when I'm using treats."

....

Food Allergies

Dog food allergies are a reaction to food that involves the body's immune system and affect about one in 10 dogs. They are the third most common canine allergy after atopy (inhaled or contact allergies) and flea bite allergies. While there's no scientific data as yet, reports from breeders and owners suggest that some German Shepherds can have adverse reactions to certain foods.

Food allergies affect males and females in equal measure as well as neutered and intact pets. They can start when your dog is five months or 12 years old - although the vast majority start when the dog is between two and six years old. It is not uncommon for dogs with food allergies to also have other types of allergies.

 Two of the breeders involved in this book have come across food allergies, and there is anecdotal evidence that chicken does not agree with all Shepherds.

If your dog is not well, how do you know if the problem lies with his food or not? Here are some common symptoms to look out for:

- Itchy skin (this is the most common). Your dog may lick or chew his paws or legs and rub his face with his paws or on the furniture, carpet, etc.

- Excessive scratching or shedding

- Ear infections

- Hot patches of skin – *"hot spots"*

- Hair loss

- Redness and inflammation on the chin and face

- Recurring skin infections

- Increased bowel movements (maybe twice as often as usual)

- Skin or ear infections that clear up with antibiotics but recur when the antibiotics run out

The problem with food allergies is that the symptoms are similar to symptoms of other issues, such as environmental or flea bite allergies, intestinal problems, mange and yeast or bacterial infections. There's also a difference between dog food *allergies* and dog food *intolerance*:

ALLERGIES = SKIN PROBLEMS AND/OR ITCHING

INTOLERANCE = DIARRHOEA AND/OR VOMITING

Dog food intolerance can be compared to people who get an upset stomach from eating spicy curries. Symptoms can be cured by changing to a milder diet. With dogs, certain ingredients are more likely to cause a reaction than others. In order of the most common triggers across the canine world in general, they are:

- Beef

- Dairy products

- Chicken

- Wheat

- Eggs

- Corn

- Soy (soya in the UK)

Unfortunately, these are also the most common ingredients in dog foods!

It is also worth noting that a dog is allergic or sensitive to an ingredient, not to a particular brand of dog food, so it is very important to read the label on the sack or tin. If your German Shepherd has a reaction to beef, for example, he will react to any food containing beef, regardless of how expensive it is or how well it has been prepared.

AVOID corn, corn meal, corn gluten meal, artificial preservatives (including BHA, BHT, Propyl Gallate, Ethoxyquin, Sodium Nitrite/Nitrate and TBHQBHA), artificial colours, sugars and sweeteners, e.g. corn syrup, sucrose and ammoniated glycyrrhizin, powdered cellulose, propylene glycol.

Food Trials

The only way to completely cure a food allergy or intolerance is complete avoidance. This is not as easy as it sounds. First you have to determine your dog DOES have an allergy to food - and not pollen, grass, etc. - and then you have to discover WHICH food is causing the reaction.

Blood tests are nowadays not thought to be reliable. Most people soldier on with trial and error, trying to eliminate certain foods and add others.

As far as I am aware, the only true way to determine exactly what your dog is allergic to, is to start a **food trial or exclusion diet.** This involves feeding one specific food for 12 weeks, something the dog has never eaten before.

Before you embark on one, you should know that food trials are a real pain-in-the-you-know-what. You have to be incredibly vigilant and determined, so only start one if you are prepared to see it through to the end, or you are wasting your time. The chosen food must be the **only thing** eaten during the trial. During the trial, your dog shouldn't roam freely, as you can't control what (s)he is eating or drinking when out of sight. Don't give:

* Treats
* Rawhide (not recommended anyway)
* Pigs' ears
* Cows' hooves
* Flavoured medications (including heartworm treatments) or supplements
* Flavoured toothpastes
* Flavoured plastic toys

A more practical, less scientific approach is to eliminate ingredients one at a time by switching diets over a period of a week or so. If you switch to home-cooked or raw, you know exactly what your dog is eating; if you choose a commercial food, a *hypoallergenic* one is a good place to start. These feeds all have the word *'hypoallergenic'* in the name and do not include wheat protein or soya. They are often based around less common ingredients like venison, duck or fish.

Grain Intolerance

Although beef is the food most likely to cause allergies in the general dog population, there is plenty of anecdotal evidence to suggest that GRAIN can also be a problem. *"Grain"* is wheat or any other cultivated cereal crop. Some dogs also react to starch, which is found in grains and potatoes, as well as bread, pasta rice, etc.

Some breeds can be prone to a build-up of yeast in the digestive system. Foods high in grains and sugar can cause an increase in unhealthy bacteria and yeast in the stomach. This crowds out the good bacteria allowing toxins to affect the immune system.

When this happens, the itchiness related to food allergies can cause secondary bacterial and yeast infections. These may show as hot spots, ear or bladder infections, excessive shedding, reddish or dark brown tear stains. You may also notice a musty smell, skin lesions or redness on the underside of the neck, belly or paws.

 Drugs like antihistamines and steroids will help temporarily, but they do not address the root cause.

Before you automatically switch to a grain-free diet, you should know that a recent study by University of California, Davis, vets found a link between a form of heart disease called taurine-deficient dilated cardiomyopathy and some popular grain-free dog foods where legumes (e.g. beans, lentil, peas, soy) or potatoes were the main ingredients.

Lead author Joshua Stern spoke of the importance of choosing: "A well-researched dog food that has a healthy nutrient profile backed by expert formulation and research is of paramount importance." He added that while many owners may not want to see *"by products"* listed in their dog's food, they often contain organ meat like heart and kidney, which are good sources of taurine.

Some of the symptoms of food allergies - particularly the scratching, licking, chewing and redness - can also be a sign of environmental allergies, caused by a reaction to pollen, grass, dust, etc. Some dogs are also allergic to flea bites. See **Chapter 13. Skin and Allergies** for more details.

 If you suspect your dog has a food problem and you've switched diet to little effect, it's time to see a vet. But remember that drugs only mask the problem and some vets promote specific brands of dog food, which may or may not be the best option for your German Shepherd. Do your research.

....

Bloat

Bloat occurs when there is too much gas in the stomach. It is known by several different names: *twisted stomach, gastric torsion* or *Gastric Dilatation-Volvulus (GDV)* and occurs mainly in larger breeds, particularly those with deep chests like the German Shepherd.

It is statistically more common in males than in females and in dogs over seven years old.

As the stomach swells with gas, it can rotate 90° to 360°. The twisting stomach traps air, food and water inside and the bloated organ stops blood flowing properly to veins in the abdomen, leading to low blood pressure, shock and even damage to internal organs. Canine Bloat is a serious medical condition that requires urgent attention. Without it, the dog can die. In fact, it is one of the leading killers of dogs after cancer.

The causes are not fully understood, but there are some well-known risk factors. One is the dog taking in a lot of air while eating - either because he is greedy and gulping the food too fast, or stressed, e.g. in kennels where there might be food competition. A dog that is fed once a day and gorges himself could be at higher risk, which is one reason why some owners feed twice a day.

Exercising straight after eating or after a big drink increases the risk - like colic in horses.

Another potential cause is diet. Fermentable foodstuffs that produce a lot of gas can cause problems for the stomach if the gas is not burped or passed into the intestines.

Symptoms

- Swollen belly
- Standing uncomfortably or hunched
- Restlessness, pacing or looking for a place to hide
- Rapid panting or difficulty breathing
- Dry retching, or excessive saliva or foam
- White or colourless gums
- Excessive drinking
- Licking the air
- General weakness or collapse

Tips to Avoid Canine Bloat

- Some owners buy a frame for food bowls so they are at chest height for the dog, other experts believe dogs should be fed from the floor – do whichever slows your GSD down
- Buy a bowl with nobbles *(pictured, above)* and moisten your dog's dry food – both of these will slow down a gulper
- Feed twice a day rather than once
- Avoid dog food with high fats or those using citric acid as a preservative, also avoid tiny pieces of kibble
- Don't let your dog drink too much water just before, during or after eating
- Stress can possibly be a trigger, with nervous and aggressive dogs being more susceptible. Maintain a peaceful environment, particularly around his mealtimes
- Avoid vigorous exercise before or after eating, allow one hour either side of mealtimes before strenuous exercise

Bloat can kill a dog in less than one hour. If you suspect your German Shepherd has Bloat, get him into the car and off to the vet IMMEDIATELY. Even with treatment, mortality rates range from 10% to 60%. With surgery, this drops to 15% to 33%.

Overweight Dogs

It is far easier to regulate your dog's weight and keep it at a healthy level than to try and slim down a voraciously hungry German Shepherd when he becomes overweight. According to James Howie, Veterinary Advisor to Lintbells, overweight and obese dogs are susceptible to a range of illnesses, including:

Joint disease – excessive body weight may increase joint stress, which is a risk factor in joint degeneration (arthrosis), as is cruciate disease (knee ligament rupture). Joint disease tends to lead to a reduction in exercise that then increases the likelihood of weight gain, further reducing exercise. A vicious cycle is created. Overfeeding young, growing German Shepherds can lead to various problems, including the worsening of hip dysplasia.

Heart and lung problems – fatty deposits within the chest cavity and excessive circulating fat play important roles in the development of cardio-respiratory and cardiovascular disease.

Diabetes – resistance to insulin has been shown to occur in overweight dogs, leading to a greater risk of diabetes mellitus.

Tumours – obesity increases the risk of mammary tumours in female dogs.

Liver disease – fat degeneration may result in liver insufficiency.

Exercise intolerance – this is also a common finding with overweight dogs, which can compound an obesity problem as fewer calories are burned off and are therefore stored, leading to further weight gain.

Reduced Lifespan - one of the most serious proven findings in obesity studies is that obesity in both humans and dogs reduces lifespan.

Most German Shepherds are extremely loyal companions and very attached to their humans. They are a part of our family. However, beware of going too far.

FACT ❯ Studies show that dogs regarded as "family members" by the owner (anthropomorphosis) are at greater risk of becoming overweight. This is because all the attention given to the dog often results in food being given as well.

If you have to put your dog on a diet, be aware that a reduced amount of food will also mean reduced nutrients, so he may need a supplement during this time.

 Remember that many of the problems associated with being overweight are reversible. Increasing exercise increases calories burned, which in turn reduces weight.

Looking the picture of health are Harro (left) and Lexi, owned by Cheryl Spurr, Reinglen German Shepherds, West Yorkshire, UK. Photo by Rob Spurr.

....

To Recap:

- ✓ Diet is extremely important for German Shepherds, but no one food is right for every dog; you must decide on the best for yours
- ✓ GSD puppies need the right balance of minerals in the right quantities
- ✓ The best test of a food is how well your dog is doing on it

If your German Shepherd is happy and healthy, interested in life, has lots of energy, is not too fat and not too thin, doesn't scratch a lot and has dark brown, firm stools, then...

Congratulations, you've got it right!

....

8. Traits and Behaviour

The importance of socialisation and training cannot be underestimated when it comes to German Shepherds. And in order to successfully train and build an excellent relationship with your GSD, you need to understand what makes him or her tick. This chapter helps you to do that, as well as sharing some techniques for dealing with unwanted behaviour.

....

Just as with humans, a dog's personality is made up of a combination of temperament and character.

Temperament is the nature – or inherited characteristics - a dog is born with; a predisposition to act or react to the world around her. Natural temperament is *extremely important* with Shepherds; this is where good breeders come into their own. Not only do they produce puppies from physically healthy dams and sires, but they also look at temperament and only breed from GSDs with good traits.

If you haven't got your pup yet, ask if the parents have passed a temperament test or the Good Citizen award. Also, think carefully about what type of Shepherd would best suit your lifestyle: one from working or show lines, West German, American, Eastern European lines - or a mixture? Different types of GSD have different natural temperament traits and drives.

Character is what develops through the dog's life and is formed by a combination of temperament and environment. How you treat your dog will have a huge effect on her personality and behaviour.

Start off on the right foot with your puppy by establishing the rules of the house and good routines. Treat her well and make lots of time for socialisation, training and, as her body matures, exercise.

FACT ❯ Socialisation means "learning to be part of society." With dogs, it means helping them learn to be comfortable living within human society; one that includes many different types of people, environments, buildings, sights, noises, smells, animals and other dogs.

All dogs need different environments, scents and experiences to keep them stimulated and well-balanced. German Shepherds are high-energy dogs that enjoy running free off the leash, swimming and activities which challenge their minds as well as their bodies.

The German Shepherd is a highly intelligent dog that was originally bred to work all day, to follow commands, but also be able to work independently. These tendencies are evident in today's Shepherd:

* **Herder** – they may round up whatever they consider their flock - this might include the kids, the cat or the hens! Without proper training, this herding instinct could lead to nipping or grabbing, which is what GSDs do to move sheep

- **Watchdog** - How many German Shepherds does it take to screw in a lightbulb? "One, but first she needs to check the perimeter for incursions!" Although German Shepherds' eyesight is nothing out of the ordinary, their senses of smell and hearing are phenomenal. Ever wondered why your GSD tilts her head when you are talking? Well, she really is trying to understand you! The tilt funnels the sound into her ears. GSDs are always on the alert and very conscious of any changes in their environment

- Bred to respond by barking or growling, both of these traits can become a nuisance without proper socialisation and training to teach a German Shepherd to distinguish between a threat and a non-threatening situation

- **Protector** – As well as herding sheep, the courageous Shepherd protected the flock and the family from predators such as robbers, foxes and even wolves. Although gentle with those she considers "her own," she is wary of strangers. Again, socialising and training a young Shepherd teaches her who to accept and who to be fierce with

- **Athlete** – Not only were German Shepherds bred to work all day, but they also required bursts of speed during herding - so they are canine sprinters as well as marathon runners. All of this energy needs channelling in a positive manner; a bored Shepherd can become destructive. The breed loves nothing better than having a task to do - whether taking part in canine competitions, playing games or working as a Service Dog. GSDs from working lines have especially high physical and mental drives

- **Player** – German Shepherds, and working lines in particular, also have a strong play and prey drive. They were originally trained to work for rewards and this is what they love doing.

Balls, toys, games and treats are great motivators for GSDs and excellent training tools - although the novelty may wear off after you have thrown that ball for the 50th time... You will definitely tire of the game before your Shepherd! Some have an almost obsessive love of their toy or ball, and many GSDs whine when they want to play or get over-excited; it's not a negative trait, just a quirk

One GSD owner adds: "My dog is an optimist; he always takes his Frisbee with him when he goes outside - even for his last pitstop of the evening!"

Because of the strong prey drive in some GSDs, always introduce other pets slowly and on neutral territory.

 When choosing a ball, buy one bigger than a tennis ball, or a ball on a rope. GSDs can choke on anything smaller.

Understanding Canine Emotions

As pet lovers, we are all too keen to ascribe human characteristics to our dogs; this is called *anthropomorphism* – "the attribution of human characteristics to anything other than a human being."

Most of us dog lovers are guilty of that, as we come to regard our pets as members of the family - and German Shepherds certainly regard themselves as members and guardians of the family.

An example of anthropomorphism might be that the owner of a male dog might not want to have him neutered because he will "miss sex," as a human might if he or she were no longer able to have sex. This is simply not true.

A male dog's impulse to mate is entirely governed by his hormones, not emotions. If he gets the scent of a bitch in heat, his hormones (which are just chemicals) tell him he has to mate with her. He does not stop to consider how attractive she is or whether she is *"the one"* to produce his puppies.

No, his reaction is entirely physical, he just wants to dive in there and get on with it!

It's the same with females. When they are in heat, a chemical impulse is triggered in their brain making them want to mate – with any male, they aren't at all fussy.

So, don't expect your little princess to be all coy when she is in heat, she is not waiting for Prince Charming to come along - the tramp down the road or any other scruffy pooch will do! It is entirely physical, not emotional.

Food is another issue. A dog will not stop to count the calories of a delicious treat – you have to do that. No, she is driven by food and just thinks about getting the treat. Most non-fussy eaters will eat far too much, given the opportunity.

German Shepherds are loving, incredibly loyal and extremely eager to please you, and if yours doesn't make you smile from time to time, you must have had a humour by-pass. All of this adds up to one thing: a beloved family member that is all too easy to spoil.

If your dog is kept indoors, it's fine to regard her as a member of the family - as long as you remember that she is a canine, not a human.

 Avoid treating your dog like a child. German Shepherds respond well to positive training methods and learn to respect the authority figure, which is you - not her! In the beginning, think of yourself as a kindly but firm teacher with a lively young student.

Learn to understand her mind, patiently train her be comfortable with her place in the household, teach her some manners and household rules – like not jumping up or growling at visitors - and you will be rewarded with a companion who is second to none and fits in beautifully with your family and lifestyle.

Dr Stanley Coren is well known for his work on canine psychology and behaviour. He and other researchers believe that in many ways a dog's emotional development is equivalent to that of a young child. Dr Coren says: "Researchers have now come to believe that the mind of a dog is roughly equivalent to that of a human who is two to two-and-a-half years old. This conclusion holds for most mental abilities as well as emotions.

"Thus, we can look to human research to see what we might expect of our dogs. Just like a two-year-old child, our dogs clearly have emotions, but many fewer kinds of emotions than found in adult humans. At birth, a human infant only has an emotion that we might call excitement. This indicates how excited he is, ranging from very calm up to a state of frenzy. Within the first weeks of life the excitement state comes to take on a varying positive or a negative flavour, so we can now detect the general emotions of contentment and distress.

"In the next couple of months, disgust, fear, and anger become detectable in the infant. Joy often does not appear until the infant is nearly six months of age and it is followed by the emergence of shyness or suspicion. True affection, the sort that it makes sense to use the label "love" for, does not fully emerge until nine or ten months of age."

So, our German Shepherds can truly love us – but we knew that already!

According to Dr Coren, dogs can't feel shame. So, if you are housetraining your puppy, don't expect her to feel ashamed if she makes a mess in the house, she can't; she simply isn't capable of feeling shame. But she will not like it when you ignore her when she's behaving badly, and will love it when you praise or reward her for relieving herself outdoors.

FACT ⟩ **She is simply responding to you with her simplified range of emotions.**

This anecdote from one UK Retriever breeder made us smile. She told us that when one of her dogs has done something naughty, she is sent to the bathroom for a couple of minutes, and now the dog has taken it a step further.

She said: "Our breeding chocolate "punishes" herself. If there is something she thinks she has done that will get her told off, she goes and sits in the bathroom – and you then have to hunt round the house to see if you can find what she thinks she has done!"

German Shepherds can certainly show empathy - *"the ability to understand and share the feelings of another"* – they are known for being intuitive and this is one reason why they work so well with humans. They can pick up on the mood and emotions of the owner.

One emotion that all dogs can experience is jealousy. It may display itself by being overly-protective of her humans, food or toys.

An interesting article was published in the PLOS (Public Library of Science) Journal in 2014 following an experiment into whether dogs get jealous. Building on research that shows that six-month old infants display jealousy, the scientists studied 36 dogs in their homes and videoed their actions when their owners showed affection to a realistic-looking stuffed canine *(pictured)*.

Over three-quarters of the dogs pushed or touched the owner when they interacted with the decoy. The envious mutts were more than three times as likely to do this for interactions with the stuffed dog, compared to when their owners gave their attention to other objects, including a book. Around a third tried to get between the owner and the plush toy, while a quarter of the put-upon pooches snapped at the dummy dog!

Professor Christine Harris from University of California in San Diego said: "Our study suggests not only that dogs do engage in what appear to be jealous behaviours, but also that they were seeking to break up the connection between the owner and a seeming rival."

The researchers believe that the dogs understood that the stuffed dog was real. The authors cite the fact that 86% of the dogs sniffed the toy's rear end during and after the experiment!

Professor Harris said: "We can't really speak of the dogs' subjective experiences, of course, but it looks as though they were motivated to protect an important social relationship. Many people have assumed that jealousy is a social construction of human beings - or that it's an emotion specifically tied to sexual and romantic relationships.

"Our results challenge these ideas, showing that animals besides ourselves display strong distress whenever a rival usurps a loved one's affection."

Typical German Shepherd Traits

Every dog is different, of course. But within the breed, there are some similarities. Here are some typical German Shepherd characteristics - some of them also apply to other types of dog, but put them all together and you have a blueprint for the German Shepherd.

1. German Shepherds are the most versatile dogs in the world. They have developed a unique bond with humans and are able to fulfil more roles to assist us than any other breed. They excel as loyal family pets and protectors, and as working dogs. They can be trained to a level as high or higher than any other breed. German Shepherds work as Service dogs, Search and Rescue dogs, Protection dogs, Scent dogs, Emotional Support dogs and Assistance dogs, helping a wide range of people, including the military, police, and people with physical disabilities or illnesses.

2. They are powerful, courageous and high-energy, with a lot of stamina and lively minds that need occupying. Working line dogs usually need more mental stimulation and exercise than show line or mixed line GSDs. Even if your Shepherd is a pet, she still has these natural instincts to some extent.

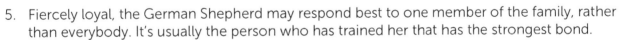

3. An under-exercised, under-stimulated German Shepherd will display poor behaviour, as any dog will.

4. This breed thrives on training and having a job to do. They also want to be involved with their owners and families. Find your dog a job or activity - or she will find one herself, and you might not like her response! A German Shepherd left alone in a house all day is a sad dog.

5. Fiercely loyal, the German Shepherd may respond best to one member of the family, rather than everybody. It's usually the person who has trained her that has the strongest bond.

6. Natural protectors, they are often wary of strangers.

7. German Shepherds are the most courageous of dogs; they will do anything for you. Don't ask your dog to do anything that would put her in danger.

8. They have an exceptionally keen sense of smell and excellent hearing. They can be trained to sniff out drugs, explosives, gas leaks, cell phones, prison contraband, bedbugs, and even hidden computer memory sticks and hard drives.

9. Once trained, German Shepherds are gentle and protective with children - although young children and dogs should always be supervised.

10. German Shepherds are eager to please their owners; they are intelligent and love rewards. They do not like rough handling or heavy-handed training.

11. The same goes for housetraining; a German Shepherd can get the hang of it in a week or two, provided you are committed in the beginning.

12. Many German Shepherds are also mentally strong. Be firm and positive when training, not nervous, as they will sense weakness and push the boundaries.

13. Young German Shepherds don't know their own strength and can be boisterous and clumsy, jumping up and knocking things over - some new owners wonder what they have let themselves in for!

14. Exercise varies from one GSD to another. Much depends on what bloodlines they come from and what they get used to as a puppy. They are, however, large, athletic dogs and the UK Kennel Club recommends two or more hours of exercise per day.

15. Most love water and are good swimmers. They have a hardy, double coat and cope well with cold water and snow. They may need air conditioning in a hot climate.

16. German Shepherds are incredibly loyal dogs that become very attached to their owners. Many GSD owners would not consider any other breed. They will steal your heart - OK, that's not very scientific, but it's true!

Cause and Effect

As you've read, when treated well, socialised and trained, German Shepherds make devoted canine companions second to none, and excellent working and competitive dogs. Once you've had one, no other dog seems quite the same. But sometimes German Shepherds, just like other breeds, can develop behaviour problems. Poor behaviour may result from a number of factors, including:

- Lack of socialisation
- Lack of training
- Poor breeding
- Boredom, due to lack of exercise or mental challenges
- Being left alone too long
- Being badly treated
- A change in living conditions
- Anxiety or insecurity
- Fear
- Being spoiled

Bad behaviour may show itself in different ways:

- Excessive barking or whining
- Growling, biting, nipping
- Aggression towards people or other dogs
- Chewing or destructive behaviour
- Snarling and lunging on the leash

- ❖ Jumping up
- ❖ Soiling or urinating inside the house
- ❖ Constantly demanding your attention

This chapter looks at some familiar behaviour problems and is geared towards German Shepherds kept as pets, rather than working dogs kennelled outside. For more information on working dogs, read **Chapters 4 and 10.**

FACT German Shepherd experts agree that the best way to avoid poor behaviour is to put in lots of time early on to socialise and train your German Shepherd, and to nip any potential problems in the bud.

If you are rehoming a Shepherd, you'll need extra time and patience to help your new arrival unlearn some bad habits.

10 Ways to Avoid Bad Behaviour

Here are some tips to help you start out on the right foot:

1. **Buy from a good breeder.** They use their expertise to match suitable breeding pairs, taking into account factors such as good temperament, health and being *"fit for function."*

2. **Start socialisation right away.** We now realise the vital role that early socialisation plays in developing a well-rounded adult dog. This is especially true of German Shepherds, as they are naturally protective and territorial. It is essential to expose your dog to other people, places, animals and experiences as soon as possible. Give her a day or so to get used to her new surroundings and then start – even if this means carrying her places until the vaccination schedule is complete.

Lack of socialisation is one of the major causes of unwanted behaviour in Shepherds. Exposing your puppy to as many different things as possible goes a long way in helping a dog become a more stable, happy and trustworthy companion.

 Socialisation does not end at puppyhood. Dogs are social creatures that thrive on sniffing, hearing, seeing, and even licking. While the foundation for good behaviour is laid down during the first few months, good owners will reinforce social skills and training throughout a dog's life.

German Shepherds love to be at the centre of the action and it is important that they learn when young that they are not also the centre of the universe. Socialisation helps them to learn their place in that universe and to become comfortable with it.

3. **Start training early** - you can't start too soon. German Shepherd

puppies can focus earlier than some other breeds and can quickly absorb a lot of new information. Start teaching your puppy to learn her own name as well as some simple commands as soon as you bring her home.

4. **Basic training should cover several areas:** housetraining, chew prevention, puppy biting, simple commands like SIT, COME, STAY and familiarising her with a collar or puppy harness and leash. Adopt a gentle approach and keep training sessions short. German Shepherds are sensitive to you and your mood and do not respond well to harsh treatment. Start with five or 10 minutes a day and build up.

Often the way a dog responds to her environment is a result of owner training and management – or lack of it. Puppy classes or adult dog obedience classes are a great way to start, but make sure you do your homework afterwards. Spend a few minutes each day reinforcing what you have both learned in class - owners need training as well as dogs!

5. **Reward your dog for good behaviour.** All behaviour training should be based on positive reinforcement; so praise and reward your dog when she does something good. German Shepherds want to learn and please their owners, and this trait speeds up the training process. The main aim of training is to build a good understanding between you and your dog.

6. **Ignore bad behaviour**, no matter how hard this may be. If, for example, your dog is chewing her way through your kitchen, shoes, or couch, jumping up or nipping the kids, remove her from the situation and then ignore her. For some dogs even negative attention is some attention. Or if she is constantly demanding your attention, ignore her. Remove her or yourself from the room so she learns that you give attention when you want to give it, **not** when she demands it.

The more time you spend praising and rewarding good behaviour, while ignoring bad behaviour, the more likely she is to respond to you. If your pup is a chewer – and most are - make sure she has plenty of durable toys to keep her occupied. German Shepherds can chew their way through flimsy toys in no time.

7. **Take the time to learn what sort of temperament your dog has.** Is she by nature nervous or confident? What was she like as a tiny puppy, did she rush forward or hang back? Does she fight to get upright when on her back or is she happy to lie there? Is she a couch potato or a ball of fire? Your puppy's temperament will affect her behaviour and how she reacts to the world. A nervous German Shepherd will certainly not respond well to a loud approach on your part, whereas an energetic, strong-willed one will require more patience and exercise, and a firm hand.

Photo courtesy of Cherly Spurr, Reinglen German Shepherds, West Yorkshire, UK.

8. **Exercise and stimulation.** A lack of either is another major reason for dogs behaving badly. Regular daily exercise, games, organised activities and toys are all ways of stopping your dog from becoming bored or frustrated.

9. **Learn to leave your dog.** Just as leaving your dog alone for too long can lead to problems, so can being with her 100% of the time. The dog

becomes over-reliant on you and then gets stressed when you leave; this is called *separation anxiety*. When your dog first arrives at your house, start by leaving her for a few minutes every day and gradually build it up so that after a while you can leave her for up to four hours.

10. **Love your German Shepherd – but don't spoil her,** however difficult that might be. You don't do your dog any favours by giving her too many treats, constantly responding to her demands for attention or allowing her to behave as she wants inside the house.

....

Separation Anxiety

It's not just dogs that experience separation anxiety - people do too. About 7% of adults and 4% of children suffer from this disorder. Typical symptoms for humans are:

* Distress at being separated from a loved one
* Fear of being left alone

Our canine companions aren't much different. When a dog leaves the litter, her owners become her new family or pack. It's estimated that as many as 10% to 15% of dogs suffer from separation anxiety. It is an exaggerated fear response caused by being apart from their owner.

Separation anxiety affects millions of dogs and is on the increase. According to behaviourists, it is the most common form of stress for dogs.

FACT ❭ Surprisingly, German Shepherds CAN suffer from it, especially if they have not spent enough time away from their owners when young. Even if your Shepherd does not have separation anxiety, becoming over-reliant on you can lead to other insecurity issues, such as becoming:

* Anxious
* Over-protective
* Too territorial
* Too aggressive with other people

Separation anxiety can be equally distressing for the owner - I know because one of our dogs suffered from it. He howled whenever we left home without him. He'd also bark if one of us got out of the car - even if other people were still inside.

Fortunately, his problem was relatively mild. If we returned after only a short while, he was usually quiet. Although if we silently sneaked back and peeked in through the letterbox, he was never asleep. Instead he'd be waiting by the door looking and listening for our return.

It could be embarrassing. Whenever I'd go to the Post Office, I'd tie him up outside and, even though he could see me through the glass door, he'd still bark his head off - so loud that the people inside couldn't make themselves heard. Luckily, the postmistress was a dog lover and, despite the large **'GUIDE DOGS ONLY'** sign outside, she'd let him in. He'd promptly dash through the door and sit down beside me...quiet as a mouse!

Tell-Tale Signs

Does your German Shepherd do any of the following?

- Follow you from room to room – even the toilet - whenever you're home?
- Get anxious or stressed when you're getting ready to leave the house?
- Howl, whine or bark when you leave?
- Tear up paper or chew things she's not supposed to?
- Dig, chew, or scratch at the carpet, doors or windows trying to join you?
- Soil or urinate inside the house, even though she is housetrained? (This **only** occurs when left alone)
- Exhibit restlessness - such as licking her coat excessively, pacing or circling?
- Greet you ecstatically every time you come home – even if you've only been out to empty the bins?
- Wait by the window or door until you return?
- Dislike spending time alone in the garden or yard?
- Refuses to eat or drink if you leave her?
- Howl or whine when one family member leaves - even though others are still in the room or car?

If so, she may suffer from separation anxiety. Fortunately, in many cases this can be cured.

....

Causes

Dogs are pack animals and being alone is not a natural state for them. Puppies should be patiently taught to get used to short periods of isolation slowly and in a structured way if they are to be comfortable with it. A puppy will emotionally latch on to her new owner, who has taken the place of her mother and siblings.

She will want to follow you everywhere initially and, although you want to shower her with love and attention, it's best to leave her, starting with a minute or two. Nobody wants an insecure Shepherd on their hands. In our case, I was working from home when we got Max. With hindsight, I should have left him alone more often in the critical first few weeks and months.

Adopted dogs may be particularly susceptible to separation anxiety. They may have been abandoned once already and fear it happening again.

One or more of these causes can trigger separation anxiety:

- Not being left alone for short periods when young
- Being left for too long by owners who are out of the house for most of the day

- Leaving a dog too long in a crate or confined space, which can also cause hip and other joint issues

- Anxiety or lack of confidence due to insufficient socialisation, training or both

- Boredom - German Shepherds are intelligent dogs and need physical and mental exercise

- Being over-indulgent with your dog; giving her too much attention

- Making too much of a fuss when you leave and return to the house

- Mistreatment in the past, a dog from a rescue centre may have insecurities and feel anxious when left alone

Separation anxiety is not uncommon in elderly dogs. Pets age and, like humans, their senses, such as scent, hearing and sight, diminish.

They can become more dependent on their owners and then more anxious when they are separated from them - or even out of view. You may find that your elderly German Shepherd reverts to puppyhood and starts to follow you around the house again.

FACT 〉 It may be very flattering that your dog wants to be with you all the time, but insecurity and separation anxiety are forms of panic, which is distressing for the dog. If she shows signs, help her to become more self-reliant and confident; she will be a happier, more relaxed dog.

So, what can you do if your dog is showing signs of canine separation anxiety? Every dog is different, but here are tried and tested techniques that have worked for some dogs.

12 Tips to Combat Separation Anxiety

1. After the first two or three days at home, practise leaving your new puppy or adult dog for short periods, starting with a minute, then two, then gradually lengthening the time you are out of sight.

2. Tire your German Shepherd out before you leave her alone. Take her for a walk, do an activity or play a game before leaving and, if you can, leave her with a view of the outside world, e.g. in a room with a patio door or low window.

3. Keep arrivals and departures low key and don't make a big fuss.

4. Leave your dog a *"security blanket,"* such as an old piece of clothing that still has your scent on it, a favourite toy, or leave a radio on softly in the room with the dog. Avoid a heavy rock station! If it will be dark when you return, leave a lamp on a timer.

5. Associate your departure with something good. As you leave, give your dog a rubber toy, like a Kong, filled with a tasty treat, or a frozen treat. This may take her mind off your departure. (Some dogs may refuse to touch the treat until you return home).

6. If your dog is used to a crate - and only if - try crating her when you go out. Many dogs feel safe there, and being in a crate can also help to reduce destructiveness. Always take her collar off first. Pretend to leave the house, but listen for a few minutes.

NEVER leave a dog in a crate with the door closed all day; two or three hours are long enough during the day. This option is more popular in the US; many UK owners prefer to give their dogs the freedom of a room or downstairs.

Warning: if your dog starts to show major signs of distress, remove her from the crate immediately as she may injure herself.

7. Structure and routine can help to reduce anxiety. Carry out regular activities, such as feeding and exercising, at the same time every day.

8. Dogs read body language very well, most German Shepherds are intuitive. They may start to fret when they think you are going to leave them. One technique is to mimic your departure routine when you have no intention of leaving.

Put your coat on, grab your car keys, go out of the door and return a few seconds later. Do this randomly and regularly and it may help to reduce your dog's stress levels when you do it for real.

9. Some dogs show anxiety in new places; get her better socialised and used to different environments, dogs and people.

10. However lovable your German Shepherd is, if she is showing early signs of anxiety when separating from you, do not shower her with attention all the time when you are there. She will become too dependent on you.

11. If you have to regularly leave the house for a few hours at a time, try to make an arrangement so the dog is not on her own all day every day during the week.

12. Getting another dog to keep the first one company can help, but first ask yourself if you have the time and money for two or more dogs. German Shepherds are not inexpensive to maintain - can you afford double the food and veterinary bills?

Sit-Stay-Down

Another technique for helping to reduce separation anxiety is to practise the common *"sit-stay"* or *"down-stay"* exercises using positive reinforcement. The goal is to be able to move briefly out of your dog's sight while she is in the *"stay"* position.

Through this, your dog learns that she can remain calmly and happily in one place while you go about your normal daily life. You have to progress slowly with this. Get your dog to sit and stay and then walk away from her for five seconds, then 10, 20, a minute and so on. Reward your dog every time she stays calm.

Then move out of sight or out of the room for a few seconds, return and give her the treat if she is calm, gradually lengthen the time you are out of sight. If you're watching TV with your dog snuggled up at your side and you get up for a snack, say *"Stay"* and leave the room. When you come back, praise her quietly. It is a good idea to practise these techniques after exercise or when your dog is a little sleepy (but not exhausted), as she is likely to be more relaxed.

 Canine separation anxiety is NOT the result of disobedience or lack of training. It's a psychological condition; your dog feels anxious and insecure.

NEVER punish your dog for showing signs of separation anxiety – even if she has chewed your best shoes. This will only make her more anxious.

NEVER leave your dog unattended in a crate for long periods or if she is frantic to get out, it can cause physical or mental harm. If you're thinking of leaving an animal all day in a crate while you are out of the house, get a rabbit or a hamster - not a German Shepherd.

Excessive Barking

There's no getting away from the fact that German Shepherds are vocal - and they have a whine that cuts right through you! If you want a dog that hardly barks, a Bulldog or Greyhound would be a better choice.

You DO want your Shepherd to bark. She will alert you to potential dangers. The trick is to get her to bark at the right times and then to stop, as incessant barking will drive you and your neighbours nuts.

Dogs, especially youngsters, sometimes behave in ways you might not want them to, until they learn that this type of unwanted behaviour doesn't earn any rewards. Young German Shepherds like the sound of their own voices and can bark too much - until they learn not to.

 The problem sometimes develops during adolescence when a dog becomes more confident. Puppies teethe until about eight months of age, so make sure she has hardy chews, and perhaps give a bone under supervision to keep her occupied and gnawing. Give her these when she is quiet, not when she is barking.

Is your dog getting enough exercise and mental stimulation? Barking can be a way of letting off steam. Or, she may be lonely, bored, attention-seeking, possessive or over-protective.

Sometimes it is the German Shepherd's alert system going into overdrive. Is she barking at people she can see through the window or coming to the door? You want an alert bark, but not a constant bark.

Your behaviour can also encourage excessive barking. If your dog barks non-stop for several seconds or minutes and then you give her a treat to quieten her, she associates her barking with getting a nice treat.

 Tone of voice is very important when trying to quieten your Shepherd. Do not use a high-pitched or semi-hysterical STOP!! or NO!! Use low, firm commands.

One method is to set up a situation where you know she is going to bark, such as somebody arriving at your house, and put her on a leash beforehand. When she starts barking like crazy, give a short, sharp tug on the leash and give the command **"Quiet"** - spoken, not shouted. Reward her when she stops barking, not before.

If she's barking to get your attention, ignore her. If that doesn't work, leave the room and don't allow her to follow you, so you deprive her of your attention. Do this as well if her barking and attention-seeking turns to nipping. Tell her to **"Stop"** in a firm voice, or use the **"ACK!"** sound, remove your hand or leg and, if necessary, leave the room.

FACT ❯ As humans, we use our voice in many different ways: to express happiness or anger, to scold, to shout a warning, and so on. Dogs are the same; different barks and whines give out different messages.

LISTEN to your dog and try and get an understanding of German Shepherd language. Learn to recognise the difference between an alert bark, an excited bark, a demanding bark, a fearful, high pitched bark, an aggressive bark or a plain *"I'm barking 'coz I can bark"* bark!

If your dog is barking at other dogs when on a leash, arm yourselves with lots of rewards and spend
time calming her down. When you see another dog approaching, give the **Sit** command and let her sniff the treat in your hand to distract her. Turn her away from the other dog so they do not make eye contact. Get her to focus on YOU and the treat.

Talk in a calm, reassuring manner and keep showing, then giving, her a treat for remaining calm and not barking while the other dog goes past. This may take many repetitions, but it is a proven technique. There are several videos on YouTube that demonstrate this method.

Speak and Shush!

The Speak and Shush technique is one way of getting a dog to quieten down. When your dog barks at an arrival at your house, gently praise her after the first few barks. If she persists, tell her **"Quiet."** Like humans, some German Shepherds can get carried away with the sound of their own voice. The Speak and Shush technique teaches your dog or puppy to bark and be quiet on command.

Get a friend to stand outside your front door and say **"Speak"** or **"Alert."** This is the cue for your accomplice to knock on the door or ring the bell – don't worry if you both feel like idiots, it will be worth the embarrassment!

When your dog barks, say **"Speak"** and praise her profusely. After a few good barks, say **"Shush"** or **"Quiet"** and then dangle a tasty treat in front of her nose. If she is food-motivated, she will stop barking as soon as she sniffs the treat, because it is **physically impossible for a dog to sniff and woof at the same time.**

Praise your dog again as she sniffs quietly and give her the treat. Repeat this routine a few times a
day and your Shepherd will quickly learn to bark whenever the doorbell rings and you ask her to **"Speak."** Eventually your dog will bark AFTER your request but BEFORE the doorbell rings, meaning she has learned to bark on command. Even better, she will learn to anticipate the likelihood of getting a treat following your **"Shush"** request and will also be quiet on command.

With Speak and Shush training, progressively increase the length of required shush time before offering a treat - at first just a couple of seconds, then three, five, 10, 20, and so on. By alternating instructions to speak and shush, the dog is praised and rewarded for barking on request and also for stopping barking on request.

In the unlikely event that you have a German Shepherd that is silent when somebody comes to the door, you can use this method to get her to bark on the command of **"Speak."** This is also a useful command to teach if you walk your dog alone, especially at night; a barking German Shepherd will keep you safe. The method is:

1. Have some treats at the ready, waiting for that rare bark.

2. Wait until she barks - for whatever reason - then say **"Speak"** or whatever word you want to use.

3. Praise her and give her a treat. At this stage, she won't know why she is receiving the treat.

4. Keep praising her every time she barks and give her a treat.

5. After you've done this for several days, hold a treat in your hand in front of her face and say **"Speak."**

6. Your dog will probably still not know what to do, but will eventually get so frustrated at not getting the treat that she will bark.

7. At which point, praise her and give the treat.

We trained a Labrador to do this in a week and then, like clockwork, he barked like mad every time anybody came to the door, or whenever we gave him the "Speak" command, knowing he would get a treat for stopping.

Dealing with Aggression

Unfortunately, the German Shepherd has got a somewhat unfair reputation as an aggressive dog among some sections of the general public.

The problem more often lies with owners who have not socialised or trained their Shepherd in order to manage the breed's natural wariness of strangers and desire to protect. Given certain situations, any dog can growl, bark or even bite.

Sometimes a Shepherd learns unwanted behaviour from another dog or dogs, but more often it is because the dog either feels insecure, or has become too territorial or protective.

FACT Puppy biting is not aggression; all puppies bite; they explore the world with their mouths and noses. But cute little pups should be trained not to bite, as they will cause injury as 90lb adults with powerful jaws.

To treat aggression, you first have to understand the cause. There are many known types of aggression, and often an aggressive dog has more than one issue. Most are rooted in either fear or dominance:

* Growling or barking at people - this may be **territorial aggression**

* Snarling or lunging at other dogs - **dog-on-dog aggression**

* Snarling and lunging on the leash - dog-on-dog aggression, which may be rooted in fear

- Growling or biting if you or another pet goes near her food - **resource guarding**
- Growling if you pet or show attention to another animal – **possessive aggression**
- Marking territory by urinating inside the house, usually males - **dominance**
- Chasing things that move - cars, joggers, strangers, etc. - **prey aggression**
- Standing in your way, blocking your path - **dominance**
- Being possessive with toys or food - **possessive aggression**

If a Shepherd has not been socialised enough around other animals and people, she may feel threatened or challenged.

Rather than being comfortable with new situations, dogs or intrusions, she responds using *"the best form of defence is attack"* philosophy and displays aggressive behaviour to anything or anyone she is not sure about and therefore perceives as a threat.

 **As well as snarling, lunging, barking or biting, look out for other physical signs such as raised hackles, top lip curled back to bare teeth, ears back or tail raised.**

An owner's treatment of a dog can be a further cause. If the owner has been too harsh with the dog, using physical violence, shouting or reprimanding the dog too often, this in turn causes poor behaviour.

Aggression breeds aggression.

And if you haven't bothered to lay down any house rules, your Shepherd will! She may come to believe that she rules the roost and start to throw her weight around. She may start to display bad behaviour or aggression towards you or other members of the family. This should not be tolerated under any circumstances

You need to start re-establishing your leadership by putting in lots of time on the training front. There is no quick fix – if you love your Shepherd, spend the time to train her.

FACT Ultimately, German Shepherds want to please you, but they can lose their way a bit when the rules of the house are unclear or non-existent.

Dogs can also become aggressive if they are consistently left alone, cooped up, under-fed or under-exercised. A bad experience with another dog or dogs can also be a cause. Some dogs are more combative on the leash. This is because once on a leash, they cannot run away.

Fight or flight.

They know they can't escape, so they make themselves as frightening as possible and warn off the other dog or person. Train your German Shepherd to be comfortable walking on the leash from an early age.

If your dog **suddenly** shows a change of behaviour or becomes aggressive, ask:

- Is she getting enough exercise?
- Is she mentally bored?

If the answer to these questions is YES followed by NO, consider getting her checked out by a vet to rule out any underlying medical reason for the crankiness, such as earache or toothache.

Raging hormones can be another reason. If the vet thinks your dog has a hormonal issue, discuss the pros and cons of spaying or neutering. A levelling-off of hormones can lead to a more laid-back dog.

A further reason is because a dog has been spoiled by her owner and has come to believe that the world revolves around her. Not spoiling your dog, teaching her what is acceptable behaviour in the first place is the best preventative measure. Early training, especially during puppyhood and adolescence - before she develops unwanted habits - can save a lot of trouble in the future.

Aggression Towards People

Desensitisation is the most common method of treating aggression. It starts by breaking down the triggers for the behaviour one small step at a time. The aim is to get the dog to associate pleasant things with the trigger, i.e. people or a specific person whom she previously feared or regarded as a threat.

This is done through using positive reinforcement, such as praise or rewards. Successful desensitisation takes time, patience and knowledge. If your dog is starting to growl at people, there are a couple of techniques you can try to break her of this bad habit while she is still young and small – and before it develops into full-blown biting.

Arrange for friends to come around, one at a time. When one arrives at your house, get him to scatter kibble in front of him on the floor, so your dog associates the arrival of people with tasty treats. As the friend moves into the house and your dog eats the kibble, praise her for being a good girl.

If your Shepherd is at all anxious around children, separate them or carefully supervise their time together. Children typically react enthusiastically to dogs and some less confident dogs may regard this as frightening or an invasion of their space.

A crate is also a useful tool for removing an aggressive dog from the situation for short periods of time, but should not be used as a regular form of punishment or imprisonment.

FACT ⟩ Many owners get GSDs intending them to be family pets AND guard dogs. Trained guard dogs do not make good pets in the home. A well-socialised, well-trained German Shepherd makes the best family guard dog.

Coprophagia (Eating Faeces)

It is hard for us to understand why a dog would want to eat her or any other animal's faeces (stools, poop or poo, call it what you will), but it does happen. There is plenty of anecdotal evidence that some dogs love the stuff. Nobody fully understands why dogs do this, it may simply be an unpleasant behaviour trait or there could be an underlying reason.

It is also thought that the inhumane and useless housetraining technique of *"sticking the dog's nose in it"* when she has eliminated inside the house can also encourage coprophagia.

If your dog eats poop from the cat litter tray, place the tray somewhere where your dog can't get to it, but the cat can. Perhaps high on a shelf, or put a guard around it, small enough for the cat to get through, but not your Shepherd.

You may find that your dog will roll in fox and other animal poop to cover the animal's scent. Try and avoid areas you know are frequented by foxes if you can, as their poop can transmit several diseases, including Canine Parvovirus or lungworm — neither of these should pose a serious health risk if your dog is up to date with vaccinations and worming medication.

Vets have found that canine diets with low levels of fibre and high levels of starch increase the likelihood of coprophagia. If your dog is exhibiting this behaviour, first check that her diet is nutritionally complete. Look at the first ingredient on the dog food packet or tin — is it corn or meat? Check that you are feeding the right amount.

If there is no underlying medical reason, try and modify your dog's behaviour. Remove cat litter trays, clean up after your dog and do not allow her to eat her own poop. If it's not there, she can't eat it.

One breeder told us of a dog that developed the habit after being allowed to soil his crate as a pup, caused by the owners not being vigilant in their housetraining. The puppy got used to eating his own faeces and then continued to do it as an adult, when it became quite a problem.

Don't reprimand a dog for eating poop. A better technique is to cause a distraction while she is in the act and then remove the offending material.

Coprophagia is sometimes seen in pups aged between six months to a year and often disappears after this age.

....

Important: This chapter provides just a general overview of German Shepherd traits and behaviour. If your dog exhibits persistent behavioural problems, particularly if he or she is aggressive towards people or other dogs, consider getting help from a reputable canine behaviourist, such as those listed the Association of Professional Dog Trainers at http://www.apdt.co.uk (UK) or https://apdt.com (US). Check your chosen trainer uses positive training methods.

9. Training a German Shepherd

Breeders' opinions may vary on the best type of food to give your dog or the most efficient grooming brush. But one topic they all 100% agree on is this: It is ABSOLUTELY ESSENTIAL for all new owners to devote lots of time to socialising and training your German Shepherd.

....

Natural Tendencies

German Shepherds are not like many other breeds that are happy to snooze in front of the fire or out in the yard most of the day. They have been selectively bred to work all day alongside humans. This is a highly intelligent, powerful, athletic breed with an active mind that thrives on stimulation and some kind of job or activity.

When you get a German Shepherd, you are allowing a dog into your life that has almost limitless capabilities. Not training or socialising such a finely-tuned canine is the equivalent of giving a loaded gun to a five-year-old. It won't end well.

People forget that genetics play a big part in a dog's natural tendencies. Over the decades, breeders have selected dogs for their breeding programmes based on certain traits. This means your GSD puppy arrives at your home hard-wired to be naturally wary of strangers with a desire to protect you and your family.

That's great, and probably one of the reasons why you chose the German Shepherd.

However, unless the GSD is integrated into society and learns to accept friendly people and animals - i.e. socialised - and trained to obey your commands, you could end up with a "loaded gun;" an unruly dog that barks too much and is aggressive with everything and everyone.

On the other hand, put in the effort early on to teach him some rules and manners and how to integrate with other people and animals, and you will be rewarded with a well-adjusted individual who will be a loyal companion and protector second to none.

Photo: The German Shepherd has an incredible intensity of focus from an early age. This focus is a powerful training tool.

....

Intelligence

The German Shepherd is extremely versatile and can be trained to the highest level. works alongside humans in more roles than any other breed.

Psychologist and canine expert Dr Stanley Coren has written a book called *"The Intelligence of Dogs"* in which he ranks the breeds. He surveyed dog trainers to compile the list and used "Understanding of New Commands" and "Obey First Command" as his standards of intelligence. He says there are three types of dog intelligence:

- ❧ Adaptive Intelligence (learning and problem-solving ability). This is specific to the individual animal and is measured by canine IQ tests

- ❧ Instinctive Intelligence. This is specific to the individual animal and is measured by canine IQ test

- ❧ Working/Obedience Intelligence. This is breed-dependent

The brainboxes of the canine world are the 10 breeds ranked in the *"Brightest Dogs"* section of his list. All dogs in this class:

Understand New Commands with Fewer than Five Repetitions

Obey a First Command 95% of the Time or Better

It will come as no surprise to anyone who has ever owned German Shepherds to know that they are the third most intelligent dogs on the planet, after the Border Collie and Poodle.

By the author's own admission, this rating scale is heavily weighted towards obedience-related behavioural traits, which are often found in working dogs like the German Shepherd, rather than understanding or creativity, which is found in hunting dogs. As a result, some breeds, such as the Bully breeds (Bulldogs, French Bulldogs, Mastiffs, Bull Terriers, Pugs, Rottweilers, etc.) are ranked quite low on the list, due to their stubborn or independent nature.

But as far as German Shepherds are concerned, it's true to say that you are starting out with a puppy that not only has the intelligence to pick up new commands very quickly, but who also really wants to learn and please you.

FACT ❭ Just look at Dr Coren's stats: your puppy understands what to do when he's only heard it three or four times. Once trained, he will obey you the first time of asking virtually every time. If that isn't incentive to train a German Shepherd, I don't know what is!

Advice from Breeders

Over the decades, **Cheryl Spurr, of Reinglen German Shepherds,** has done all kinds of training, including Agility, Obedience and Therapy Dog, and is currently involved with KC Obedience and IGP (formerly Schutzhund).

She says: "It is very important that people realise how much work they are potentially taking on with a GSD. They often see well-trained ones and want one like that, but don't think about the training involved. Training is vital; you can't have a dog like a GSD taking control of your life.

"I often get asked when I'm walking my four together: "How do you manage it?" and: "Why won't my dog do that?" I reply you get back what you put in. I spend a lot of time teaching my dogs how to behave in different situations and that I am in charge and they don't need to protect or look after me; I will tell them if I need that. They don't need to worry about anything, I have everything under control.

"One of the things I say to my new puppy owners is: "Socialising your dog does not mean letting it play with every dog it sees; it means teaching your dog to fit into your lifestyle and society around you. Your dog doesn't need to go up to every dog it sees, it should want to stay with you, come to you when you call, stay calm in strange situations and ignore other dogs.

"Do you go up to every person you meet and say: "Hello, do you want to come and play?" No, and neither should your dog."

Cheryl's photo shows Harro vom Heiligental of Reinglen doing protection training.

"You are the big motivator for your dog! GSDs love their families, they love to work, they are happy when they have a job, and that can be any kind of task. Food and toys are great training aids. *I always tell new owners to hand-feed the puppy to build a strong bond quickly.*

"GSDs go through fear stages in their puppyhood and these need to be managed calmly. Don't mollycoddle and reassure unwanted behaviour, but dismiss it so they get over it quickly - and reward the good stuff."

Marie Donahue, of Rodina Straze German Shepherds, breeds and trains working dogs, and says: "I find the GSD very intelligent and easy to train. The working line dogs do need a job as they love to work and can become difficult or destructive if not kept busy.

"Training is very important for all dogs. It can never start too early as it builds your relationship with your dog. GSDs love to train and use their minds; they also love to interact with their people. Start training immediately and find fun things you enjoy that you can do with your dog.

"They excel in Obedience, Scent Work, Agility; pretty much anything you want to do, they are happy to oblige. I compete my dogs in Schutzund, now called IGP. It is a protection sport with three phases – Tracking, Obedience and Protection; it was historically the GSD breed test. I also compete in Scent Work, Dock Diving, Barn Hunt, Rally, Agility and my dogs are in the National Top 10 in Fast Cat."

Jaqueline Levy, of Crosskeys K9, also breeds and trains working GSDs: "The German Shepherd is a highly intelligent and trainable dog. The more time and effort you invest in that relationship, the better that relationship will be. Training is essential. Ten minutes a day, twice a day, is really the bare minimum.

"GSDs naturally want to learn. They are very inquisitive and sensitive to their surroundings. We tell clients to work with their dogs at least twice a day for short periods, gradually extending the time each day, but not so much so that the dog is overstimulated, overwhelmed or loses interest.

"Every puppy that leaves here goes with recommendations for trainers in their areas. Working with a professional trainer is really key to maximise the capabilities of the dog and prevent or address behaviour problems.

"Early and often socialisation is absolutely critical to your dog's adaptation to the world. Socialise with different people of different cultures, different shapes and sizes, unique situations and noises/sounds, textures and other stimuli to increase the resilience of your dog and the ability to tolerate and handle a variety of situations, people, and places."

Stef Millington, of CunAnnun German Shepherds: "Training any dog is of the utmost importance. An untrained dog is not well-mannered and can turn into a nuisance, especially in a large breed like a Shepherd. If you want a GSD as a pet, basic obedience is essential but specialist training is not needed.

"Obviously, I always advise owners to go to puppy classes, as it is also essential to socialise your puppy with other breeds, small and large. If you get the bug and want to do further training, then there are plenty of specialised classes, like Obedience, Agility, Flyball, Ring Craft classes, as well as Search training or Schutzhund – or IGP, as they call it today. I exhibit most of my dogs. They are all Ring Craft-trained with monthly refreshers for all and do basic obedience training to make sure they are well-mannered in public. My adults are also lightly-trained in personal protection, at which German Shepherds are absolute naturals.

"First and foremost, it's the love for his owner and the anticipation for praise and play that motivates a GSD. Shepherds have a great drive and an unrivalled eagerness to please and thrive with positive training."

Tammey Tilton, Tiltonhaus German Shepherds: "I have always been attracted to German Shepherds; I was raised around them from the time I was a very young child. They are loyal, protective and loving, and my family and I are having a blast raising, training and breeding dogs we dearly love."

Photo of SG1 Miss Ella von Morgen Haus IPO1, aged five, courtesy of Tammey.

"Training is so very important! I believe that people are more apt to keep their German Shepherd if they train them, either by going to training class or training them at home. It creates more of a bond between the dog and the owner - and living with an obedient German Shepherd is a lot more enjoyable.

"We love **Marker Training,** where you use a sound or a word to tell your dog he or she did something right, followed by a reward, such as a treat or praise.

"German Shepherds are motivated by lots and lots of praise throughout the training. Keep the training upbeat and fun so your German Shepherd will stay engaged and not get bored. Move around; use a lot of verbal praise in addition to the food and toy treats. Your German Shepherd will look forward to and get very excited when it is time to train with you if you make training fun!

"Our dogs have won titles in IGP, Scent Work and Nosework, Canine Good Citizen and Conformation. We are members of Lilac City Dog Training Club in Spokane, Washington, and spend a lot of time there training our dogs to become well-behaved German Shepherds. I also have a service dog that I've trained myself and have been teaching her different tricks to perform in hopes of making her a therapy dog in the near future too"

Donna Bonney, Hirten Bray Hugel: "Training is extremely important for GSDs as they need a "job."

"If they get bored, they destroy things! I always say "A tired puppy is a good puppy!" Training is not a cookie cutter plan; every dog is different. What works for one dog may not work for another, but they are motivated by their willingness to please."

Bobbi King, RVT, of Redwood Runs, has bred GSDs for 40 years and says: "Training is an ABSOLUTE MUST with German Shepherds. Start training as soon as you bring your puppy home. Train a bit more if he or she gets into trouble, then even more as the dog gets a little older. Always continue training; stay a step ahead of your dog.

"Couple loads of love with absolute firmness. Training is a great way to exercise your dog - and there are certificates for everything –Obedience, Agility, Frisbee, stockwork, running or biking with your dog, Scent Work, personal protection, IGP... the list goes on! Your GSD can become a great hobby."

Bobbi's photo shows Declan's Astro of Redwood Runs, not yet four months old, proudly displaying his AKC STAR Puppy Award, trained by 12-year-old Declan.

Teresa Mapp, UK hobby breeder: "We have all our prospective owners meet all our six dogs; if they can deal with them, they can deal with one pup. All of our dogs live and play together from about four weeks, this helps the pups learn and be socialised.

"GSDs are loyal, devoted, affectionate and intelligent, and many people are surprised to find that they also love to make their owners laugh. They will rise to any challenge and work things out; they adore children and are very protective. They can be cheeky and, when young, love to push boundaries - just like humans! We have found they will try their boundaries at about 18 to 24 months of age, equivalent to their teenage years!

"They are also extremely intelligent. They usually come third or fourth in surveys for intelligence, but the people doing these surveys have not met some of ours! In some respect they are easy to train because they are so intelligent, but this can also make them difficult. One of my sister's boys would watch what was expected when doing Agility, then work out an easier way around the course because he was quite a lazy chap!

"Early socialisation is important for a pup and puppy classes are a good idea. KC Good Citizen training is also good for building a bond between pup and owner. In fact, any training is good for developing the relationship and also keeping a GSD busy.

"Some dogs are food-motivated and will do anything for a treat. Beware of over feeding, if they get a lot of treats, their food should be adjusted accordingly or you could end up with a chunky dog. Other dogs respond better to praise and most of ours love nothing more than a ball."

Wendy Sharp, Sharphouse's German Shepherds: "German Shepherd Dogs should be trained with kindness and positive reinforcement. Love and games is how to train to get a confident dog.

"Start training from a young age to prevent mouthing and jumping. Ignore bad behaviour and praise good behaviour, just like you would a child. If you practise consistent rules and positive reinforcement, GSDs will respond quickly and training will be very rewarding. Keep things calm and do not over-tire or over-excite.

"I believe every GSD should be trained to at least KC Silver Award certificate; German Shepherds are big and can be a liability if untrained or treated badly. Training should be fun. Reward with games and a favourite toy or a treat; praise and hugs if the dog is to be a pet. If it is for a job of work, specialist training is required.

"I show my German Shepherds in Ring Craft Championship dog shows, and have qualified for Crufts in 2019 and 2020. I have two dogs who have reached Obedience Level Gold in the Good Citizen certificates, and one dog has passed the test for being a PAT (Pets as Therapy) dog.

"German Shepherds are good with children if raised from pups with good socialisation with children, and they will adapt to different situations if trained with kindness and love."

Larry Yates started breeding Lornstone German Shepherds way back in the 1960s. Bert, the great-grandfather of Larry's current puppies, became the oldest dog ever to pass his Breed Survey Class One at the age of 10 and was described as "a credit to the breed."

I could write a whole book about the care Larry and his wife, Diane, put into choosing the right mate when they decide to produce a litter – including several trips a year to Germany. He also hand-writes the Lornstone pedigree (in addition to the Kennel Club registration) with details of every ancestor's DNA health tests and qualifications, which takes around four hours for each puppy.

Larry says: "We vet the owners, sit down with them and give them as much help then and later as we can. But, at the end of the day, it is up to the owner to put in the time, training and socialisation to mould the dog into the finished article."

He adds: "Each dog is different. What is important is to understand that what you have is a dog and we, as humans, need to see life from their point of view. You haven't to be heavy-handed with a German Shepherd; it will destroy the temperament."

Training Tips for GSDs

1. **Start training immediately.** German Shepherds learn quickly and, compared with other breeds, puppies have good focus from an early age. Intelligent, lively minds need channelling in a positive manner. Simple daily repetition of basic commands will stay with the dog if reinforced periodically throughout life.

2. **Puppy training starts with five to 10 minutes per day, twice a day every day, increasing as the dog grows.**

3. **German Shepherds do not respond well to heavy-handed training.** Aggression breeds aggression. Keep training sessions short, positive and fun, so the whole experience is enjoyable for you and him.

4. **Be firm.** German Shepherds do best when they know their place in the world. They respect leadership. Your aim as a trainer is **to establish authority over your GSD in a calm manner using reward-based training methods.** Do not be nervous or timid around the dog or he may take advantage of your weakness.

5. **They respond well to rewards.** GSDs can be trained as Service dogs with just a ball or toy for reward. Don't think you have to give treats all the time. Praise, toys, balls, games are all great rewards for a German Shepherd.

Photo: Donna Bonney, Hirten Bray Hugel.

6. **German Shepherds are born to serve.** They are fiercely loyal and love nothing better than performing a task for their owner - and this includes training.

7. **Your voice is a very important training tool.** Your dog should learn to understand your language. Commands should be issued in a calm, authoritative voice - not shouted. Praise should be given in a happy, encouraging voice. If your dog has done something wrong, use a stern voice, not a harsh shriek. This applies even if your German Shepherd is unresponsive at the beginning.

8. **Use your dog's name often when he arrives home.** He won't know what it means in the beginning, but it won't take him long to realise you're talking to him.

9. **Only use his name for positive things.** Don't fall into the trap of shouting the dog's name and saying **"NO!"** when he has done something wrong. He should believe that every time he hears you say his name, something good will follow. Using his name to reprimand could encourage him to switch off when he hears it.

10. **Have a negative sound.** Use words such as **"Ack!"** or **"Bad Boy/Girl"** in a stern (not shouted) voice. Some parents prefer not to use "No" with their dog, as they use it often around their kids and it can confuse the pup! When a puppy is corrected by his mother, e.g. – if he bites her – she growls at him to warn him not to do it again. Using a short sharp sound like **"Ack!"** can work surprisingly well.

11. **Avoid giving your dog commands you know you can't enforce.** Every time you give a command that you don't enforce, he learns that commands are optional. Give your dog only one command - twice maximum - then gently enforce it. Repeating or nagging will make your German Shepherd tune out. They also teach him that the first few commands are a bluff. Telling your dog to **"SIT, SIT, SIT, SIT!!!"** is neither efficient nor effective. Give him a single **"SIT"** command, gently place him in the sit position and then praise him.

12. **Begin your training around the house, garden or yard.** How well your dog responds to you at home affects his behaviour away from the home. If he doesn't respond well at home, he certainly won't respond any better when he's out and about where there are 101 distractions, such as other dogs, people, cats, food scraps, interesting scents, etc.

13. **Mealtimes are a great time to start training your puppy.** Teach him to sit and stay at breakfast and dinnertime, rather than just putting the dish down and letting him dash over immediately. Initially, he won't know what you mean, so gently place him into the sit position while you say **"Sit."** Place a hand on his chest during the **"Stay"** command - gradually letting go – and then give him the command to eat his dinner, followed by encouraging praise - he'll soon get the idea.

NOTE: Don't physically manipulate a poorly-trained adult or adolescent German Shepherd, as he may react badly to being pushed around.

14. **Don't give your puppy lots of attention when he misbehaves.** Dogs like attention. If yours gets lots when he jumps up on you, his bad behaviour is being reinforced. If he jumps up, push him away, use the command **"Down"** and then ignore him.

15. **Give your dog attention when YOU want to – not when he wants it.** When you are training, give your puppy lots of positive attention when he is good. But if he starts jumping up, nudging you constantly or barking to demand your attention, ignore him. Don't give in to his demands. Wait a while and pat him when you want and AFTER he has stopped demanding your attention. If he won't stop, remove yourself or the dog from the room.

16. **Timing is critical.** When your puppy does something right, praise him immediately. If you wait a while he will have no idea what he has done right. Similarly, when he does something wrong, correct him straight away. For example, if he relieved himself in the house, don't shout and certainly don't rub his nose in it; this will only make things worse. If you catch him in the act, use your **"Ack"** sound and immediately carry him out of the house. Then use the toilet command (whichever word you have chosen) and praise your pup or give him a treat when he performs. If your pup is constantly eliminating indoors, you are not keeping a close enough eye on him.

17. **Start as you mean to go on.** In terms of rules and training, treat your cute little pup as though he were a fully-grown German Shepherd and introduce the rules you want him to live by as an adult. If you don't want your dog to take over your couch or bed or jump up at people when he is an adult, train him not to do it when he is small. You can't have one set of rules for a pup and one set for a fully-grown dog, he won't understand.

18. **Make sure that everybody in the household sticks to the same commands and rules.** Use the same words and don't send mixed messages in terms of what he's allowed and not allowed to do, otherwise he won't learn.

19. **Don't give up during the adolescent phase!** Shepherds may try to impose their will on the household during their rebellious teenage years, between one and two years old. Extra time may be needed to reinforce the training your dog has already learned, but seems to forget as he pushes the boundaries – and your buttons!

20. **If you're struggling, get professional help.** There is no shame is seeking the assistance of a professional dog trainer if you feel you are not making any headway. A few sessions with an expert can help to build a better understanding between the pet Shepherd and owner. And professional, specialised training is recommended for all working Shepherds.

 TREATS: Get your pup used to a small piece of carrot or apple as a healthy, low-calorie alternative. In general, start off with low-value treats and work your way up to your best treats as training progresses!

Training should be a positive learning experience for you both. Bawling at the top of your voice, hitting or rough handling should play no part. Establishing the natural order of things is not something forced on a dog through shouting or violence; it is brought about by mutual consent and good training, which in turn deepens the bonds between owner and dog.

If you have a high spirited, high energy German Shepherd, use your brain to think of ways to make training fun and to persuade your dog that what YOU want him to do is actually what HE wants to do. With time and patience, he will realise that when he does as you ask, something good is going to happen – verbal praise, pats, a toy or treat, playtime, etc.

Socialisation is a very important aspect of training. Your puppy's breeder should have already begun this process with the litter and then it's up to you to keep it going when the pup arrives home. Up to around 16 weeks' old pups can absorb a great deal of information, but they are also vulnerable to bad experiences.

Don't just leave your dog at home in the early days, take him out and about with you, get him used to new people, places and noises. German Shepherds that are not sufficiently exposed to different situations can find them frightening when they do finally encounter them later. They may react badly by barking, growling, lunging or biting.

Chewing can be an issue with many young German Shepherds. Some will chew through anything – including wires, phone chargers, remote controls, bedding, etc. And Shepherds are not infrequent visitors to veterinary clinics to have "foreign objects" removed from their stomachs. Train your puppy only to chew the things you give him – so don't give him your old slippers, an old piece of carpet or anything that resembles something you don't want him to chew. Buy purpose-made long-lasting chew toys or give a bone, supervised.

Jumping up is another issue, it's often a natural reaction when young dogs see somebody they like. You don't, however, want your fully-grown Shepherd to jump up on Grandma when he has just come back from a romp through the muddy woods and a swim in a dirty pond. Teach him while he is still small not to jump up!

....

Teaching Basic Commands

Sit - Teaching the Sit command to your German Shepherd is relatively easy. Teaching a young pup to sit still for a few seconds is a bit more difficult! In the beginning you may want to put your protégé on a leash to hold his attention.

Stand facing each other and hold a treat between your thumb and fingers an inch or so above his head. Don't let your fingers and the treat get much further away or you might have trouble getting him to move his body into a sitting position. If your dog jumps up, you're probably holding your hand too far away from his nose.

If your dog backs up, practise with a wall behind him.

As he reaches up to sniff it, move the treat upwards and back over the dog towards his tail at the same time as saying **"Sit."** Most dogs will track the treat with their eyes and follow it with their noses, causing their snouts to point straight up.

As his head moves up toward the treat, his rear end should automatically go down towards the floor. *TaDa! (drum roll!)*

As soon as he sits, say **"YES"** (or GOOD BOY/GOOD GIRL), give him the treat. Stroke and praise him for as long as he stays in the sitting position. If he jumps up on his back legs and paws you while you are moving the treat, be patient and start all over again.

Another method: Put one hand on his chest and with your other hand, gently push down on his rear end until he is sitting, while saying **"Sit."** Give him a treat and praise, even though you have made him do it, he will eventually associate the position with the command **"Sit."**

Once your puppy catches on, leave the treat in your pocket or have it in your other hand. Repeat the sequence, but this time your dog will just follow your empty hand. Say **"Sit"** and bring your empty hand in front of your dog's nose, holding your fingers as if you had a treat. Move your hand exactly as you did when you held the treat.

When your dog sits, say **"YES!"** and give him a treat from your other hand or your pocket.

Gradually lessen the amount of movement with your hand. First, say **"Sit"** then hold your hand eight to 10 inches above your dog's face and wait a moment. Most likely, he will sit. If he doesn't, help him by moving your hand back over his head, like you did before, but make a smaller movement this time. Then try again. Your goal is to eventually just say **"Sit"** without having to move or extend your hand at all.

Jumping Up - Once your dog reliably sits on cue, you can ask him to sit whenever you meet and talk to people - admittedly, it may not work straight away, but it should help to calm him down a bit. The key is anticipation. Give your German Shepherd the cue before he gets too excited to hear you and before he starts jumping up on the person just arrived.

Generously reward your dog the instant he sits. Say "YES" and give him treats every few seconds while he holds the Sit.

Whenever possible, ask the person you're greeting to help you out by walking away if your dog gets up from the sit and lunges or jumps towards him or her. With many consistent repetitions of this exercise, your dog will learn that lunging or jumping makes people go away, and polite sitting makes them stay and give him attention.

Photo: With plenty of training and socialisation, your puppy will learn to be as relaxed and integrated as this lovely old Shepherd.

You can practise by arranging for a friend to come round, then for him or her to come in and out of the house several times. Each time, show the treat, give the Sit command - initially, don't ask your dog to hold the sit for any length of time - and then allow him to greet your friend. Ask your friend to bend down to pat your dog, rather than standing straight and encouraging the dog to jump up for a greeting.

 If your dog is still jumping up, use a puppy harness and leash inside the house to physically prevent him from jumping up at people, while still training him to Sit when someone arrives. You can also use the "Off" command when you want your dog NOT to jump up at a person, or not to jump on furniture.

"Sit" can be used in a number of different situations. For example, when you are putting his leash on, while you are preparing his meal, when he returned the ball you have just thrown, when he is jumping up, demanding attention or getting over-excited.

....

Come or The Recall - Teaching **"The Recall"** is a must. A Shepherd who responds quickly and consistently can enjoy freedoms that other dogs cannot. Although you might spend more time teaching this command than any other, it is worth the effort.

 "Come" or a similar word is better than "Here" if you intend using the "Heel" command, as "Here" and "Heel" sound too similar.

Whether you're teaching a young puppy or an older German Shepherd, the first step is to establish that coming to you is the best thing he can do. Any time your dog comes to you whether you've called him or not, acknowledge that you appreciate it with praise, affection or other rewards. This consistent reinforcement ensures that your dog will continue to *check in* with you frequently.

1. Say your dog's name followed by the command "Come!" in an enthusiastic voice. You'll usually be more successful if you walk or run away from him while you call. Dogs find it hard to resist chasing after a running person, especially their owner.

2. He should run towards you.

FACT ❯ Dogs tend to tune us out if we talk to them all the time. Whether you're training or out for an off-leash walk, refrain from constantly chattering to your Shepherd - no matter how much of a brilliant conversationalist you are! If you're quiet much of the time, he is more likely to pay attention when you call him.

❖ Outdoors, a young dog will often start running towards you but then get distracted and head off in another direction. Pre-empt this situation by praising your puppy, cheer him on when he starts to come to you before he has a chance to get distracted!

Your praise will keep him focused so that he'll be more likely to come all the way to you. If he stops or turns away, you can give him feedback by saying **"Oh-oh!"** or **"Hey!"** in an unpleasantly surprised tone of voice. When he looks at you again, call him and praise him as he approaches.

Progress your dog's training in baby steps. If he's learned to come when called in your kitchen, you can't expect him to be able to do it straight away at the park or on the beach when he's surrounded by distractions.

When you first try this outdoors, make sure there are minimal distractions. Consider using a long training leash initially - or to do the training within a safe, fenced area. Only when your dog has mastered the recall in a number of locations and in the face of various distractions can you expect him to come to you regularly.

....

Down - There are a number of different ways to teach your dog to lie down. If you are teaching the "Down," use "Off" to teach your dog not to jump up. Being down does not come naturally to a young pup, so it may take a while for him to master the Down.

 Don't make it a battle of wills and, although you may gently push him down, don't physically force him down against his will. This will be seen as you asserting dominance in an aggressive manner and your German Shepherd will not like it.

1. Give the 'Sit' command.

2. When your dog sits, don't give him the treat immediately, but keep it in your closed hand. Slowly move your hand straight down toward the floor, between his front legs. As your dog's nose follows the treat, just like a magnet, his head will bend all the way down to the floor.

3. When the treat is on the floor between your dog's paws, start to move it away from him, like you're drawing a line along the floor. The entire luring motion forms an L-shape.

4. At the same time say "Down" in a firm manner.

5. **To continue to follow the treat, your dog will probably ease himself into the Down position.** The instant his elbows touch the floor, say **"YES!"** and immediately let him eat the treat. If your dog doesn't automatically stand up after eating the treat, just move a step or two away to encourage him to move out of the Down position. Then repeat the sequence several times. Aim for two short sessions of five minutes or so per day.

If your dog's back end pops up when you try to lure him into a Down, quickly snatch the treat away. Then immediately ask him to sit and try again. It may help to let him nibble on the treat as you move it toward the floor. If you've tried to lure your dog into a Down, but he still seems confused or reluctant, try what I call the *Tent Trick*:

1. Sit down on the floor with your legs straight out in front of you with your dog at your side. Keep your legs together, your feet on the floor and bend your knees to make a tent shape.

2. Hold a treat right in front of your dog's nose. As he licks and sniffs the treat, slowly move it down to the floor and then underneath your legs. Continue to lure him until he has to crouch down to keep following the treat, giving the Down command.

3. The instant his belly touches the floor, say **"YES!"** and let him eat the treat. If your dog seems nervous about following the treat under your legs, make a trail of treats for him to eat along the way.

Some dogs find it easier to follow a treat into the Down from a standing position.

 Hold the treat right in front of your dog's nose, and then slowly move it straight down to the floor, right between his front paws. His nose will follow the treat

 If you let him lick the treat as you continue to hold it still on the floor, your dog will probably plop into the Down position

 The moment he does, say **"YES!"** and let him eat the treat

FACT ❯ Some dogs are reluctant to lie on a cold, hard surface. It may be easier to teach the Down on a carpet or grass.

The next step is to introduce a hand signal. You'll still reward him with treats, though, so keep them nearby or hidden behind your back.

1. **Start with your dog in a Sit**

2. **Say "Down"**

3. **Without a treat in your fingers, use the same hand motion you did before**

4. As soon as your dog's elbows touch the floor, say "Yes!" and immediately get a treat to give him. Important: Even though you're not using a treat to lure your dog into position, you must still give him a reward when he lies down. You want your dog to learn that he doesn't have to see a treat to get one.

5. **Clap your hands or take a few steps away to encourage him to stand up.** Then repeat the sequence from the beginning several times for a week or two. When your dog readily lies down as soon as you say the cue and then use your new hand signal, you're ready for the next step.

You probably don't want to keep bending all the way down to the floor to make your German Shepherd lie down. To make things more convenient, gradually shrink the signal to a small movement. Progress slowly.

6.   **Repeat the hand signal,** but instead of guiding your dog into the Down by moving your hand all the way to the floor, move it almost all the way down. Stop moving your hand when it's an inch or two above the floor. Practise the Down exercise for a day or two, using this slightly smaller hand signal. Then you can make your movement an inch or two smaller, stopping your hand three or four inches above the floor.

7.   **After practising for another couple of days, you can shrink the signal again.** As you continue to gradually stop your hand signal further and further from the floor, you'll bend over less and less. Eventually, you won't have to bend over at all. You'll be able to stand up straight, say **"Down,"** and then just point to the floor.

Your next job is a bit harder – it is to practise your dog's new skill in many different situations and locations so that he can lie down whenever and wherever you ask him to.

Slowly increase the level of distraction; for example, first practise in calm places, like different rooms in your house or in your garden, when there's no one else around. Then increase the distractions; practise at home when family members are moving around, on walks and then at friends' houses, too.

....

Stay - This is another essential command, but it's not so easy to teach a lively young Shepherd to stay still for any length of time. Here is a simple method to get your dog to stay; don't ask a puppy to stay for more than a few seconds at the beginning.

 This requires some concentration from your dog, so pick a time when he's relaxed and well exercised, mealtimes or just after a game - but not exhausted when he is too tired to concentrate.

1.   Command your dog to sit or lie down, but instead of giving a treat as soon as he hits the floor, hold off for one second. Then say **"YES!"** in an enthusiastic voice and give him a treat. If your dog bounces up again instantly, have two treats ready. Feed one right away, before he has time to move; then say **"YES!"** and feed the second treat.

2.   You need a release word or phrase. It might be **"Free!"** or **"Here!"** or a word that you only use to release your dog from this command. Once you've given the treat, immediately give your release cue and encourage your dog to get up. Repeat the exercise several times in one training session, gradually wait a tiny bit longer before releasing the treat. (You can delay the first treat for a moment if your dog bounces up).

3.   A common mistake is to hold the treat high and then give the reward slowly. As your dog doesn't know the command yet, he sees the treat coming and gets up to meet the food. Instead, bring the treat toward your dog quickly - the best place to deliver it is right between his front paws. If you're working on a Sit-Stay, give the treat at chest height.

4.   When your dog can stay for several seconds, start to add a little distance. At first, you'll walk backwards, because your German Shepherd is more likely to get up to follow you if you turn away from him. Take one single step away, then step back towards your dog and say **"YES!"** and give the treat. Give him the signal to get up immediately, even if five seconds haven't passed.

FACT ❯ The Stay gets harder for your dog depending on how far away you are, how long it is, and what else is going on around him. Trainer shorthand is "Distance, Duration, Distraction." Only increase one at a time.

5. For best success in teaching a Stay, work on one factor at a time. Whenever you make one factor more difficult, such as distance, ease up on the others at first, then build them back up. So, when you take that first step back from your dog, adding distance, you should cut the duration of the stay.

6. Now your dog has mastered the Stay with you alone at home, move the training on so that he learns to do the same with distractions. Have someone walk into the room, or squeak a toy or bounce a ball once. A rock-solid stay is mostly a matter of working slowly and patiently to start with. Don't go too fast.

If he does get up, take a breather and then give him a short refresher, starting at a point easier than whatever you were working on when he cracked. If you think he's tired or had enough, leave it for the day and come back later – just finish off on a positive note by giving one very easy command you know he will obey, followed by a treat reward.

 Don't use the Stay command in situations stressful for your dog. For instance, avoid saying "Stay" as you close the door behind you on your way to work. And don't use the command to hold him in a scary situation, such as when he may feel threatened by other dogs or people.

Dealing with Puppy Biting and Jumping Up

German Shepherd puppies are naturally **"mouthy."** They spend a lot of time chewing; it's natural for them to use their mouths and needle-sharp teeth to investigate the world.

When puppies play with people, they often bite, chew and mouth on people's hands, limbs and clothing. Play biting is normal for puppies; they do it all the time with their littermates. They also bite moving targets with their sharp teeth; it's a great game!

FACT When they arrive in your home, they have to be taught that human skin is sensitive and body parts are not suitable biting material. Biting is not acceptable, not even from a puppy.

When your puppy bites, he is playing and investigating; he is NOT being aggressive. But puppy biting can develop into aggressive rough play if not checked. Initially, this can be a problem if you have children. The kids wind the puppy up and vice versa, both get over-excited and accidents can happen.

Keep the play controlled and the puppy's teeth away from children's faces until the pup has learned not to nip.

 Puppy biting training should start as soon as the pup comes home. Don't wait until he has nipped you a few times before you start teaching him not to.

Here are some tips to reduce the risk of, and deal with, puppy biting:

1. **Puppies growl and bite more when they are excited.** Don't allow things to escalate, so remove your pup from the situation before he gets too excited by putting him (or the kids!) in a crate or pen.

2. **Don't put your hand or finger into your pup's mouth to nibble;** this promotes biting.

3. **Limit your children's play time with pup** - and always supervise the sessions in the beginning. Teach them to gently play with and stroke your puppy, not to wind him up.

4. **Don't let the kids (or adults) run around the house with the puppy chasing** – this is an open invitation to nip at the ankles.

5. **If the puppy bites you, say "OUCH!" or "ACK!" loudly,** pull your hand or limb away quickly and rub the area – even if it doesn't hurt, pretend that it does. Shepherds are intuitive; your pup doesn't intend to hurt you and will probably be shocked that he has. He may come over to investigate, and even try to lick it better.

6. **Have a soft toy nearby every time you have a play session,** and when he starts to chew your hand or feet, clench your fingers (or toes!) to make it more difficult and distract him with a soft toy in your other hand. Keep the game interesting by moving the toy around or rolling it around in front of him. (He may be too young to fetch it back if you throw it). He may continue to chew you, but will eventually realise that the toy is far more interesting and livelier than your boring hand.

7. **If he becomes over-excited and too aggressive with the toy, if he growls a lot, stop playing with him and walk away.** When you walk away, don't say anything or make eye or physical contact with your puppy. Simply ignore him.

8. **If your pup is more persistent and tries to bite your legs as you walk away, thinking this is another fantastic game, stand still and ignore him.**

9. **If he still persists, tell him "NO!" in a very stern voice,** then praise him when he lets go.

10. **If you have to physically remove him from your trouser leg or shoe, leave him alone in the room for a while and ignore his demands for attention, even if he starts barking.**

Although you might find puppy biting quite cute and funny, it should be discouraged at all costs. You don't want an adolescent or adult German Shepherd doing this, when he can inadvertently cause serious injury.

Data compiled by the AVMA (American Veterinary Medical Association), found that German Shepherds are very high on the list of causing injury by biting: http://bit.ly/1jrLz5n

Jacque Lynn Schultz, CPTD, author and Companion Animal Programs Adviser, National Outreach, Petfinder, says: "Every year in the United States, 800,000 dog bites are severe enough to need medical treatment... Fifty per cent of all American children are bitten by a dog before the age of 13. Literally every dog has the potential to bite. Luckily for us, most don't."

However, she adds: "Some dogs believe the only way to protect their valuables is through an act of aggression. A dog's list of valuables may include food, toys, territory (a house or a car) or even their human family members. Dogs have been known to "protect" one family member from another, driving crying children away from their mothers or chasing amorous husbands out of bedrooms.

"The protection of territory is most often seen in males of guarding/herding breeds, such as German shepherds and rottweilers, while certain cocker spaniels and Labrador retrievers – females more often than males – put on ferocious displays over toys and chews, resulting in punishing bites to hands and faces."

The report states: "Responsible ownership and supervision is key to minimizing the risk of dog bites."

You may also think about keeping the toys you use to play with your puppy separate from other toys he has on his own. That way he will associate certain toys with having fun with you and will work harder to please you.

German Shepherds love playing and you can use this to your advantage by teaching your dog how to play nicely with you and the toy and then by using playtime as a reward for good behaviour.

....

Breeders' Advice

"GSDs are very oral dogs and like to play tug and mouth. Try to redirect the mouthing to a toy. They need to be taught very young not to put you in their mouths! Puppies should be taught to sit to receive attention or to be petted; jumping should be discouraged."

"My advice is persistent training so they know biting and jumping up are unacceptable, and rewards such a small marrow bone to help with the teething process. Turn your back on them so they realise attention is given only when they are seated."

"Mouthing is probably the hardest thing to deal with a German Shepherd puppy. Although, each puppy is unique and what works for one might not work for another, I have the most success with using one finger and lightly tapping the puppy on the nose and say **"No bite"** when they are mouthing me. I then offer them a toy and as soon as they are biting on the toy, I say, **"Good puppy."**

"To help stop a puppy from jumping up on you; never pet your puppy or pick them up if they are jumping up, wait until they are sitting nicely before you give them any attention. It will not take them long to learn that the only way they are going to get attention from you is to sit nicely and wait."

"Puppies that mouth, in my opinion, are doing what toddlers do. They don't have hands; they use their mouth to explore. The puppy needs to understand that teeth on skin is not acceptable, you would teach a toddler by saying: "No, don't touch, have your toy instead." Do the same with your dog: say **"No"** then offer a toy.

"If they insist on biting you, put your finger to the back of the jawline to where there are no teeth and they can't bite. It's uncomfortable, so they don't want your hand in there. This is only in extreme cases; most respond to a **"No"** and then a toy."

"Mouthing puppies get the same treatment from me that they would get from their mother. She uses her mouth to hold the puppy's mouth shut if the puppy was trying to mouth her. I do the same using my hand, gently holding the puppy's mouth shut without pressure. The puppy usually stops mouthing within a couple of failed attempts of him or her trying to mouth me. I find this the gentlest and most effective way.

"As for jumping up, I try and ignore it, don't touch, just turn my back and walk away. It is a difficult one as jumping up is what puppies naturally do to encourage mum to regurgitate, but by encouraging your puppy to stand (show dogs) or sit for their food and ignore undesired behaviour such as jumping up, the puppy will soon learn not to jump up.

"When a pup mouths, I tell people to redirect the puppy to a toy or something that is OK for them to bite."

The situation is slightly different with working GSD puppies. One breeder of working Shepherds said: "For a dog going into protection, we don't discourage the mouthiness, because the dogs have to learn how to bite, when to bite, where to bite. Any puppy that is discouraged from biting is going to be hesitant to bite as a protection dog.

"If it is an unwanted behaviour - and that is the case in most situations - then we advise the client to correct the dog verbally, redirect the puppy's attention to a proper item to mouth on, such as a bully stick or toy. Jumping up on people has to be curbed early and often or you will eventually have a dog that jumps on people and no one likes that. We turn our backs to the dog, ignore the dog, and reward the dog when all four feet are on the floor."

Clicker Training

Clicker training is a method of training that uses a sound - a click - to tell a dog when he does something right. The clicker is a tiny plastic box held in the palm of your hand, with a metal tongue that you push quickly to make the sound.

The clicker creates an efficient language between a human trainer and a trainee. First, the trainer teaches the dog that every time he hears the click, he gets a treat. Once the dog understands that clicks are always followed by treats, the click becomes a powerful training tool.

When this happens, the trainer can use the click to mark the instant the dog performs the right behaviour. For example, if a trainer wants to teach a dog to sit, she'll click the instant his rump hits the floor and then deliver a tasty treat. With repetition, the dog learns that sitting earns rewards.

So, the click takes on huge meaning. To the animal it means: "What I was doing the moment my trainer clicked, that's what she wants me to do."

The clicker in animal training is like the winning buzzer on a game show that tells a contestant he's just won the money! Through the clicker, the trainer communicates precisely with the dog, and that speeds up training.

Although the clicker is ideal because it makes a unique, consistent sound, you do need a spare hand to hold it. For that reason, some trainers prefer to keep both hands free and instead use a one-syllable word like **"Yes!"** or **"Good!"** to mark the desired behaviour. In the steps below, you can substitute the word in place of the click to teach your pet what the sound means.

It's easy to introduce the clicker to your German Shepherd. Spend half an hour or so teaching him that the sound of the click means **"Treat"** or **"Reward!"** Here's how:

1. **Sit and watch TV or read a book with your dog in the room. Have a container of treats within reach.**

2. **Place one treat in your hand and the clicker in the other**. (If your dog smells the treat and tries to get it by pawing, sniffing, mouthing or barking at you, just close your hand around the treat and wait until he gives up and leaves you alone).

3. **Click once and immediately open your hand to give your dog the treat.** Put another treat in your closed hand and resume watching TV or reading. Ignore your dog.

4. Several minutes later, click again and offer another treat.

5. Continue to repeat the click-and-treat combination at varying intervals, sometimes after one minute, sometimes after five minutes. Make sure you vary the time so that your dog doesn't know exactly when the next click is coming. Eventually, he'll start to turn toward you and look expectantly when he hears the click—which means he understands that the sound of the clicker means a treat is coming his way.

If your dog runs away when he hears the click, make the sound softer by putting it in your pocket or wrapping a towel around your hand that's holding the clicker. You can also try using a different sound, like the click of a retractable pen.

Clicker Training Basics

Once your dog seems to understand the connection between the click and the treat, you're ready to get started.

1. **Click just once, right when your dog does what you want him to do.** Think of it like pressing the shutter of a camera to take a picture of the behaviour.

2. **Remember to follow every click with a treat.** After you click, deliver the treat to your dog's mouth as quickly as possible.

3. **It's fine to switch between practising two or three behaviours within a session, but work on one command at a time.** For example, say you're teaching your German Shepherd to sit, lie down and raise his paw. You can do 10 repetitions of sit and take a quick play break. Then do 10 repetitions of down, and take another quick break. Then do 10 repetitions of stay, and so on. Keep training sessions short and stop before you or your dog gets tired of the game.

4. **End training sessions on a good note, when your dog has succeeded with what you're working on.** If necessary, ask him to do something you know he can do well at the end.

....

Collar and Leash Training

You have to train your Shepherd to get used to a collar and leash (lead), and then to walk nicely on the leash. Teaching these manners can be challenging because young German Shepherds are lively and quite strong, and they don't necessarily want to walk at the same pace as you.

FACT ❯ All dogs will pull on a leash initially. This isn't because they want to show you who's boss, it's because they are excited to be outdoors and are forging ahead.

If you are worried about pulling on your young protégé's neck, you might prefer to use a body harness to start off with. Harnesses work well with some puppies; they take the pressure away from a dog's sensitive neck area and distribute it more evenly around the body.

Generally, collars are best for training, but harnesses with a chest ring for the leash can also be effective; when your dog pulls, the harness turns him around.

Another option is to start your dog on a padded collar and then change to a harness once he has learned some leash etiquette – although padded collars can be quite heavy. Some dogs don't mind collars; some will try to fight them, while others will slump to the floor like you have hung a two-ton weight around their necks!

 Be patient and calm and proceed at a pace comfortable to him; don't fight your dog and don't force the collar on.

1. **Buy a collar that fits your puppy now** - not one he is going to grow into - so choose a small lightweight one that he will hardly notice. Consider getting one that snaps together to start with, rather than fiddling with buckles.

2. **Give a treat once the collar is on, not after you have taken it off.** Then gradually increase the length of time you leave the collar on. IMPORTANT: If you leave your dog in a crate, or alone in the house, take off the collar.

3. **Put the collar on when there are other things that will occupy him,** like when he is going outside with you, or in the home when you are interacting with him. Or put it on at mealtimes.

4. **Don't put the collar on too tight, you want him to forget it's there.** If yours scratches the collar, get his attention by encouraging him to follow you or play with a toy to forget the irritation.

5. **Once your puppy is happy wearing the collar, introduce the leash.** Buy a fixed-length leash around six feet long. Start off in the house or garden.

 Think of the leash as a safety device to stop him running off, not something to drag him around with. You want a dog that doesn't pull, so don't start by pulling him around; you don't want to get into a tug-of-war contest.

6. **Attach the leash to the collar and give him a treat while you put it on.** The minute it is attached, use the treats (instead of pulling on the leash) to lure him beside you so he gets used to walking with the collar and leash. You can use a favourite toy instead of treats and start off indoors.

Walking around the house with your dog on a leash might feel a bit odd, but it's a good way for your pup to develop a positive relationship with the collar and leash – just hope the neighbours aren't watching!

Some dogs react the moment they feel some tension on the leash – a bit like when a horse is being broken in. Drop the leash and allow him to run around the house or yard, dragging it after him. Try to make him forget about it by playing or starting a short fun training routine with treats.

7. **While he is concentrating on the new task, occasionally pick up the leash and call him to you.** Do it in an encouraging tone.

8. **The most important thing is not to yank on the leash.** If it is gets tight, just lure him back beside you with a treat or a toy while walking. Keep your hand holding the treat or toy down so your dog doesn't get the habit of jumping up at you.

9. **Let him gain confidence in you, and then in the leash and then himself.**

Some young dogs can sit down and refuse to move! If this happens, walk a few steps away, go down on one knee and encourage him to come to you using a treat or toy, then walk off again.

For some pups, the collar and leash can be restricting and they initially react with resistance. Present it as an exciting new game for your Shepherd. Proceed in tiny steps if that is what your puppy is happy with, don't over face him, but stick at it if you are met with resistance.

With training, your puppy WILL learn to walk nicely on a leash; it is a question of WHEN, not IF.

Walking on a Leash

There are different methods, but we have found the following one to be successful for quick results. Initially, the leash should be kept fairly loose. Have a treat in your hand as you walk, it will encourage your dog to sniff the treat as he walks alongside. He will not pull ahead as he will want to remain near the treat.

Give him the command **"Walk"** or **"Heel"** and then proceed with treat in hand, giving him a treat every few steps initially, then gradually extend the time between treats. Eventually, you should be able to walk with your hand comfortably at your side, periodically (every minute or so) reaching into your pocket to grab a treat to reward your dog.

If your dog starts pulling ahead, give him a **"No"** or **"Steady"** warning. If he slows down, give him a treat. But if he continues to pull ahead so that your arm becomes fully extended, stop walking. Wait for him to stop pulling and to look up at you.

At this point reward him for good behaviour before carrying on. Be sure to reward or praise him **quickly** any time he doesn't pull and walks alongside you with some slack in the leash.

If you have a lively young pup who is dashing all over the place on the leash, start training sessions when he is already a little bit tired - after play or exercise – but not exhausted.

Another way is what dog trainer Victoria Stillwell describes as the *"Reverse Direction Technique."* When your dog pulls, say **"Let's Go!"** in an encouraging manner, then turn away from him and walk off in the other direction, without jerking on the lead.

When he is following you and the leash is slack, turn back and continue on your original way. It may take a few repetitions, but your words and body language will make it clear that pulling will not get your dog anywhere, whereas walking calmly by your side - or even slightly in front of you - on a loose leash will get him where he wants to go.

There is an excellent video (in front of her beautiful house!) that shows Victoria demonstrating this technique and highlights just how easy it is with a dog that's easy to please.

It only lasts three minutes and is well worth watching: https://positively.com/dog-behavior/basic-cues/loose-leash-walking or Google *"Victoria Stillwell Loose Leash Walking."*

Teaching Tricks

German Shepherd breeder **Bobbi King, RVT, of Redwood Runs Pet Resort, California,** has this advice for teaching tricks and adds: "While they are just "tricks," they set the foundation for other things! The key to teaching your dog tricks is a lot of repetition and rewards. It is important to reward your dog with praises and/or treats when he is learning how to perform a new trick. Positive reinforcement is key. Only practise tricks for a few minutes at a time, your dog may become tired or frustrated because repeating tricks over and over may cause your dog's muscles to become fatigued. After each session reward your dog with a fun play session."

Paw

This is a fairly easy trick to teach your dog. The paw trick is your dog shaking your hand. Start by having your dog sit and simply reach your hand out and take hold of your dog's paw while saying **"Paw."** After a while all you have to do is reach out your hand and say **"Paw"** and your dog will put his paw in your hand.

Catch

Catch is probably one of the easiest tricks you can teach since it'll come naturally to most dogs. Simply toss a treat - small enough so that they won't choke on it and big enough for them to see it - into the air and when your dog sees it, he will grab it before it hits the ground. This may take a little while for your dog to get this trick so keep on practising by tossing up treats.

Fetch

Fetch is another trick that comes naturally for most dogs. Simply throw a ball or another object that you want your dog to retrieve and he'll go get it and return it to you. If you dog doesn't fetch the object, throw the ball and run with your dog to retrieve the object.

Give your dog a treat every time you retrieve the object. (You can cut a slit into a ball, place treats inside the ball and take them out of the ball when retrieved for a stronger association). After a while, slowly wean your dog off the treats by only giving them a treat every other retrieval, then every three retrievals, and so on.

Bow

This trick is where your dog looks like he is taking a bow by bringing his head to the floor. To start out with, get your dog in a standing position. Hold a treat in front of your dog's nose and bring it downward, his head should follow the treat while his body should stay off the ground (if he lays down simply place your hand underneath your dog to keep him from laying down and continue with the trick) and give him the treat after a couple seconds and say bow. After a while your dog will learn to bow whenever you give the **"Bow"** command.

....

GENERAL NOTE: If your puppy is in a hyperactive mood or extremely tired, he is not likely to be very receptive to training.

CREDIT: With thanks to the American Society for the Prevention of Cruelty to Animals for assistance with parts of this chapter. The ASPCA has a great deal of good advice and training tips on **its website at: www.aspca.org**

....

10. Working K9s

There is lots of information elsewhere in this book for owners whose German Shepherds live in the home as pets and companions.

In this chapter, Jacqueline Levy, of Cross Keys K9, based in Williamstown, New Jersey, gives an insight into what goes into the successful breeding, training and placement of working line German Shepherds.

....

Starting Out

My early experiences with German Shepherds began with my father's family, with whom I was very close. His brother had a black Shepherd named Shadow, and my Great Aunt kept several Shepherds, some of which they brought back with them from Germany, where my Great Uncle was stationed during and after World War II.

As a child, my neighbor and schoolmate had a Shepherd, Bondi, then later Bodi; both dogs seemed to know it was their duty to keep an eye on us children while we played outside. It was a nice neighborhood, but not crime-free. Dogs were security and fun to love.

When I met my partner, Steve LaFlamme, 10 years ago, he had two beautiful young German Shepherds from mixed American Show lines. These are show lines developed in the United States and Europe; dogs that are titled in conformation. American Show lines are markedly different from European Show lines – they tend to be larger and their bodies are more angular. Mixed Show lines could be a combination of American and European or mixed European lines (show dogs from Western, middle and Eastern Europe).

Photo: Kane, Explosive Detector Dog, with his handler and handler's wife after getting certified.

Show line dogs may also be mixed with working line dogs, depending on the breeder - although this is not a practice we utilize. All our dogs have either working titles or have been breed-surveyed for conformation if they or their ancestors came from overseas.

Steve and I discussed our likes and dislikes of the breed. Health, aptitude, and workability were the overarching set of objectives that eventually defined and developed our breeding program.

He had extensive experience of breeding and showing champion miniature horses and Keeshonds when he was younger, then keeping and considering breeding German Shepherds. We decided we wanted to breed functional, intelligent and healthy German Shepherds from European Working lines.

We knew we needed a stud. Money was tight and we needed to make the right decisions. After reviewing several options, he found a wildcard stud, Shelby – the thickest, blackest, fluffiest bear/wolf-like creature with a massive head and an equally large personality and intellect.

Shelby had nice dogs in his pedigree; he was bred in the United States from working line dogs going back to the older German, Dutch, Czech and Belgian working dogs of the late 20th century. Moreover, Shelby came with a solid health history and an amazing level of focus and engagement, which has become one of the hallmarks of our breeding program.

I'd been offered a place on a university program in the veterinary field, but turned it down after we found Shelby. I wanted to set up a breeding and consulting program, with the goal of providing additional first-class services for working K9s.

We then chose Sascha, a beautiful sable female from West and East German Working lines with a strong working pedigree. I received a lot of history and paperwork with the pedigrees – the German SV certification system is far more rigorous than here in the US.

It stated where her ancestors came from and what they were bred for, as well as hip histories and DM (Degenerative Myelopathy) status. We decided early on that DM was not going to be a part of our breeding program.

As we added females that met our criteria for breeding and potential offspring, we discovered in one of these, amazing scent capabilities in bloodlines largely known for personal protection dogs, as well as dogs with good longevity, solid nerves and excellent temperaments. Service dogs for the disabled was another strength in our puppies that we honed and continue to produce.

....

Why We Health Test

In my opinion, health testing should be a factor in any breeding program. All dogs are prone to illness and disease, and if you know what is in your bloodlines, you have a better understanding of what outcomes to expect.

I do not think enough breeders pay attention to it. I also think that it is possible to lose good dogs in the gene pool that might have more positives than negatives if you discriminate based on the results of one genetic test.

All GSD puppy buyers should ask to see the health testing results for the puppy's parents, and a history of health problems in the bloodlines. Any breeder who tells a prospective buyer that the dogs in the pedigree are clear and that there are no problems is not telling the entire truth.

Photo: "This is Wolf, our newest stud who is nearly two. The puppy isn't his, but Wolf gets along with everyone; he is one of our demo dogs. He is my dream dog. His father is a very well-known former Slovakian police dog named Clif Vicona."

All dogs have faults, whether visible or invisible and, without health testing, we have no way of guaranteeing that the offspring will not be affected.

As well as what the health guarantees are, a prospective buyer should understand their recourse with the breeder if the puppy is defective in one way or another.

No dog is perfect, but no health testing or history of testing in the lines is a recipe for disaster.

Health is primary for us. Clients who spend thousands on a dog with training for a working capacity need to know that their dogs are healthy, come from healthy, tested stock and will likely work for at least seven to 10 years.

We are a DM-clear kennel, meaning we do not breed dogs that test at risk or as carriers for the gene mutation that causes DM. This is the one test and requirement that first and foremost must include the pairing of two dogs that have two normal copies of the gene, despite my personal feelings that one should take into consideration the entire dog when considering a candidate for a breeding program.

The disease is like ALS (or Lou Gehrig's disease in humans), where the dog's back end starts to deteriorate and it travels up the spine, cripples and eventually kills the dog.

We do genetic testing for diseases that are relevant to German Shepherds including, but not limited to, blood clotting diseases, kidney diseases, hip and elbow dysplasia.

....

Differences in Working and Show Lines

As we added females that met our criteria for breeding and potential offspring, we also knew we needed another stud to add to the father and son we had been using, albeit with great success in the puppies produced.

That put me on a search for a new stud, one we would raise and train and test for health and temperament. I now became the consumer looking at a newer online marketplace than what had existed five years earlier. Things evolve.

It is challenging selecting a good breeder with good lines and healthy dogs; breeders who will stand behind their dogs if there is a problem. I lucked out with the best puppy with the ideal temperament and great health clearances. From Eastern and Western European lines, he has become quite the sire we'd hoped he would be.

The drive levels are different between the Central and East European dogs and the American dogs. Here we also see the divide between the working lines and the show lines that has been brewing since the inception of the breed, but became more pronounced in the American Show lines with barrel chests, roached backs, sharp rear angulations, odd gaits and usually the typical black and tan or black and red dog that looks beautiful, but may not be practical in a working or active home, which is the typical client for us.

In show lines you have the dogs that excel in conformation and compete in AKC-sanctioned events and there you will see *"Champion Bloodlines."* Dogs that are not show quality are deemed *"pet quality."*

In working dogs, you will see a variety of titles most notably from IGP (the former IPO or Schutzhund, testing Tracking, Obedience and Protection). There's also Agility, Scent Work, Tracking, Utility, Obedience and a slew of other events that can challenge the German Shepherd.

German Shepherds are appealing in a variety of ways and for a variety of reasons. I find the show line conformation to be compromised by its exaggerated characteristics, although for many that is the quintessential German Shepherd.

In the working lines you see longer coats, which are a fault in the show lines (in the US), as well as sables with thick double coats, and various colors including solid black, which is highly desirable, and other colors such as solid white, liver, bi-color, blanket backs which are mostly black - more black overall than the typical black and tan, or black with another collar saddle pattern

The coat and how active the dog is often affects where you can keep your dog so it can be comfortable and have space to be outside. German Shepherds are comfortable at approximately 40 degrees (4.5 degrees Celsius).

Anything under freezing and the dog should have access to indoors with heating and ventilation, proper access to food and water, and/or a warm kennel or crate set-up. Most of my dogs love to be outside when it's cold and find the heat oppressive. In the summertime, every dog is indoors in the air conditioning.

Our Working Lines

We breed strictly working line dogs. These are dogs that become active or working companions, service dogs for people with disabilities, or get certified for scent work and or patrol work.

A Single Purpose Dog is a working dog that is trained in either scent or patrol. A Scent Dog might be trained in explosives, narcotics, cell phones, prison contraband, bedbugs, leaks in gas lines, or thumb drives and hard drives often used by pedophiles to store and hide child pornography or details of human trafficking.

Search and Rescue dogs are trained to find either a) live targets or b) cadavers. During the aftermath of September 11, the emergency services used mainly cadaver dogs because the operation quickly went from a rescue to a recovery effort. The rescue dogs were sometimes provided with live targets (rescuers who hid), so the dogs could find them and realize some success for their efforts.

Photo: Blaze, aged two. "He is astonishingly beautiful and sweet and now lives as a family dog with a teacher and her husband in Virginia."

Working dogs are trained in a variety of methods, but there is always a reward in some shape or form for the dog, which is the dog's incentive to work. This might a ball, Kong, or decoy sleeve. Another methodology is that the dogs eat only when they are working and training, so the objective is that the dog will work for food.

A couple of our dogs have show titles in their pedigrees; those titles were obtained overseas, and those are working lines that have been breed surveyed by the European breed wardens. We prefer and look for working titles wherever possible, preferably deep into the pedigrees of the parents, along with whatever historical health and longevity data we have accumulated over the years.

The working dog is bred for function, health and successful placement of the puppies with owner/handlers that are a mutually beneficial fit.

We try and approximate the Breed Standard as best we can, but sometimes the client needs something that exceeds or is smaller than what a standard-sized Shepherd has to offer.

Smaller dogs make for better military applications, because, in some cases, the handler may need to carry the dog and/or the dog can get into tight spaces. Larger dogs might be better as man-stoppers for law enforcement or might be better suited to a tall handler.

For example, I have clients that are well over 6'3" and need dogs for mobility assistance. I am breeding my male of Slovakian/German descent because he is taller than my other males and breeding him with a female that is also taller than my other females.

The bark of the Shepherd is enough to deter most people; some are downright scary in their appearance. It is wonderful to have that extra pair of high-performance ears and nose on alert, adding an additional level of security.

Most of our clients are looking for house/estate/family dogs. Dogs that don't go into working capacities are house dogs; pets and companions that are naturally protective of their owners, their property, and the perimeter of that property. These dogs are excellent deterrents for people with bad intentions and double as comfort/therapy dogs, providing intelligent active company for their owners and handlers. A trained protection dog adds another level of defence and offense if necessary.

Most Shepherds will usually detect the presence of other people through sounds or smells. The Shepherd has adequate vision, but their scent and hearing capabilities are superlative. Most of our dogs go through training that will capitalize on these abilities and cultivate them for particular purposes.

Temperament

Temperament testing, such as the Volhard Method, can help determine the nature of the puppies and if they might be a good fit.

Potential is hard to gauge at such an early age, but there are things you can look for in a puppy that might indicate he may have potential as a service dog, scent dog, protection dog, or something in between.

We produce a significant number of service dogs for people in a variety of situations with a variety of needs. Service dogs cannot and should not be protective. Their temperaments and capabilities need to be extremely stable and secure.

As for temperament, we look for:

- Clear head, intelligence, aptitude, adaptability and resilience
- Great eye contact and responsiveness; follows directions
- Eager to please the handler and complete the tasks, or
- A supreme ball drive that indicates that the dog can be taught several things using the ball (or a towel or a Kong rubber toy) as the incentive

Dogs that are suitable for service work for people with disabilities should be confident and focussed in temperament, meaning nothing distracts them from the task at hand. They have to be good with people of all types and sizes, environmentally socialized to different sounds, textures, places and situations.

They also need to be smart and not aggressive, with a touch of civil disobedience to decide if the handler or owner needs help.

A prime example of this might be a blind person who is walking across a street with their service dog. The service dog needs to let the handler know to stop walking if there is a car coming. The handler may persist, but the dog must know that it is more important NOT to let the handler proceed in the wake of danger, despite the handler wanting to continue.

Another example is a person who has a service dog for medical alert, and might have a seizure in public. The dog cannot be protective of the handler if the handler is down. The dog may be trained to leave the handler and go search for help. It is largely dependent on the needs of the client, and the training the dog has to do its job correctly.

Photo: Law enforcement service dog, Kane, bred by Jacqui, goes everywhere with his handler.

Diet and Activity

The level of activity of the GSD can also determine what diet would be appropriate. Shepherds are known for allergies and food intolerances. They can also have digestive disorders such as irritable bowel syndrome, megaesophagus, etc.

As a large breed dog, they need to be fed a balanced food that provides calcium and phosphorus in a 1 to 1 ratio, so that the puppy grows into a dog at a commensurate rate. Upsetting this balance can create growing pains, such as panosteitus.

It takes two years for the growth plates to close in a GSD puppy. For that we recommend spay and neuter at around the age of two.

Some people feed raw and that is great for keeping a working dog lean, and it has been shown that raw-fed dogs shed less. Dogs that donate blood are not allowed to be on a raw diet.

I utilize good quality kibble supplemented with whole foods such as small fish like sardines in olive oil or water, mackerel, krill, beef, chicken, some vegetables, and wholesome table scraps depending on how you eat.

Dogs that are more active will need a diet that includes higher levels of protein. Higher levels of protein can be a heavy load on a dog's kidneys and liver, so owners should check with their veterinarians or consult with canine nutrition specialists.

During this time of development, it is important to start training your dog. Working with or under the direction of a professional trainer will help you identify and correct problems early. House manners, crate and potty training, simple courtesies and commands. Then basic and advanced obedience, off leash, and into a task or achievement-based training.

Seller's Remorse

The goal for breeding Working Line shepherds is function over form, but they also happen to be magnificently beautiful dogs.

It is bittersweet when the puppies leave. I get very attached, and I spend most of my days with them for early environmental socialization and the ability to handle the dog early on. I have seller's remorse for many dogs that I have placed from here!

Some dogs have gone on to save lives and to give people a reason to live. They are part of my reason to live. A dog gets you out of your head; the bond can be incredible.

He or she may be able to sense differences and changes in your body chemistry; some can create a buffer zone for people with hyper-vigilance, and the possibilities in scent work are incredible.

My goal is to continue to explore these opportunities as they arise and breed dogs that fill the need for explosive detection, chemical detection, narcotics and/or provide security and protection services to a family or business.

Each dog comes with a personality, from aloof and stoic with strangers to dogs that get along with everyone and most dogs they meet. The German Shepherd, no matter whether it is from show lines or working lines, is always going to be more appealing than other breeds from an intelligence and abilities standpoint. Their loyalty is unmatched once you have developed a bond.

There is simply no other dog like the awesome German Shepherd.

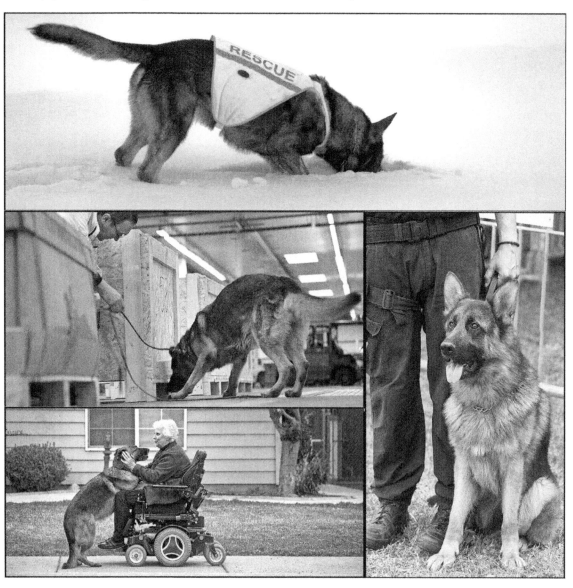

Library photos showing German Shepherds working in a variety of roles.

11. Exercise

There's no getting away from the fact that the German Shepherd is a big, active breed that needs a lot of daily exercise. The Kennel Club recommends a minimum of two hours per day. How your GSD gets this will depend on a number of factors, including your lifestyle, whether he is from show or working lines, and whether you take part in any canine activities.

The Importance of Exercise

One thing all dogs have in common – including every German Shepherd ever born - is the need for daily exercise. It helps to keep your dog content, healthy, free from disease, and exercise:

- ❧ Strengthens respiratory and circulatory systems
- ❧ Helps get oxygen to tissue cells
- ❧ Helps to keep Shepherds mentally stimulated and socialised
- ❧ Keeps muscles toned and joints flexible
- ❧ Wards off obesity
- ❧ Aids digestion
- ❧ Releases endorphins that trigger positive feelings

 **The amount of exercise an individual dog needs varies according to** temperament, natural energy levels, your living conditions, whether he is kept with other dogs and, importantly, what he gets used to.

Another major factor is whether your dog is bred from show, working or mixed lines. There are, of course, variations from one dog to another, but working dogs generally have a higher drive than German Shepherds bred for showing or as pets.

It makes sense. A Shepherd whose ancestors worked all day will have higher physical and mental demands than one bred to have a calmer nature for the show ring or home. That's not to say German Shepherds don't love snuggling up with you; they do - they just need their exercise as well.

ALL GSDs, whether from show, working or mixed lines, require considerable exercise and mental challenges. They are not small dogs; they were not bred as companions; they were developed to do a job alongside humans all day long - and all breeds with working backgrounds need daily physical and mental stimulation.

When we talk about "exercising" a German Shepherd, most people think this means taking the dog out for a walk two or three times a day - and it does for many owners. However, there are many other forms of exercise for Shepherds.

 Mental exercise is extremely important for German Shepherds.

They love a challenge. They will fetch a ball or toy for hours on end; some become almost obsessive about games or toys. Daily training, hiding objects and rewarding your dog with praise when he finds them, setting up a mini agility course in your yard or garden, or providing interactive toys that make dogs use their brains to get the treat will all help to keep your GSD stimulated.

Playing in the garden or yard with toys or balls is also a great way to burn off steam (for both of you!). But Frisbee isn't recommended for growing GSDs, as high-impact jumping can lead to joint issues later in life.

A fenced garden or yard should not be seen as a replacement for daily exercise away from the home, where a dog can experience new places, scents, people and dogs. Your dog will enjoy going for walks on the leash, but will enjoy it far more when he is allowed to run free, once you have taught him The Recall.

Owning more than one dog - or having friends with dogs - is a great way for well-socialised German Shepherds to get lots of exercise. A couple of dogs running around together get far more exercise than one dog on his own.

A German Shepherd is a great choice for active families. Once trained, they make excellent jogging and cycling companions – if you are cycling, gradually build up distance and make sure your dog is not struggling to keep up. These incredibly loyal dogs will run until they drop. You can hike all day with a fit German Shepherd and you won't tire him out.

Most enjoy swimming and this is a great form of exercise – particularly for older dogs as it does not place any stress on joints. Many veterinary practices now use water tanks for remedial therapy as well as canine recreation.

German Shepherds will dash in and out of the water all day long if you'll let them, but remember that swimming is a lot more strenuous for a dog than walking or even running. Don't constantly throw that stick or ball into the water - overstretching him could place a strain on his heart; all dogs should exercise within their limits. We also advise gently drying your GSD's ears after swimming to reduce the risk of ear infections.

 Training your Shepherd to Canine Good Citizen level is an excellent start.

GSDs excel in obedience events and canine competitions, and the list of potential events is as long as your arm, including: Agility, Showing, Working Trials, Flyball, Rally Obedience, Herding, Tracking, Nose Work, Barn Hunt, Dock Diving, Lure Coursing, Trick Dog, IGP (Schutzhund). Read about some of the activities Marie Donahue does with her Shepherds in **Chapter 4.**

An under-exercised or bored German Shepherd will find something to occupy him - and it could well involve destructive behaviour inside the house or yard. Leaving the dog in a crate too often is NOT the solution, as an over-crated Shepherd is likely to develop anxiety issues. The answer is more exercise and mental stimulation.

These are big dogs in every sense of the word; they are not dogs to be ignored all day. If you haven't the time or energy levels to devote a couple of hours a day to a German Shepherd, consider getting a smaller non-working breed with a lower drive.

Exercising Puppies

There are strict guidelines to stick to with puppies; it is important not to over-exercise young pups. Their bones and joints are quick-growing and cannot tolerate a great deal of stress until their skeletons are fully developed.

German Shepherds are prone to hip dysplasia and other joint and spine issues. Allowing a young pup to run up and down stairs, jump on and off the couch or play Fetch or Frisbee for hours on end are all asking for trouble. You could end up with a damaged dog and a pile of vet's bills.

(Tip) **The golden rule is to start slowly and build it up. The worst case scenario for GSD puppies is a combination of over-exercise and overweight.**

Do not take your pup out of the yard or garden until he has got the all-clear after his vaccinations, unless you carry him around to start the socialisation process. Then start with short daily walks on the leash. Shepherd puppies are extremely curious and have a highly-developed sense of smell, so get yours used to being outside the home environment and experiencing new scents, situations, sights, etc. as soon as possible. The general guideline is:

Five minutes of on-leash exercise per month of age until the puppy is fully grown.

That means a total of:

- 🐾 15 minutes when he is three months (13 weeks) old
- 🐾 30 minutes when six months (26 weeks) old, and so on

This does not include time he spends running freely around playing on grass or indoors.

Slowly increase the time as he gets used to being exercised and this will gradually build up his muscles and stamina.

It is, however, OK for your young pup to have free run of your garden or yard (once you have plugged any gaps in the fence), provided it has a soft surface such as grass, not concrete. He will take things at his own pace and stop to sniff or rest.

If you have other dogs, restrict the time the pup is allowed to play with them, as he won't know when he's had enough.

Once he is a year old, your dog can go out for much longer walks. And when your little pup has grown into a stunning adult German Shepherd with a skeleton capable of carrying him through a long and healthy life, it will have been worth all the effort.

A long, healthy life is best started slowly.

Establish a Routine

Establish an exercise regime early in your dog's life. Get him used to walks at the same time every day, at a time that fits in with your daily routine – even if it is only five-minute puppy walks. Whatever routine you decide on, stick to it. If you begin by taking your dog out three times a day and then suddenly stop, he will become restless, attention-seeking and possibly destructive because he has been used to more exercise. Conversely, don't expect a dog used to very little exercise to suddenly go on day-long hikes; he will struggle. Such strenuous exercise should not be started until your GSD is at least one year old.

Owning a German Shepherd requires a big commitment from owners – you are looking at lots of daily exercise for a decade! Older dogs still need exercise to keep their body, joints and systems functioning properly. They need a less strenuous regime – they are usually happier with shorter or slower walks - still enough to keep them physically and mentally active. Again, every dog is different, some are happy to keep running right until the end.

Regular exercise can add months or even years to a dog's life. The exception is if your old or sick dog is struggling – he will show you that he doesn't feel well enough to walk far by stopping and looking at you or sitting down and refusing to move.

 Most German Shepherds love to go out whatever the weather – rain, snow, hail! So, when you get your German Shepherd, invest in a good set of boots and outdoor clothing!

Exercise Tips

❖ German Shepherds are intelligent and love a challenge. They like to use their brains, particularly working GSDs. Make time for daily training and games - even elderly German Shepherds like to play

❖ Don't strenuously exercise your dog straight after or within an hour of a meal as this can be a cause of Bloat. A dog can go into shock and then cardiac arrest within hours. If you suspect this is happening, get your dog to a vet IMMEDIATELY

❖ While Shepherds do well in cold weather, they can struggle when temperatures soar. If you live in a hot climate, save strenuous exercise for early mornings or evenings when it's cooler

❖ Do not throw a ball or toy repeatedly for a dog if he shows signs of over-exertion; the same goes for swimming. Your loyal German Shepherd will fetch to please you. Stop the activity after a while - no matter how much he begs you to throw it again

❖ Some dogs, particularly adolescent ones, may try to push the boundaries when out walking on the leash. If yours stops dead and stares at you or tries to pull you in another direction, ignore him. Do not return his stare, just continue along the way you want to go, not his way

❖ Vary your exercise route – it will be more interesting for both of you

❖ Exercise older dogs more gently - especially in cold weather when it is harder to get their bodies moving. Have a cool-down period at the end of the exercise to reduce stiffness and soreness; it helps to remove lactic acids from the dog's body, and our 12-year-old loves a body massage

❖ Make sure your dog has constant access to fresh water. Dogs can't sweat much; they need to drink water to cool down

Exercise helps you: bond with your dog, keep fit, see different places and meet new companions - both canine and human. In short, it enhances both your lives.

Your German Shepherd will get used to an exercise regime. If you over-stimulate and constantly exercise him as a puppy, he will think this is the norm.

This may not be such an attractive prospect when your fully-grown German Shepherd constantly needs and demands your attention a year or two later, or your work patterns change and you have less time to devote to him. The key is to start a routine that you can stick to.

Socialisation

Your adult dog's character will depend largely on two things: his temperament, which he is born with, and his environment, or how you bring him up and treat him. In other words, it's a combination of **nature and nurture.**

And one absolutely essential aspect of nurture is socialisation: *"the process of learning to behave in a way that is acceptable to society."*

When we talk about socialising puppies, it means helping them to be comfortable within a human society that includes many different types of people, animals, environments, situations, buildings, traffic, sights, noises, smells, etc. Scientists have come to realise the importance that socialisation plays in a dog's life. We also now know that there is a fairly small window that is the *optimum* time for socialisation - and this is up to the age of four months or so.

FACT 〉 This does not mean that owners shouldn't socialise their Shepherds after this age; far from it. Socialisation should continue throughout a dog's life, but it is particularly important with young German Shepherds.

Most young animals, including dogs, are naturally able to get used to their everyday environment until they reach a certain age. When they reach this age, they become more suspicious of things they haven't yet experienced. This is why it often takes longer to train an older dog.

The age-specific natural development allows a puppy to get comfortable with the

normal people, animals, scents, sights and sounds, that will be a part of his life. It ensures that he doesn't spend his life growling or barking at every visitor or other animal.

The suspicion that dogs develop in later puppyhood – after the critical window - also ensures that they react with a healthy dose of caution to new things that could really be dangerous - Mother Nature is clever!

Socialisation will give your dog confidence and teach him not to be afraid of new experiences. The ultimate goal is to have a happy, well-adjusted dog that you can take anywhere. Ever seen a therapy German Shepherd in action and noticed how incredibly well-adjusted to life they are? This is no coincidence. These dogs have been extensively socialised and are ready and able to deal in a calm manner with whatever situation they encounter. They are relaxed and comfortable in their own skin - just like you want your dog to be.

Developing the Well-Rounded Adult Dog

Well-socialised German Shepherds develop into safer, more relaxed and enjoyable adult dogs with less fear or aggression towards other people and dogs. This is because they're more comfortable in a wider variety of situations than poorly socialised canines.

German Shepherds who are relaxed about people, animals, honking horns, joggers, cyclists, veterinary examinations, crowds, traffic, noise, etc. are easier to live with than GSDs who find these situations challenging or frightening. Well-socialised dogs live more relaxed, peaceful and happy lives than dogs that are constantly stressed by their environment.

Tip And if you are planning on showing your dog or taking part in canine competitions, get him used to the buzz of these events early on.

Socialisation isn't *"all or nothing,"* it's an ongoing process. The wider the range of experiences you expose him to when young, the better his chances are of becoming a more relaxed adult. Don't over-face your little puppy. Socialisation should never be forced, but approached systematically and in a manner that builds confidence and curious interaction. If your pup finds a new experience frightening, take a step back, introduce him to the scary situation much more gradually, and make a big effort to do something he loves during the situation or right afterwards.

For example, if your puppy seems to be frightened by noise and vehicles at a busy road, a good method would be to go to a quiet road, sit with the dog away from - but within sight of - the traffic. Every time he looks towards the traffic say **"YES"** and reward him with a treat. If he is still stressed, move further away. When your dog takes the food in a calm manner, he is becoming more relaxed and getting used to traffic sounds, so you can edge a bit nearer - but still just for short periods until he becomes totally relaxed. Keep each session short and positive.

Meeting Other Dogs

When you take your beautiful pup to meet other dogs for the first few times, you are bound to be a bit nervous. To start with, introduce your puppy to just one other dog – one you know to be friendly, rather than taking him straight to the park where there are lots of dogs of all sizes racing around, which might frighten the life out of your little bundle of instinct.

1. Always make the initial introductions on neutral ground, so as not to trigger territorial behaviour. You want your German Shepherd to approach other dogs with confidence, not fear.

2. Help both dogs experience good things when they're in each other's presence. Let them sniff each other briefly, which is normal canine greeting behaviour.

3. As they do, talk to them in a happy, friendly tone of voice; never use a threatening tone. Don't allow them to sniff each other for too long as this may escalate to an aggressive response.

4. After a short time, get the attention of both dogs and give each a treat in return for obeying a simple command, such as **"Sit"** or **"Stay."** Continue with the **"happy talk,"** treats and simple commands.

Of course, if you have more than one dog or a number of working German Shepherds, your puppy will learn to socialise within the pack. However, you should still spend time introducing him to new sights, sounds and animals. Here are some signs of fear to look out for when your dog interacts with other canines:

- 🐾 Running away
- 🐾 Freezing on the spot
- 🐾 Frantic/nervous behaviour, such as excessive sniffing, drinking or playing with a toy frenetically
- 🐾 A lowered body stance or crouching
- 🐾 Lying on his back with his paws in the air – this is a submissive gesture
- 🐾 Lowering of the head, or turning the head away
- 🐾 Lips pulled back baring teeth and/or growling
- 🐾 Hair raised on his back (hackles)
- 🐾 Tail lifted in the air
- 🐾 Ears high on the head

Some of these responses are normal. A pup may well crouch on the ground or roll on to his back to show other dogs he is not a threat.

Tip Try not to be nervous or over-protective, your puppy has to learn how to interact with other dogs. But if the situation looks like escalating into something more aggressive, calmly distract the dogs or remove your puppy – don't shout or shriek. Dogs pick up on fear and this in itself could trigger an unpleasant situation.

Another sign to look out for is **eyeballing.** In the canine world, staring a dog in the eyes is a challenge and may trigger an aggressive response. This is more relevant to adult dogs, as a young pup will soon be put in his place by bigger or older dogs; it is how they learn.

The rule of thumb with puppy socialisation is to keep a close eye on your pup's reaction to whatever you expose him to, so that you can tone things down if he seems at all frightened. Always follow up a socialisation experience with praise, petting, a fun game or a special treat.

One positive sign from a dog is **the play bow** when he goes down on to his front elbows but keeps his backside up in the air, *pictured.* This is a sign that he is feeling friendly towards the other dog and wants to play.

Aggression is often grounded in fear, and a dog that mixes easily is less likely to be aggressive. Take your new dog everywhere you can. You want him to feel relaxed and calm in any situation, even noisy and crowded ones. Take treats with you and praise him when he reacts calmly to new situations.

Introduce him to your friends and teach him not to bite or jump up. If you have young children, it is not only the dog that needs socialising! Youngsters also need training on how to act around dogs, so both parties learn to respect the other.

Tip An excellent way of getting your new puppy to meet other dogs in a safe environment is at a puppy class.

Ask around if any classes are being run locally. Some vets and dog trainers run puppy classes for very junior pups who have had all their vaccinations to help pups get used to other dogs of a similar age. In some areas, there are even classes specifically for German Shepherds; check if your local German Shepherd club is running any.

Breeders on Exercise

We asked the breeders involved in this book how long they exercise their dogs for and this is what they said: "Each dog gets about two hours of exercise a day, more if they want it. Early and proper socialisation is mandatory for puppies to become well-adjusted."

"I exercise mine for one to two hours a day, but they also have the run of the whole of my yard as well as the garden to play and run around at will. I find mental stimulation as important for a GSD as the exercise, I use a lot of puzzle feeders, hide bones and treats for search games, or even hide toys and balls to find."

"The essential advice I have is do not over-exercise your puppy. It will take the first year of the puppy for the joints to fully develop so over-exercising could do a lot of damage at this stage. If you add a couple of 10-minute play sessions a day to exercise sessions, it will already start to mount up."

"A good two hours a day." "Mine all go out for about a 45-minute walk together each day plus training, I do have a large garden too." "As much as possible, at least one hour."

Photo courtesy of Cheryl Spurr, Reinglen German Shepherds.

"Make sure your puppy gets lots of positive experiences, the more they get early on, the more confident they will be when they are adult. I have heard people say you don't want a confident GSD, as that will make it aggressive. But the opposite is true; the more confident they are, the less likely they are to react to anything."

"My dogs are trained daily for short sessions about 10 to 15 minutes each session. They are then exercised, either playing ball, Frisbee or treadmilled for short durations (working Shepherds)."

"We live on a smallholding (small farm). My dogs run outside all day and I do believe that is why they are so content and fulfilled. Young pups should not be exercised too much as their bones are soft and damage can be done if too much exercise is encouraged too early."

"It's hard to say on a daily basis. When we are not spending time training them, hiking, bike riding, swimming, playing fetch and so many other activities we enjoy with them, they have the freedom to lay around our house or run around and play by themselves with our other German Shepherds."

"We are fortunate in that we have six dogs and during work-time, they do keep each other company and play together. We also have a large field as well as the garden so we are up there two to three times a day for at least half an hour, playing ball, fetching and retrieving. They also spend quite a bit of time chasing each other and sniffing round the field checking out who has visited during the day or overnight. A good sniff can be as stimulating as a short walk.

"While a pup should not be over-worked, two to six-year-olds are is in their prime and should have enough exercise and stimulation to make them tired."

Many of the breeders also take part in organised activities with their German Shepherds.

12. German Shepherd Health

Health has a major impact on an animal's quality of life and should always be a major consideration when choosing and raising a dog. The first step is to select a puppy from a breeder producing German Shepherds that are sound in both body and temperament – and this involves health screening - and secondly, to play your part in keeping your dog healthy throughout his or her life.

NOTE: This chapter is intended to be used as a medical encyclopaedia to help you to identify potential health issues and act promptly in the best interests of your dog. Please don't read it thinking your German Shepherd will get lots of these ailments – he or she WON'T!

....

It is becoming increasingly evident that genetics can have a huge influence on a person's health and even life expectancy, with a great deal of time and money currently being devoted to genetic research. A human is more likely to suffer from a hereditary illness if the gene or genes for that disorder is passed on from parents or grandparents. That person is said to have a *"predisposition"* to the ailment if the gene is in the family's bloodline. Well, the same is true of dogs.

There is not a single breed without the potential for some genetic weakness. For example, 30% of Dalmatians have problems with their hearing and a quarter of all West Highland White Terriers have a hereditary itchy skin disease.

A German Shepherd or a Westie from unscreened parents will be more likely to suffer from these disorders than one from health-tested parents.

The 2015 UK scientific study *The Challenges of Pedigree Dog Health: Approaches to Combating Inherited Disease* states: "The development of (such) pedigree dog breeds can be both a blessing and a curse: desirable features are rigidly retained, but sometimes, undesirable disease-causing genes can be inadvertently fixed within the breed."

In other words, bad genes can be inherited along with good ones.

 In the same study, the German Shepherd is listed at the top of the table with more potentially inheritable diseases than any other breed – a whopping 77.

To read the full study, type the title into Google and click on Table 1 at the bottom to view individual breed statistics.

UFAW, Universities Federation for Animal Welfare, www.ufaw.org.uk, says this about Hip Dysplasia: "Figures for the proportion of German Shepherds affected vary from study to study, but range from 18 to 49%, and the breed appears to have significantly higher risk of hip dysplasia than Dobermanns, Labradors and Rottweilers."

The AKC (American Kennel Club) still only lists the average GSD lifespan at seven to 10 years, while in the UK, the average is 10 to 11 years. Some German Shepherds even live into their teens. And if you already have your German Shepherd, there is plenty you can do to help your dog live a long and healthy life.

Health Certificates

The good news is that anyone thinking of getting a German Shepherd puppy today can reduce the chance of their dog having a genetic disease by choosing a puppy from healthy bloodlines.

If you're looking for a puppy, you might be considering a breeder based on the look or colour of her dogs, or their success at sporting competitions or in the show ring, but consider the health of the puppy's parents and ancestors as well. Could they have passed on unhealthy genes along with the good genes for all those features you are attracted to?

Check these health tests for the parents and ask to see original certificates where relevant - a good breeder will be happy to provide them:

UK:

- ❧ **Hip Dysplasia** - *compulsory* for AKC Assured Breeders. BVA/KC Hip Dysplasia Scheme
- ❧ The Kennel Club (KC) also *recommends* the following tests:
- ❧ **Elbows** - BVA/KC/ISDS Elbow Dysplasia Scheme
- ❧ **Eyes** - BVA/KC Eye Scheme for various eye diseases
- ❧ **DM** - Degenerative Myelopathy
- ❧ **Haemophilia** – testing for males only
- ❧ **Age** - No stud dog to be under 18 months old; females under two years old should not produce a litter

USA:

To achieve the German Shepherd Dog Club of America's (GSDCA) Health Award of Merit, breeders have to carry out the following tests:

- ❧ Hips and Elbows – OFA or SV
- ❧ **Heart** – OFA
- ❧ Thyroid – OFA
- ❧ **DM** – (Optional)
- ❧ **Temperament** - GSDCA Temperament Test

The AKC has a ***Bred with H.E.A.R.T. program*** and all member breeders have to ensure that: "You certify that your breeding stock is health tested in accordance with the recommendations of their breed's AKC Breed Parent Club." You can find a list of these committed breeders on the AKC website.

UK breeder Stephanie Millington, of CunAnnun German Shepherds, Norfolk, says: "More DNA tests are developed every year, and I strongly believe that if one has the possibility to test for certain hereditary issues, then one should do so - rather than turning a blind eye for whatever reason.

For most breeders it's not wanting to spend money on it, as well as the fear of losing their breeding stock. The German Kennel Club eliminated the eye disease PRA from their registered stock of Dachshunds 10 years ago by ONLY registering puppies from PRA-clear parentage. In Holland, they are starting to do the same with brachycephalic (flat-faced) breeds. In German Shepherds, we have one of the largest gene pools in purebred dogs all over the world, so eliminating hereditary diseases could be easily done."

Jacqueline Levy, of Cross Keys K9, New Jersey, US, says: "GSDs are prone to a variety of disorders such as Degenerative Myelopathy, Hip Dysplasia, Elbow Dysplasia, spine issues such as stenosis, perianal fistulas (anal furunculosis), irritable bowels, skin issues and allergies and cancer.

"Prospective buyers should look for DM-tested parents with hips and elbows radiographed for dysplasia, transitional vertebrae, osteoarthritis and/or hip laxity using the PennHIP method. OFA certifications are subjective, but can be reliable ways to evaluate overall hips and elbows, and propensities for dysplasia. OFA also maintains a database of tests on dogs — we like to do thyroid and cardiac certifications to make sure we don't have issues."

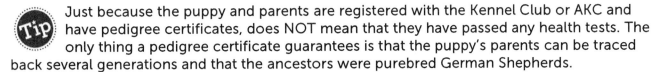 **Just because the puppy and parents are registered with the Kennel Club or AKC and have pedigree certificates, does NOT mean that they have passed any health tests. The only thing a pedigree certificate guarantees is that the puppy's parents can be traced back several generations and that the ancestors were purebred German Shepherds.**

Prospective buyers should always find out **exactly** what health screening the sire and dam (mother and father) have undergone. As well as physically seeing certificates, ask what health guarantees, if any, the breeder is offering with the puppy.

FACT ❯ **If a puppy is sold as "Vet Checked," it does not mean that the parents have been health screened. It means that a vet has given the puppy a brief physical and visual examination, worming and inoculations are up to date, and the pup appears to be in good health on the day of the examination.**

If you have already got your dog, don't worry! There is plenty of advice in this book on how to take good care of your German Shepherd. Feeding a quality food, monitoring your dog's weight, regular grooming and check-overs, plenty of exercise, socialisation and stimulation will all help to keep him or her in tiptop condition. Good owners can certainly help to extend the life of their GSD.

Controversy

The German Shepherd was one of the breeds highlighted in the 2008 BBC documentary *Pedigree Dogs Exposed*, which said that critics described the breed as "half dog, half frog." The documentary investigated health issues in several breeds and caused a stir around the world. The UK Kennel Club was criticised for allowing Breed Standards, judging standards and breeding practices to compromise the health of pedigree dogs.

The issue highlighted with German Shepherds was rear angulation, or a sloping topline (or back), which had become desirable in the show ring - although many working GSDs have remained closer to the original Breed Standard with straighter backs.

There was controversy again in 2016 when three-year-old Cruaghaire Catoria (*pictured*) won Best of Breed at Crufts. The dog had an extremely sloping back and appeared to be moving unnaturally around the show ring. The Kennel Club received hundreds of complaints from people who described the dog as *"deformed."*

The RSPCA was *"shocked and appalled"* to see a German shepherd with *"such poor conformation that it could not move freely, winning Best of Breed."* KC Secretary, Caroline Kisko, said: "It's very disheartening to see one breed looking so very peculiarly out-of-step with the others."

Later in 2016, the following paragraph was added to the UK Breed Standard: *"Characteristics: Versatile working dog, balanced and free from exaggeration. Must be capable of standing comfortably and calmly, freely and unsupported in any way, in structural balance, whilst both rear pasterns are vertical. Attentive, alert, resilient and tireless with keen scenting ability."*

The sloping or **roach** back is something that has crept into show lines of German Shepherds since the 1980's. Up to that point, both working lines and show lines had the straight back of the original working German Shepherd Dog developed by Max von Stephanitz.

Dogs with SV after their name are registered with the German *Verein für deutsche Schäferhunde,* or German Shepherd Association, the breed club founded in 1899 by von Stephanitz. The health standards of these dogs tend to be higher, with the average lifespan being 10 to 12 years.

 Try to avoid show puppies from parents with exaggerated sloping backs and extreme rear angulation, as these features can cause orthopaedic issues in some dogs.

German Shepherd Insurance

Insurance is another point to consider for a new puppy or adult dog. The best time to get pet insurance is BEFORE you bring your German Shepherd home and before any health issues develop. Don't wait until you need to seek veterinary help - bite the bullet and take out annual insurance.

If you can afford it, take out life cover. This may be more expensive, but will cover your dog throughout his or her lifetime - including for chronic (recurring and/or long term) ailments, such as joint, heart or eye problems, ear infections, epilepsy and cancer.

Insuring a healthy puppy or adult dog is the only sure-fire way to ensure vets' bills are covered before anything unforeseen happens - and you'd be a rare owner if you didn't use your policy at least once during your dog's lifetime.

Costs in the UK range from around £15 a month for Accident Only to around £30-£60 for Lifetime Cover, depending on where you live, how much excess you are willing to pay and the total in pounds covered per year.

I ran a few examples for US pet insurance on a three-month-old German Shepherd pup with a deductible of $100 and came back with quotes from $36 to $65, depending on location, the excess and amount of coverage per year in dollars.

With advances in veterinary science, there is so much more vets can do to help an ailing dog - but at a cost.

Surgical procedures can rack up bills of thousands of pounds or dollars. According to www.PetInsuranceQuotes.com these are some of the most common ailments affecting German Shepherds and typical treatment costs:

Hip Dysplasia $4,000-$6,000, Hemivertebrae $2,500-$7,000, Luxating Patella $1,500-$3,000 Canine Cancer $5,000-$20,000,

Spinal Stenosis $2,500-$5,000, Bloat $1,500- $7,500, Epilepsy $200-$15,000, Cardiac Issues $1,000-$20,000, Cataracts $2,000-$3,000, Degenerative Myelopathy-Costs Vary, Elbow Dysplasia $3,000-$5,000. ($1.3 = approximately £1 at the time of writing).

Pet Insurance Quotes rated US insurance companies based on coverage, cost, customer satisfaction and the company itself and came up with a top eight: 1.Healthy Paws, 2.Trupanion, 3.Embrace, 4. ASPCA, 5.Nationwide, 6.Pets Best, 7.Petplan, 8.Figo.

Of course, if you make a claim, your monthly premium will increase, but if you have a decent insurance policy BEFORE a recurring health problem starts, your dog should continue to be covered if the ailment returns. You have to decide whether insurance is worth the money. On the plus side, you'll have:

1. Peace of mind financially if your beloved German Shepherd falls ill, and

2. You know exactly how much hard cash to part with each month, so no nasty surprises.

....

Three Health Tips

1. **Buy a well-bred puppy** - Good German Shepherd breeders select their stock based on:

   * General health and the DNA test of the parents

   * Temperament

   * Conformation (physical structure)

Although well-bred puppies are not cheap, believe it or not, committed German Shepherd breeders are not in it for the money, often incurring high bills for health screening, stud fees, veterinary costs, specialised food, etc. Their main concern is to produce healthy, handsome puppies with good temperaments and instincts that are *"fit for function"* – whether from working or show lines.

2. **Get pet insurance as soon as you get your dog** - Don't wait until your dog has a health issue and needs to see a vet. Most insurers will exclude all pre-existing conditions on their policies. Check the small print to make sure that all conditions are covered and that if the problem is recurring, it will continue to be covered year after year.

When working out costs of a dog, factor in annual or monthly pet insurance fees and trips to a vet for check-ups, annual vaccinations, etc. Some breeders provide free insurance for the first few weeks in their Puppy Pack - ask yours if this is the case.

3. **Find a good vet** - Ask around your pet-owning friends, rather than just going to the first one you find. A vet that knows your dog from his or her puppy vaccinations and then right through their life is more likely to understand your dog and diagnose quickly and correctly when something is wrong. If you visit a big veterinary practice, ask for the vet by name when you make an appointment.

We all want our dogs to be healthy - so how can you tell if yours is? Well, here are some positive things to look for in a healthy German Shepherd:

Signs of a Healthy German Shepherd

1. **Eyes -** A German Shepherd's eyes should be clear with an intelligent, alert expression, *as illustrated here by two-year-old Janet, courtesy of Wendy Sharp, Sharphouse's German Shepherds, Kent, UK.*

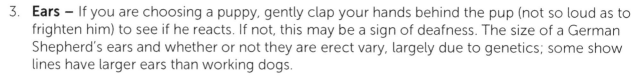

They should be almond-shaped and brown with very dark rims. Paleness around the eyeball (conjunctiva) could be a sign of underlying problems. A red swelling in the corner of one or both eyes could be cherry eye, and a cloudy eye could be a sign of cataracts. Sometimes the dog's third eyelid (nictating membrane) is visible at the eye's inside corner - this is normal. There should be no thick, green or yellow discharge from the eyes.

2. **Nose –** A dog's nose is an indicator of health. Normal nose colour is black; a pink nose can be a sign of allergies or other health issues.

A pink *"snow nose"* may appear in winter due to a lack of Vitamin D, but usually returns to black during summer. Some dogs' noses turn pinkish with age, due to their bodies producing less pigment and is not a cause for concern. Regardless of colour, the nose should be moist and cold to the touch as well as free from clear, watery secretions. Any yellow, green or foul-smelling discharge is not normal - in younger dogs this can be a sign of canine distemper.

3. **Ears –** If you are choosing a puppy, gently clap your hands behind the pup (not so loud as to frighten him) to see if he reacts. If not, this may be a sign of deafness. The size of a German Shepherd's ears and whether or not they are erect vary, largely due to genetics; some show lines have larger ears than working dogs.

Pricked-up ears allow air to circulate, keeping bacteria and mites at bay. Often pups have floppy ears that prick up before they are one year old. Although floppy ears are considered a fault in the show ring, they are not a health defect; it's nature.

4. **Mouth –** German Shepherd gums should be black with pink areas. Paleness or whiteness can be a sign of anaemia, Bloat or lack of oxygen due to heart or breathing problems (this is harder to see with black gums). Blue gums or tongue are a sign that your dog is not breathing properly. Red, inflamed gums can be a sign of gingivitis or other tooth disease.

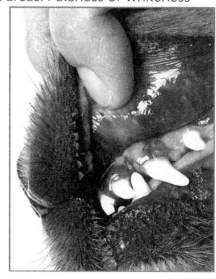

Young dogs have sparkling white teeth, whereas older dogs have darker teeth, but they should not have any hard white, yellow, green or brown bits. Your dog's breath should smell OK.

5. **Coat and Skin –** These are easy-to-monitor indicators of a healthy dog. Most German Shepherds have a double coat: an undercoat with a short, medium or long topcoat that sheds. Any dandruff, bald spots, a dull, lifeless, discoloured or oily coat, or one that loses excessive hair,

can all be signs that something is amiss. Skin should be smooth without redness. If a dog is scratching, licking or biting a lot, he may have a condition that needs addressing. Open sores, scales, scabs, red patches or growths can be a sign of a skin issue or allergy. Signs of fleas, ticks and other external parasites should be treated immediately; check for small black specks, which may be fleas, on the coat or bedding.

6. **Weight –** Your GSD's stomach should be above the bottom of his rib cage when standing, and you should be able to feel his ribs beneath his coat without too much effort. If the stomach is level or hangs below, your dog is overweight - or may have a pot belly, which can also be a symptom of other conditions.

7. **Temperature –** The normal temperature of a dog is 101°F to 102.5°F. (A human's is 98.6°F). Excited or exercising dogs may run a slightly higher temperature. Anything above 103°F or below 100°F should be checked out. The exceptions are female dogs about to give birth that will often have a temperature of 99°F. If you take your dog's temperature, make sure he is relaxed and *always* use a purpose-made canine thermometer.

8. **Stools -** Poo, poop, business, faeces - call it what you will - it's the stuff that comes out of the less appealing end of your German Shepherd on a daily basis! It should be firm and brown, not runny, with no signs of worms or parasites. Watery stools or a dog not eliminating regularly are both signs of an upset stomach or other ailments. If it continues for a couple of days, consult your vet. If puppies have diarrhoea they need checking out much quicker as they can quickly dehydrate.

9. **Energy –** The German Shepherd is the ultimate working breed and are alert, engaged dogs. Yours should have good amounts of energy with fluid and pain-free movements. Lack of energy or lethargy could be a sign of an underlying problem.

10. **Smell –** If there is a musty, 'off' or generally unpleasant smell coming from your German Shepherd's body, it could be a sign of a yeast infection. There can be a number of reasons for this; the ears may require attention or it could be a food allergy. Another not uncommon cause with the breed is an anal issue. Whatever the cause, you need to get to the root of the problem quickly before it develops into something more serious.

11. **Attitude –** A generally positive attitude is a sign of good health. German Shepherds are energetic and engaged, so symptoms of illness may include one or all of the following: a general lack of interest in his or her surroundings, tail not wagging, lethargy, not eating food and sleeping a lot (more than normal). The important thing is to look out for any behaviour that is out of the ordinary for your individual dog.

So now you know some of the signs of a healthy dog – what are the signs of an unhealthy one? There are many different symptoms that can indicate your canine companion isn't feeling great. If you don't yet know your dog, his habits, temperament and behaviour patterns, then spend some time getting acquainted with them.

What are his normal character and temperament? Lively or calm, playful or serious, a joker or an introvert, bold or nervous, happy to be left alone or loves to be with people, a keen appetite or a fussy eater? How often does he empty his bowels, does he ever vomit? (Dogs will often eat grass to make themselves sick, this is perfectly normal and a natural way of cleansing the digestive system).

You may think your German Shepherd can't talk, **but he can!** If you really know your dog, his character and habits, then he CAN tell you when he's not well. He does this by changing his patterns. Some symptoms are physical, some emotional and others are behavioural. It's important to be able to recognise these changes, as early treatment can be the key to keeping a simple problem from snowballing into something more serious.

If you think your dog is unwell, it is useful to keep an accurate and detailed account of his symptoms to give to the vet, perhaps even take a video of him on your mobile phone. This will help the vet to correctly diagnose and effectively treat your dog.

....

Four Vital Signs of Illness

1) **Heart Rate -** You can feel your German Shepherd's heartbeat by placing your hand on his lower ribcage – just behind the elbow. Don't be alarmed if the heartbeat seems irregular compared to that of a human; it IS often irregular in dogs. Your dog will probably love the attention, so it should be quite easy to check his heartbeat. Just lay him on his side and bend his left front leg at the elbow, bring the elbow in to his chest and place your fingers on this area and count the beats. The larger the dog, the slower the heartbeat.

   ❧ A Shepherd's resting heartbeat should be 70-120 beats per minute

   ❧ A young puppy has a heartbeat of around 220 beats per minute

   ❧ An older dog has a slower heartbeat

2) **Temperature -** A new-born puppy has a temperature of 94-97°F. This reaches the normal adult body temperature of around 101°F at four weeks old. A vet takes a dog's temperature reading via the rectum. If you do this, only do it with a special digital rectal thermometer (not glass), get someone to hold the dog and be very careful. Ear thermometers *(pictured)* are now widely available for home use.

NOTE: Exercise or excitement can cause temperature to rise by 2°F to 3°F when your dog is actually in good health, so wait until he is relaxed before taking his temperature. If it is above or below the norms and the dog seems under par, give your vet a call.

3) **Respiratory Rate -** Another symptom of illness is a change in breathing patterns. This varies a lot depending on the size and weight of the dog. An adult dog will have a respiratory rate of 15-25 breaths per minute when resting. You can easily check this by counting your dog's breaths for a minute with a stopwatch handy. Don't do this if he is panting; it doesn't count.

4) **Behaviour Changes -** Classic symptoms of illness are any inexplicable behaviour changes. If there has NOT been a change in the household atmosphere, such as another new pet, a new baby, moving home, the absence of a family member or the loss of another dog, then the following symptoms may well be a sign that all is not well:

   ❧ Depression or lethargy

   ❧ Anxiety and/or trembling

   ❧ Falling or stumbling

   ❧ Loss of appetite

   ❧ Walking in circles

   ❧ Being more vocal - grunting, whining or whimpering

- Aggression
- Tiredness - sleeping more than normal or not wanting to exercise
- Abnormal posture

If any of them appear for the first time or worse than usual, you need to keep him under close watch for a few hours or even days. Quite often he will return to normal of his own accord. Like humans, dogs have off-days too.

If he is showing any of the above symptoms, then don't over-exercise him, and avoid stressful situations and hot or cold places. Make sure he has access to clean water. There are many other signals of ill health, but these are four of the most important. Keep a record for your vet, if your dog does need professional medical attention, most vets will want to know:

WHEN the symptoms first appeared in your dog

WHETHER they are getting better or worse, and

HOW FREQUENT the symptoms are - intermittent, continuous or increasing?

Hip Dysplasia

Hip Dysplasia (HD) - or Canine Hip Dysplasia (CHD) as it is also called - is the most common inherited orthopaedic problem in dogs of all breeds — and particularly of the German Shepherd. It is also the biggest cause of hind leg lameness.

The hips are the uppermost joints on the rear legs of a dog, either side of the tail, and *"Dysplasia"* means *"abnormal development."* Dogs with this condition develop painful degenerative arthritis of the hip joints.

 According to America's OFA (Orthopedic Foundation for Animals), of the 125,422 German Shepherds evaluated, 20.5% had abnormal hips: *www.ofa.org/diseases/breed-statistics#detail*

The hip is a ball and socket joint. Hip dysplasia is caused when the head of the femur, or thigh bone, fits loosely into a shallow and poorly developed socket in the pelvis.

Most dogs with dysplasia are born with normal hips, but due to their genetic make-up, and sometimes worsened by factors such as diet, obesity or over-exercising when young, the soft tissues that surround the joint develop abnormally.

The joint carrying the weight of the dog becomes loose and unstable, muscle growth slows and degenerative joint disease often follows.

Symptoms often start to show at five to 18 months of age. Occasionally, an affected dog will display no symptoms at all, while others may experience anything from mild discomfort to extreme pain. Diagnosis is made by X-ray, and an early diagnosis gives a vet the best chance to tackle HD, minimising the chance of arthritis developing.

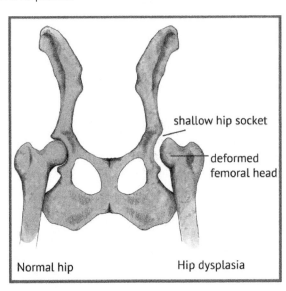

shallow hip socket

deformed femoral head

Normal hip   Hip dysplasia

Look Out For:

- 🐾 Hind leg lameness, particularly after exercise
- 🐾 Difficulty or stiffness when getting up, climbing stairs or walking uphill
- 🐾 A reluctance to jump, exercise or climb stairs
- 🐾 A "bunny hop" gait or waddling gait
- 🐾 A painful reaction to stretching the hind legs, resulting in a short stride
- 🐾 Side-to-side swaying of the croup (area above the tail)
- 🐾 Wastage of the thigh muscles

While hip dysplasia is usually inherited, other factors can trigger or worsen it, including:

- 🐾 Too much exercise, especially while the dog is still growing
- 🐾 Extended periods without exercise
- 🐾 Overfeeding, especially on a diet high in protein and calories, or too much calcium
- 🐾 Obesity
- 🐾 Damp or cold weather

 During their first year or so of life, it is very important that German Shepherd puppies are fed a diet containing the right balance of calories, minerals and protein. Too much impact exercise for puppies can also be a trigger. The key is moderate, low impact exercise for young dogs.

High impact activities that apply a lot of force to the joint - such as jumping and catching Frisbees, are not recommended, however energetic young German Shepherds are. See **Chapter 11. Exercise** and <u>www.bva.co.uk/Canine-Health-Schemes/Hip-Scheme</u> for more information.

Prevention and Treatment

The most common cause of hip dysplasia is genetic. There is, however, a system called *hip scoring*, which is run by the BVA (British Veterinary Association) and Kennel Club in the UK and PennHIP in the USA. A UK dog's hips are X-rayed at a minimum age of 12 months; in the US, dogs must be 24 months old before they can receive their final hip certification.

In the UK, the X-rays are submitted to a specialist panel at the BVA who assess nine features of each hip, giving each feature a score. **The lower the score, the better the hips,** so the range can be from **0** CLEAR to **106** BADLY DYSPLASTIC. A hip certificate shows the individual score for each hip.

It is far better if the dog has evenly matched hips, rather than a low score for one and a high score for the other. Listed here are the American ratings, with the UK ratings in brackets:

Excellent (0-4, with no hip higher than 3)

Good (5-10, with no hip higher than 6)

Fair (11-18) *This is the breed average*

Borderline (19-25)

Mild (26-35)

Moderate (36-50)

Severe (51-106)

The *Breed Mean Score (BMS),* or average, is currently 14.5 for German Shepherds. The *Median Score* is 11, which means that 50% of GSDs have better scores than 11 and 50% have worse scores.

The BVA says: "Ideally, breeders should choose breeding stock with hip scores WELL BELOW the Breed Mean Score (BMS) and ideally below the Median for their breed."

This section of BVA certificate, pictured, shows a hip score of 10

Section C – TO BE COMPLETED BY SCRUTINEERS

CERTIFICATE OF SCORING

HIP JOINT	Score Range	Right	Left
Norberg angle	0-6	O	1
Subluxation	0-6	2	3
Cranial acetabular edge	0-6	2	2
Dorsal acetabular edge	0-6	—	—
Cranial effective acetabular rim	0-6	—	—
Acetabular fossa	0-6	—	—
Caudal acetabular edge	0-5	—	—
Femoral head/neck exostosis	0-6	—	—
Femoral head recontouring	0-6	—	—
TOTALS (max possible 53 per column)		4	6	10

One UK breeder added: "I test for hip scores, but hip scores should not be looked at on their own. They should be looked at with the Kennel Club tool called Estimated Breeding Values, where you can put the name of the dog into the box and the estimated value will be shown. This is a more accurate indicator of the risk of dogs passing on genes for hip and elbow dysplasia.

"Hip and elbow score is important, but so are many other things, and we need to keep things in perspective. Character is also important, and there is no scoring system for that."

 Ask the breeder to show you certificates for both dam and sire. You are ideally looking for parents with below average hip scores; avoid buying a puppy from parents with high combined or individual hip scores.

There is no 100% guarantee that a puppy from low scoring parents will not develop hip dysplasia, as the condition is caused by a combination of genes, rather than just a one. However, the chances are significantly reduced with good hip scores.

Treatment is geared towards preventing the hip joint getting worse. Vets usually recommend restricting exercise, keeping body weight down and managing pain with analgesics and anti-inflammatory drugs. Various medical and surgical treatments are now available to ease discomfort and restore some mobility. They depend on factors such as age, how bad the problem is and, sadly, sometimes how much money you can afford – another reason for taking out early insurance.

Cortisone can be injected directly into the affected hip to provide almost immediate relief for a tender, swollen joint. In severe cases, surgery may be an option.

Elbow Dysplasia

The elbow is at the top of a dog's front leg, near the body, and bends backwards. Elbow Dysplasia is a broad term to describe a complex genetic disorder that occurs when cells, tissue or bone don't develop correctly. This causes the joint to form abnormally then to degenerate. All breeding German Shepherds should be screened for Elbow Dysplasia. Results are graded from 0 (best) to 3 (most severe).

FACT 》 Latest figures from the BVA show that 82% of UK German Shepherds were graded 0, and 18% were graded 1, 2 or 3. Results (graded I, II and III) are very similar in the USA, where OFA tested nearly 49,000 GSDs and found that 19% had abnormal elbows.

Elbow dysplasia is the most common cause of elbow pain and one of the main reasons for front leg lameness in big breeds. It affects more males than females, possibly due to their increased size and weight. Along with the German Shepherd, other at-risk breeds include the Newfoundland, Labrador Retriever, Golden Retriever, Rottweiler and Bernese Mountain Dog.

Symptoms begin during puppyhood, typically at four to 10 months of age, although not all young dogs show signs. Look out for:

❧ Stiffness followed by temporary or permanent lameness aggravated by exercise

❧ Pain when extending or flexing the elbow

❧ Holding the affected leg away from the body

❧ Groaning when getting up

❧ Swelling around the joint

❧ In advanced cases, grating of bone and joint when moving

There are several types of Elbow Dysplasia, including Humeral Condylar Osteochondrosis, or HCO, which occurs when cartilage in one part of the elbow joint thickens and starts flaking off.

Another is Ununited Anconeal Process, in which a bony protuberance within the elbow becomes detached from the ulna (lower foreleg bone). This loose, bony fragment damages the elbow, causing pain and lameness. In all cases of Elbow Dysplasia, the joint becomes stiff, painful and prone to osteoarthritis.

Diagnosis is made by a veterinary examination and X-rays, requiring the dog to be anaesthetised. Treatment depends on age and severity, and may involve Non-steroidal Anti-inflammatory Drugs (NSAIDs) or injections. An elbow brace *(pictured, below)* can help to reduce pain in some cases. Thanks to advances in veterinary medicine, surgery is now an option for many dogs. According to Embrace Pet Insurance, it costs $1,500-$4,000, and results in partial or full improvement in the vast majority of cases.

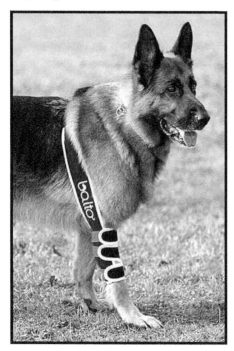

As with Hip Dysplasia and other joint diseases, feeding the right diet and keeping your dog's weight in check are important. Supplements such as omega-3-fatty acids, glucosamine and chondroitin sulphate can also help to relieve pain and stiffness.

Another joint issue that can affect growing German Shepherds and other large breed puppies is *Panosteitis,* a painful inflammation of the long leg bones.

Also called *growing pains, wandering lameness, Pano* or *Eo-Pan*, it usually starts suddenly - often at five to 14 months old – when a dog becomes partially or fully lame for days or weeks. The pain can move from one leg to another after an apparent recovery.

Rehabilitation exercises, pain and anti-inflammatory drugs can help a dog through the flare-ups. Vigorous exercise should be avoided. The cause is unknown, but genetics, stress, infection, metabolism or the autoimmune system may be factors.

Most dogs simply grow out of it and make a full recovery.

Degenerative Myelopathy (DM)

Inside the spine is the spinal cord containing the central nervous system, or bundles of nerve tissue that connect the brain to nearly all other parts of the body. The white matter inside is like wiring for the central nervous system.

Degenerative Myelopathy (DM) occurs when the white matter starts to deteriorate and can no longer transmit messages from the dog's brain to the limbs. Although it is not painful for the dog, it is both incurable and progressive. It usually affects dogs, both male and female, aged between eight and 14 years.

Symptoms start gradually with loss of co-ordination at the rear end, wobbling or the dragging of rear feet. Owners may notice their dogs squatting to poop, having difficulty climbing stairs or getting into the car.

Diagnosis is not always straightforward. A vet may use X-rays, a CT scan, MRI or myelogram to rule out other possible causes, such as a herniated disc, tumour, cyst, infection, trauma or stroke.

Mobility slings and devices, *pictured,* physiotherapy, hydrotherapy and acupuncture can all help a dog with DM.

Eventually, the hind legs weaken further and the front legs become affected until the dog can no longer walk and incontinence sets in. This often takes six months to a year, but can take up to several years in some dogs. At this stage, euthanasia may be the kindest course of action.

DM is caused by a genetic mutation, and the good news is that a DNA test is now available. Kennel Clubs and German Shepherd clubs recommend that all breeding GSDs are tested for DM.

 The gene mutation is Autosomal Recessive. Here are all possible outcomes. They are the same for all other autosomal recessive genetic diseases:

PARENT CLEAR + PARENT CLEAR = pups clear

PARENT CLEAR + PARENT CARRIER = 50% will carry the disease, 50% will be clear

PARENT CLEAR + PARENT AFFECTED = 100% will be carriers

PARENT CARRIER + PARENT CLEAR = 50% will carry disease, 50% will be clear

PARENT CARRIER + PARENT CARRIER = 25% clear, 25% affected and 50% carry disease

PARENT CARRIER + PARENT AFFECTED = 50% affected and 50% carry disease

PARENT AFFECTED + PARENT CLEAR = 100% will carry disease

PARENT AFFECTED + PARENT CARRIER = 50% affected and 50% carry disease

PARENT AFFECTED + PARENT AFFECTED = 100% affected

Pituitary Dwarfism is another autosomal recessive genetic disease. It is thought that as many as 11% of European GSDs are carriers, as well as American dogs bred from certain European bloodlines. Caused by a defect in the pituitary gland, this disease stunts the growth of German Shepherds.

Unlike some other affected breeds, German Shepherds are usually well-proportioned, just a fraction of the normal size, making some look like puppies. Unfortunately, they also have problems affecting the kidneys, liver, heart and nerves. They develop alopecia (baldness) and are prone to skin infections.

Life expectancy is usually only four to five years - although with hormone treatment, some dogs may live a little longer. A DNA test called NAH can detect Pituitary Dwarfism in breeding GSDs and is 99% accurate. Carriers and Affected dogs should not be bred.

A spine issues that can affect German Shepherds is *Stenosis*, or *Degenerative Lumbosacral Stenosis* to give it its full title. Affected dogs suffer from pain in the lower back, in one or both hind legs and/or the tail. They may appear stiff, show lameness in their hind legs and have difficulty getting up after lying down, jumping, climbing or sitting. They may not be able to wag their tail.

Lumbosacral Stenosis is a painful narrowing of the spinal column, which puts pressure on the spinal cord. It could be caused by degeneration or a birth defect, and is difficult to diagnose - especially in older dogs, as the common symptoms are similar to symptoms of old age.

Once a diagnosis is made, treatment varies according to the severity. Mild cases are treated with painkillers (NSAIDs) and a restricted exercise regime. In more severe cases, surgery is the typical treatment and it is often successful. Surgery is always a serious procedure and should first be discussed thoroughly with your vet.

Intervertebral Disc Disease (IVDD) has also been reported in German Shepherds. This occurs when the jelly-like cushion between one or more vertebrae slips or bursts, causing the disc to press on the spinal cord. If your dog is suddenly unable or unwilling to jump or go upstairs, is reluctant to move around, has a hunched back, yelps, or refuses to eat or poop, he is probably in pain. He may even experience sudden paralysis, dragging his back feet or be unable to get up.

If that's the case, get him to a vet straight away. Surgery for ruptured discs has best results if carried out within 24 hours of the onset of symptoms. In milder cases, rest and medication may resolve the problem.

As you have read, German Shepherds can suffer from a number of musculoskeletal issues. Buy a pup from health-tested parents. Once home, feed a high quality, balanced diet, avoid high-impact exercise while he's still growing, and keep his weight in check.

All of these measures will reduce the chances of an issue developing - and if it does, they will lessen the effects.

The Heart

Heart issues are relatively common among the canine population in general. Heart failure, or *Congestive Heart Failure (CHF),* occurs when the heart is not able to pump blood around the dog's body properly. The heart is a mechanical pump. It receives blood in one half and forces it through the lungs, then the other half pumps the blood through the entire body.

The most common disorder affecting German Shepherds is *Dilated Cardiomyopathy (DCM),* also known as *"enlarged heart," pictured.* The ventricles, or heart chambers, become larger and the cardiac muscle surrounding them becomes thinner, causing the heart to change shape. This then restricts muscle contractions and the effectiveness of the valves, which can lead to irregular heartbeats and the backflow or leakage of blood through the valves.

In people, heart disease usually involves the arteries that supply blood to the heart muscle becoming hardened over time, causing the heart muscles to receive less blood than they need. Starved of oxygen, the result is often a heart attack.

FACT ❯ **In dogs, hardening of the arteries (arteriosclerosis) and heart attacks are very rare. However, heart disease is quite common, and in dogs it is often seen as heart failure, which means that the muscles "give out."**

This is usually caused by one chamber or side of the heart being required to do more than it is physically able to do. It may be that excessive force is required to pump the blood through an area and over time the muscles fail. Unlike a heart attack in humans, *heart failure in a dog is a slow process* that occurs over months or years. Once symptoms appear, they usually worsen over time until the dog requires treatment.

Symptoms and Treatment

- Tiredness
- Decreased activity levels
- Restlessness, pacing around instead of settling down to sleep
- Intermittent coughing - during exertion or excitement, at night or when he wakes up in the morning - in an attempt to clear the lungs

As the condition progresses, other symptoms may appear:

- Lack of appetite
- Rapid breathing
- Abdominal swelling (due to fluid)
- Noticeable loss of weight
- Fainting (syncope)
- Paleness

A vet will carry out tests that may include listening to the heart, chest X-rays, blood tests, electrocardiogram (a record of your dog's heartbeat) or an echocardiogram. If the heart problem is due to an enlarged heart or valve disease, the condition cannot be reversed.

Treatment focuses on managing exercise and various medications, which may change over time as the condition progresses. The vet may also prescribe a special low salt diet, as sodium determines the amount of water in the blood.

 There is some evidence that vitamin and other supplements may be beneficial; discuss this with your vet.

The prognosis for dogs with congestive heart failure depends on the cause and severity, as well as their response to treatment. A dog can't recover from congestive heart failure, but once diagnosed, he can live a longer, more comfortable life with the right medication and regular check-ups.

Subvalvular Aortic Stenosis (SAS)

SAS occurs when there is a narrowing, or *stenosis,* caused by a ridge of abnormal tissue that restricts blood flow from the heart to the aorta. This narrowing is classified as *Mild, Moderate* or *Severe.* Dogs may show no clear signs of the illness, and diagnosis is often made when a vet finds a heart murmur during a routine check-up. When present, typical symptoms are:

- ❖ Exercise intolerance
- ❖ Difficulty breathing
- ❖ Weakness
- ❖ Fainting, especially when excited
- ❖ In extreme cases, sudden death

According to Purina Pro Club, the median survival age for dogs receiving treatment is 19 months, and for those dogs receiving medical therapy (consisting of beta blockers to help slow the heart) it is 56 months.

Dogs with mild to moderate cases of SAS typically live much longer, possibly having normal lifespans - although this has yet to be confirmed by hard scientific evidence. SAS will show up on a cardiac exam and dogs with hereditary heart disease generally should not be bred.

Heart Murmurs

Heart murmurs are not uncommon in dogs. One of our dogs was diagnosed with a Grade 2 murmur several years ago and, of course, your heart sinks when the vet gives you the terrible news.

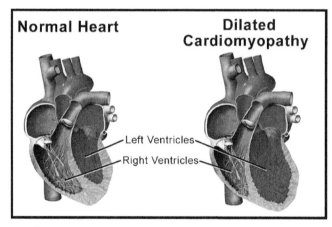

But once the shock is over, it's important to realise that there are several different severities of the condition and, at its mildest, it is no great cause for concern. Our dog lived an active, healthy life and died at the age of 13.

Literally, a heart murmur is a specific sound heard through a stethoscope, which results from the blood flowing faster than normal within the heart itself or in one of the two major arteries. Instead of the normal *"lubb dupp"* noise, an additional sound can be heard that can vary from a mild *"pshhh"* to a loud *"whoosh."* The different grades are:

- ❖ **Grade 1** - barely audible
- ❖ **Grade 2** - soft, but easily heard with a stethoscope
- ❖ **Grade 3** - intermediate loudness; most murmurs that are related to the mechanics of blood circulation are at least Grade 3
- ❖ **Grade 4** - loud murmur that radiates widely, often including opposite side of chest
- ❖ **Grade 5 and Grade 6 -** very loud, audible with the stethoscope barely touching the chest; the vibration is strong enough to be felt through the dog's chest wall

Murmurs are caused by a number of factors; it may be a problem with the heart valves or could be due to some other condition, such as hyperthyroidism, anaemia or heartworm.

In puppies, there are two major types of heart murmurs, and they will probably be detected by your vet at the first or second vaccinations. The most common type is called an innocent *"flow murmur."* This type of murmur is soft - typically Grade 2 or less - and is not caused by underlying heart disease. An innocent flow murmur typically disappears by four to five months of age.

However, if a puppy has a loud murmur - Grade 3 or louder - or if the heart murmur is still easily heard with a stethoscope after four or five months of age, it is more likely that the puppy has an underlying heart problem.

The thought of a puppy having congenital heart disease is worrying, but it is important to remember that the disease will not affect all puppies' life expectancy or quality of life. A heart murmur can also develop suddenly in an adult dog with no prior history of the problem. This is typically due to heart disease that develops with age.

In Toy and small breeds, a heart murmur may develop in middle-aged dogs due to an age-related thickening and degeneration of the mitral valve. This thickening prevents the valve from closing properly, and it starts to leak. This is known as **Mitral Valve Disease,** whereas Dilated Cardiomyopathy (DCM) more commonly affects larger breeds in middle age.

Hypothyroidism

Hypothyroidism is a common hormonal disorder in dogs and is nearly always due to an under-active thyroid gland. It happens when the glands, located on either side of a dog's windpipe, don't produce enough of the hormone called thyroxine.

Thyroxine controls the speed of the metabolism, or the speed at which the body turns food into fuel, so dogs with very low thyroid levels have a slow metabolic rate. Hypothyroidism occurs most frequently in larger dogs aged over five, males and females alike. There is a genetic link and dogs with thyroid disease should not be used for breeding. Most forms of hypothyroidism are diagnosed with a simple blood test and OFA provides a registry for thyroid screening in the USA.

The good news is that it is not life-threatening and can usually be easily treated with a single, inexpensive daily hormone-replacement tablet.

Symptoms

These often happen quite gradually and vary according to breed. In German Shepherds, the common signs to look out for are:

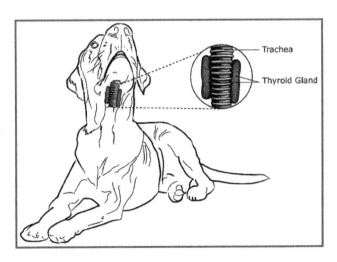

- Lack of energy
- Rapid weight gain or obesity
- Coat becoming dry, thin, coarse and brittle
- Excessive shedding
- High blood cholesterol
- Darkening of the skin (25% of cases)
- Intolerance to cold (15% of cases)

NOTE: **Hyper**thyroidism (as opposed to **hypo**thyroidism) is caused by the thyroid gland producing too much thyroid hormone. It is quite rare in dogs, more usually seen in cats. A common symptom is the dog being ravenously hungry, but losing weight.

Eyes

There is a range of eye conditions that can affect dogs of all breeds, including German Shepherds. All breeding stock should be examined annually by certified veterinary ophthalmologists, so ask to see the parents' up-to-date certificates if you haven't bought your German Shepherd puppy yet.

In the UK it's the BVA/KC/ISDS Eye Scheme, and in the US it's OFA, who also maintain the Companion Animal Eye Registry (CAER), where breeders can check the eye test results of possible mates for their dog.

Progressive Retinal Atrophy (PRA)

PRA and CPRA (Central Progressive Retinal Atrophy) are progressive diseases that lead to blindness. First recognised at the beginning of the 20th century in Gordon Setters, PRA has been documented in over 100 breeds and is the most common eye disease to affect German Shepherds.

It can develop from one year old to middle age, although is often seen at around two years old in German Shepherds. PRA causes cells in the retina at the back of the eye to degenerate and die, even though the cells seem to develop normally early in life. The main cause is genetic, although trauma and other diseases can also cause PRA, and the wrong diet can worsen it.

A dog's rod cells operate in low light levels and are the first to lose normal function. If your dog has PRA, you may first notice that he lacks confidence in low light, is perhaps reluctant to go down stairs or along a dark hallway. If you look closely into his eyes, you may see the pupils dilating (becoming bigger) or the reflection of greenish light from the back of his eyes. As the condition worsens, he might then start bumping into things, first at night and then in the daytime too.

 PRA is not painful and the eyes often appear normal - without redness, tearing or squinting. The lenses may become opaque or cloudy in some dogs.

As yet there is no treatment and most affected dogs will eventually go blind. However, dogs do not rely on sight as much as humans, and PRA develops slowly. This allows the dog to gradually adjust to life without sight, and other senses, such as hearing and smell, will be heightened. A balanced, low-fat diet may help.

Pannus (Chronic Superficial Keratitis)

This is an autoimmune disease that affects the cornea, the transparent layer covering the pupil and iris. Pannus can occur in any dog, but German Shepherds are more prone to it than most other breeds, leading experts to believe that there is a genetic link. UV rays make it worse and may even be part of the initial cause.

First signs are a pink lump towards the inside (nose) side of the eye in one or both eyes. The third eyelid, seen in the inner corner of the eye, may be thickened and inflamed. As Pannus progresses, the lump darkens, flattens and spreads out, causing scarring to spread over the cornea. There may also be a yellow mucus around the eye. It's important to spot the signs quickly as early treatment can save a dog's sight. If left untreated, a dog will become blind. Be particularly vigilant about checking your dog's eyes in summer, when most incidences occur. Look for reddening, thickening and mucus around the eye.

Treatment involves using corticosteroid ointments applied to the eye and immune-suppressing drugs, such as cyclosporine. Sometimes a vet will also give a steroid injection, and antibiotics will be prescribed in cases where a secondary infection has taken hold. He or she may also suggest doggie sunglasses *(pictured)* to protect your dog's eyes from harmful UV rays.

Surgery can improve sight in severe cases. However, if caught early, most German Shepherds respond well to treatment and, with a bit of extra care and medication, live normal lives.

Cataracts

The lens is transparent and its job is to focus rays of light to form an image on the retina at the back of the eye. A cataract occurs when the lens becomes cloudy. Then less light enters the eye, images become blurry and the dog's sight diminishes as the cataract becomes larger.

Cataracts are one of the most common eye problems for all breeds and there are three main types:

- Congenital Cataracts, present from birth
- Juvenile or Early Onset Cataracts, which affects puppies
- Senile or Late Onset Cataracts, which usually develop after six years of age

Most German Shepherd cataracts are hereditary, they develop at the back of both eyes and may lead to blindness. However, cataracts can also be caused by diabetes, eye inflammation, low levels of calcium (hypocalcaemia), old age or injury. Some dogs live perfectly happily with a small cataract, actually managing to "see around" it, but more severe cases result in blindness.

Depending on the cause and type of cataract, surgery is an option for some dogs; the lens is removed and replaced with a plastic substitute. It costs around $2,700-$4,000 (around £2,500-£3,500 in the UK) per eye, but, if the dog is a suitable candidate, is successful in 90% of cases.

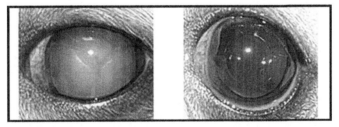

Left: eye with cataracts. Right: same eye with artificial lens

There is no such thing as laser treatment for dogs. However, in some cases, particularly in older dogs, eye drops may help - but beware of miracle cures!

 If you do try drops, look for some containing the effective ingredient N-Acetyl Carnosine, or NAC. German Shepherd Dog Rescue in the UK recommends a relatively inexpensive product called Cataract Clear, available from https://costcuttersrus.com

As well as a cloudy eye, other signs are the dog bumping into things, especially in dimly-lit situations, squinting or pawing at the eye, eye redness or an inflamed eye socket, or a bulging eye. If you suspect your German Shepherd has cataracts, get him or her to the vet for an examination as soon as possible. Early intervention can prevent complications such as glaucoma developing.

Cherry Eye

Humans have two eyelids, but dogs have a third eyelid, called a nictating membrane. This is a thin, opaque tissue with a tear gland that rests in the inner corner of the eye. It provides extra protection for the eye and spreads tears over the eyeball.

Usually it is retracted and therefore you can't see it, although you may notice it when your dog is relaxed and falling asleep. When the third eyelid becomes visible it may be a sign of illness or a painful eye.

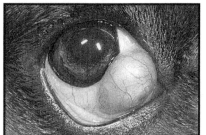

Cherry Eye is a prolapse of the gland of the third eyelid. The exact cause is not known, but it's thought to be due to a weakness of the fibrous tissue that attaches the gland to the surrounding eye.

This weakness allows the gland to fall down, or **prolapse.** Once this has happened and the gland is exposed to the dry air and irritants, it can become infected and/or begin to swell.

There is sometimes a mucous discharge and if the dog rubs or scratches it, he can further damage the gland and even possibly create an ulcer on the surface of the eye. Although it looks sore, it is not generally painful.

Mild cases are treated with a steroid ointment to try and get the gland back to its normal position, and antibiotics to prevent infection. If that doesn't work, surgery to reposition the gland should be considered. A simple stitch or two can tack the gland down into the conjunctiva.

....

Anal Glands

German Shepherds are prone to a painful, long-term condition known as **Anal Furunculosis** or **Perianal Fistula,** which occurs most commonly in dogs aged seven or older. An anal fistula is a small tunnel that develops between the end of the bowel and the skin near the anus (where poop leaves the body).

They're usually the result of an infection inside the anus. To combat this, the dog's body creates **fistulas**, or tubes, to allow the pus to drain outside the body. These are visible externally as **"pinholes"** around the dog's anus and the area becomes inflamed or develops sores, while the infected mass grows internally. Symptoms include:

- ❖ A nasty, fishy smell from the rear end
- ❖ Redness or swelling around the anus
- ❖ Constipation or diarrhoea
- ❖ Straining or apparent pain when pooping
- ❖ Biting or licking the rear end or paws
- ❖ Reluctance to sit

Sadly, it can be difficult to treat and requires lifelong medications, prescription food, and sometimes even surgery. Antibiotics are not effective. However, if it is diagnosed early, many Shepherds can live a comfortable life to old age.

There is an excellent website dedicate to the disease, with details of treatments, medication and doses at http://members.tripod.com/~perianal-fistulas

While we're discussing the less attractive end of your Shepherd, let's get **impacted anal glands** out of the way as well! The two anal glands are located either side of your dog's anus, just under the skin. They secrete a smelly, oily substance that dogs use for identification and marking territory - which is why when two dogs meet for the first time, the first place they sniff is the bottom.

Dogs of all breeds can suffer from impacted anal glands, which means that one or both get blocked and they need *"expressing"* or squeezing – either by a vet, groomer or you, if you know what you are doing. There are various videos on the internet that show you how to do it, but we prefer to have our dogs' glands checked by the vet (or groomer, of you have one) during routine check-ups

Symptoms are similar to Perianal Fistula, but often without the external redness and swelling – and scooting, or dragging the rear end along the ground, which can also be a sign of worms.

We had a dog that had one anal sac removed after surgery for cancer on his rear end - and he managed perfectly well with just one.

Prevention includes feeding the right diet, and keeping the area clean. In a hairy German Shepherd, this may include trimming some of the fur under the tail to stop poop getting stuck.

Exocrine Pancreatic Insufficiency (EPI)

This digestive illness affects German Shepherds more than most other breeds. GSDs and their crossbreeds account for 50% of all cases. EPI can be potentially life-threatening if not treated, but dogs normally respond well to medication and a change of diet.

The pancreas has two jobs: producing enzymes to help food digestion and regulating blood sugar. In simple terms, EPI occurs when the pancreas stops producing the enzymes needed to absorb the goodness from food. Symptoms are:

- Wasting away while being voraciously hungry
- Pooping a lot – often runny, yellow or grey stools like cow pats
- Eating their own poop (Coprophagia)
- Gas and stomach gurgling
- Dry and flaky coat
- Some dogs undergo a personality change

A dog may show only one of these symptoms, or none at all. Treatment varies from one dog to another, but usually involves switching to a grain-free diet low in fibre, enzyme replacements in every meal, and Vitamin B12 injections.

Cushing's Disease

This complex ailment, also known as **hyperadrenocorticism,** is caused when a dog produces too much Cortisol hormone. It develops over a period of time, which is why it is more often seen in middle-aged or senior dogs. German Shepherds are more susceptible than many other breeds.

Cortisol is released by the adrenal gland located near the kidneys. Normally it is produced during times of stress to prepare the body for strenuous activity. Think of an adrenaline rush.

While this hormone is essential for the effective functioning of cells and organs, too much of it can be dangerous. The disease can be difficult to diagnose, as the most common symptoms are similar to those for old age. A dog may display one or more:

- A ravenous appetite

- Drinking excessive amounts of water
- Urinating frequently and possible urinary incontinence
- Hair loss or recurring skin issues
- Pot belly
- Thin skin
- Muscle wastage
- Insomnia
- Lack of energy, general lethargy
- Panting a lot

Cushing's disease cannot be cured, but it can be managed and controlled with medication, giving the dog a longer, happier life. Some dogs with mild symptoms do not require treatment, but should be closely monitored for signs of them worsening. Lysodren (mitotane) or Vetoryl (trilostane) are usually prescribed by vets to treat the most common pituitary-dependent Cushing's disease. Both have a number of side effects – so your dog needs monitoring - and the dog remains on the medication for his or her lifetime. If you suspect your dog has Cushing's disease, contact your vet immediately.

Haemophilia

Known as the bleeding disease, haemophilia occurs when dogs do not produce a protein essential for blood clotting. There are two types that can affect German Shepherds: *Haemophilia A* and *von Willebrand's Disease (vWD),* and both are genetic. The main symptom is excessive bleeding:

- Nosebleeds
- Blood in the urine or faeces (black or bright red blood)
- Bleeding from the gums
- Females bleeding excessively from the vagina
- Bruising of skin
- Prolonged bleeding after surgery or an injury
- Lameness or stiffness if the bleeding is in a joint
- Anaemia following prolonged bleeding

Haemophilia A affects German Shepherds more than other breeds, and normally males. It's highly unusual for females to suffer from the disease, although they are the carriers – much like the 19th century English Royal Family, when Queen Victoria passed haemophilia on to three of her nine children.

In the Royal case - and probably that of the GSD - the disease entered bloodlines through interbreeding of closely-related pairs. Following the marriages of Prince William to Kate, and Prince Harry to Meghan, nobody could accuse the Royal Family of that today!

Affected dogs usually show only mild to moderate symptoms. There is no cure, the only way to eradicate this disease is by DNA testing and NOT breeding from dogs that test as *AFFECTED.* The test cannot detect the disease in females, however, it can in males. The German Shepherd Dog Breed Council of Great Britain recommends blood screening of all males before breeding and keeps a database of results.

von Willebrand's Disease can affect lots of breeds, including the German Shepherd. It affects male and female dogs alike. Again, there is no cure. Some dogs may have only mild symptoms and live a normal life. In serious cases, the only proven treatment is transfusions of blood from healthy dogs, followed by the owner keeping a close eye on the dog.

Epilepsy

Epilepsy means repeated seizures (also called fits or convulsions) due to abnormal electrical activity in the brain. All breeds are affected by epilepsy. Across the canine population, it affects around four or five dogs in every 100, and slightly more German Shepherds.

The type that can affect German Shepherds is called *Idiopathic Epilepsy*.

FACT 〉 According to UFAW (Universities Federation for Animal Welfare), the majority of epileptic GSDs have their first seizure between one and four years old, and males are more commonly affected than females. Idiopathic Epilepsy is hereditary in German Shepherds - probably caused by more than one faulty gene - although the exact genes have yet to be identified.

Affected dogs behave normally between seizures. In some cases, the gap between seizures is relatively constant, in others it can be very irregular with several occurring over a short period of time, but with long intervals between *"clusters."* If they occur because of a problem somewhere else in the body, such as heart disease (which stops oxygen reaching the brain), this is not epilepsy.

Anyone who has witnessed their dog having a seizure knows how frightening it can be. Seizures are not uncommon, and many dogs only ever have one. If your dog has had more than one, it may be that he is epileptic. The good news is that, just as with people, there are medications to control epilepsy in dogs, allowing them to live relatively normal lives with normal lifespans.

Symptoms

Some dogs seem to know when they are about to have a seizure and may behave in a certain way. You will come to recognise these signs as meaning that an episode is likely. Often dogs just seek out their owner's company and come to sit beside them. There are two main types of seizure:

- **Petit Mal**, also called a Focal or Partial Seizure, which is the lesser of the two as it only affects one half of the brain.

  This may involve facial twitching, staring into space with a fixed glaze and/or upward eye movement, walking as if drunk, snapping at imaginary flies, and/or running or hiding for no reason. Sometimes this is accompanied by urination, and the dog is conscious throughout.

❖ **Grand Mal,** or Generalised Seizure affects both hemispheres of the brain and is more often what we think of when we talk about a seizure. Most dogs become stiff, fall onto their side and make running movements with their legs. Sometimes they will cry out and may lose control of their bowels, bladder or both.

FACT ❯ The dog is unconscious once the seizure starts – he cannot hear or respond to you. While it is distressing to watch, the dog is not in any pain - even if howling.

It's not uncommon for an episode to begin as Petit Mal, but progress into Grand Mal. Sometimes, the progression is pretty clear - there may be twitching or jerking of one body part that gradually increases in intensity and progresses to include the entire body – other times the progression happens very fast.

Most seizures last between one and three minutes - it is worth making a note of the time the seizure starts and ends – or record it on your phone because it often seems that it goes on for a lot longer than it actually does.

If you are not sure whether or not your dog has had a seizure, look on YouTube, where there are many videos of dogs having epileptic seizures.

Afterwards dogs behave in different ways. Some just get up and carry on with what they were doing, while others appear dazed and confused for up to 24 hours afterwards. Most commonly, dogs will be disorientated for only 10 to 15 minutes before returning to their old self.

FACT ❯ Most seizures occur while the dog is relaxed and resting quietly, often in the evening or at night; it rarely happens during exercise. In a few dogs, seizures seem to be triggered by particular events or stress.

They often have a set pattern of behaviour that they follow - for example going for a drink of water or asking to go outside to the toilet. If your dog has had more than one seizure, you may well start to notice a pattern of behaviour that is typically repeated.

The most important thing is to **STAY CALM**. Remember that your dog is unconscious during the seizure and is not in pain or distressed. It is probably more distressing for you than for him. Make sure that he is not in a position to injure himself, for example by falling down the stairs, but otherwise do not try to interfere with him. NEVER try to put your hand inside his mouth during a seizure or you are very likely to get bitten.

It is very rare for dogs to injure themselves during a seizure. Occasionally, they may bite their tongue and there may appear to be a lot of blood, but it's unlikely to be serious; your dog will not swallow his tongue.

If it goes on for a very long time (more than 10 minutes), his body temperature will rise, which can cause damage to the liver, kidneys or brain. In very extreme cases, some dogs may be left in a coma after severe seizures. Repeated seizures can cause cumulative brain damage, which can result in early senility (with loss of learned behaviour and housetraining, or behavioural changes).

When Should I Contact the Vet?

Generally, if your dog has a seizure lasting more than five minutes, or is having more than two or three a day, you should contact your vet. When your dog starts fitting, make a note of the time. If he comes out of it within five minutes, allow him time to recover quietly before contacting your vet. It is far better for him to recover quietly at home rather than be bundled into the car and carted off to the vet right away.

However, if your dog does not come out of the seizure within five minutes, or has repeated seizures close together, contact your vet immediately, as he or she will want to see your dog as soon as possible. If this is his first seizure, the vet may ask you to bring him in for a check-up and some routine blood tests. Call the vet before setting off to make sure there is someone who can help when you arrive.

There are many things other than epilepsy that cause seizures in dogs. It's unlikely that the vet will see your dog during a seizure, so it is **vital** that you're able to describe in some detail just what happens. Your vet may need to run a range of tests to ensure that there is no other cause of the seizures. These may include blood tests, possibly X-rays, and maybe even an MRI scan of your dog's brain. If no other cause can be found, then a diagnosis of epilepsy may be made. If your German Shepherd already has epilepsy, remember these key points:

- Don't change or stop any medication without consulting your vet

- See your vet at least once a year for follow-up visits

- Be sceptical of *"magic cure"* treatments

Treatment

As yet, it is not possible to cure epilepsy, so medication is used to control seizures – in some cases even a well-controlled epileptic may have occasional fits. There are many drugs available; two of the most common are Phenobarbital and Potassium Bromide (some dogs can have negative results with Phenobarbital). There are also a number of holistic remedies advertised, but we have no experience of them or any idea if any are effective.

 FACT Factors that have proved useful in some cases are: avoiding dog food containing preservatives, adding vitamins, minerals and/or enzymes to the diet and ensuring drinking water is free of fluoride.

Each epileptic dog is an individual and a treatment plan will be designed specifically for him, based on the severity and frequency of seizures and how he responds to different medications. Many epileptic dogs require a combination of one or more types of drug for best results.

Keep a record of events in your dog's life, note down dates and times of episodes and record when you have given medication. Each time you visit your vet, take this diary along with you so he or she can see how your dog has been since his last check-up. If seizures are becoming more frequent, it may be necessary to change the medication.

Tip Owners of epileptic dogs need patience and vigilance. Treatment success often depends on owners keeping a close eye on the dog and reporting any physical or behavioural changes to the vet.

It is also important that medication is given at the same time each day, as he becomes dependent on the levels of drug in his blood to control seizures. If a single dose of treatment is missed, blood levels can drop, which may be enough to trigger a seizure.

It is not common for epileptic dogs to stop having seizures altogether. However, provided your dog is checked regularly by your vet, *there is a good chance that he will live a full and happy life, as most epileptic dogs have far more good days than bad ones.*

Thanks to www.canineepilepsy.co.uk for assistance with this article. If your German Shepherd has epilepsy, we recommend reading this website to gain a greater understanding of the illness.

Canine Diabetes

Diabetes can affect dogs of all breeds, sizes and both genders, as well as obese dogs. There are two types: *diabetes mellitus* and *diabetes insipidus. Diabetes insipidus* is caused by a lack of vasopressin, a hormone that controls the kidneys' absorption of water. *Diabetes mellitus* occurs when the dog's body does not produce enough insulin and therefore cannot successfully process sugars.

Dogs, like us, get their energy by converting the food they eat into sugars, mainly glucose. This travels in the bloodstream and then, using a protein called *insulin,* cells remove some of the glucose from the blood to use for energy. Almost all diabetic dogs have Type 1 diabetes; their pancreas does not produce any insulin. Without it, the cells can't use the glucose that is in the bloodstream, so they *"starve"* while the glucose level in the blood rises.

Diabetes mellitus (sugar diabetes) is the most common form and affects mostly middle-aged and older dogs. Both males and females can develop it, although unspayed females have a slightly higher risk. Vets take blood and urine samples in order to diagnose diabetes. Early treatment helps to prevent further complications developing.

FACT ❭ The condition is treatable and need not shorten a dog's lifespan or interfere greatly with quality of life. Due to advances in veterinary science, diabetic dogs undergoing treatment now have the same life expectancy as non-diabetic dogs of the same age and gender.

Symptoms of Diabetes Mellitus:

- Extreme thirst
- Excessive urination
- Weight loss
- Increased appetite
- Coat in poor condition
- Lethargy
- Vision problems due to cataracts

If left untreated, diabetes can lead to cataracts or other ailments.

Treatment and Exercise

Many cases of canine diabetes can be successfully treated with a combination of a diet low in fat and sugars and medication, while more severe cases may require insulin injections. In the newly-diagnosed dog, insulin therapy begins at home after a vet has explained how to prepare and inject insulin.

Normally, after a week of treatment, you return to the vet for a series of blood sugar tests over a 12 to 14-hour period to see when the blood glucose peaks and troughs. Adjustments are made to the dosage and timing of the injections. You may also be asked to collect urine samples using a test strip of paper that indicates the glucose levels in urine.

 If your dog is already having insulin injections, beware of a "miracle cure" offered on the internet. It does not exist. There is no diet or vitamin supplement that can reduce a dog's dependence on insulin injections, because vitamins and minerals cannot do what insulin does in the dog's body.

If you think that your dog needs a supplement, discuss it with your vet first to make sure that it does not interfere with any other medication.

Managing a dog's diabetes also means managing his activity level. Exercise burns up blood glucose the same way that insulin does. If your dog is on insulin, any active exercise on top of the insulin might cause him to have a severe low blood glucose episode, called *"hypoglycaemia."* Keep your dog on a reasonably consistent exercise routine. Your usual insulin dose will take that amount of exercise into account. If you plan to take your dog out for some demanding exercise, such as running around with other dogs, you may need to reduce his usual insulin dose.

Tips

- Specially-formulated diabetes dog food is available from most vets

- Feed the same type and amount of food at the same times every day

- Most vets recommend twice-a-day feeding for diabetic pets (it's OK if your dog prefers to eat more often)

- Help your dog to achieve the best possible blood glucose control by not feeding table scraps or treats between meals

- Watch for signs that your dog is starting to drink more water than usual. Call the vet if you see this happening, as it may mean that the insulin dose needs adjusting

Food raises blood glucose - Insulin and exercise lower blood glucose - Keep them in balance

For more information visit www.caninediabetes.org

Canine Cancer

This is the biggest single killer and will claim the lives of one in four dogs, regardless of breed. It is the cause of nearly half the deaths of all dogs aged 10 years and older, according to the American Veterinary Medical Association.

A study of more than 15,000 dogs of different breeds found that the German Shepherd is prone to certain types of cancer. One such is *Hemangiosarcoma*, a malignant cancer in the blood vessel walls, most commonly found in the spleen or heart. Symptoms include:

- Pale gums

- Disorientation, tiredness or collapse

- Rapid breathing

- Extreme thirst

- Lack of appetite

Unfortunately, many GSDs with Hemangiosarcoma die from internal bleeding or the cancer spreading to other parts of the body. In some cases, however, if the cancer is in the spleen and discovered early, the spleen may be removed before the malignant cells spread to other organs.

Symptoms of other types of cancer include:

- Swellings anywhere on the body or around the anus
- Sores that don't heal
- Weight loss
- Lameness, which may be a sign of bone cancer, with or without a visible lump
- Laboured breathing
- Changes in exercise or stamina level
- Change in bowel or bladder habits
- Increased drinking or urination
- Bad breath, which can be a sign of oral cancer
- Poor appetite, difficulty swallowing or excessive drooling
- Vomiting

If your dog has been spayed or neutered, there is evidence that the risk of certain cancers decreases. These cancers include uterine and breast/mammary cancer in females, and testicular cancer in males, if the dog was neutered before he was six months old. However, recent studies also show that some dogs may have a higher risk of certain cancers after early neutering. Spaying prevents mammary cancer in female dogs, which is fatal in about 50% of all cases.

Treatment and Reducing the Risk

Just because your dog has a skin growth doesn't mean that it's cancerous. Your vet will probably confirm the tumour using X-rays, blood tests or a biopsy. Often these are benign (harmless), but if you discover one you should get it checked out by a vet, as they can sometimes be malignant (cancerous).

If your dog is diagnosed with cancer, there is hope. Advances in veterinary medicine and technology offer various treatment options, including chemotherapy, radiation and surgery. Unlike with humans, a dog's hair does not fall out with chemotherapy.

We have all become aware of the risk factors for human cancer - stopping smoking, protecting ourselves from over-exposure to strong sunlight and eating a healthy, balanced diet all help to reduce cancer rates. We know to keep a close eye on ourselves, go for regular health checks and report any lumps to our doctors as soon as they appear. *The same is true with your dog.*

 Every time you groom your dog, get into the habit of lifting his top lip to check for signs of paleness or whiteness in the gums. Also check his body for lumps. As with any illness, early detection often leads to a better outcome.

If you notice any new lumps, for example, monitor them for the next few days to see if there is any change in their appearance or size. If there is, then make an appointment to see your vet as soon as possible. It might only be a cyst, but better to be safe than sorry. Many older dogs develop fatty lumps, or *lipomas,* which are often harmless, but it's still advisable to have the first one checked.

The outcome depends on the type of cancer, treatment used and, importantly, how early the tumour is found. The sooner treatment begins, the greater the chances of success.

While it is impossible to completely prevent cancer, the following points may help to reduce the risk:

- Feed a healthy diet with few or no preservatives

- Consider dietary supplements, such as antioxidants, Vitamins, A, C, E, beta carotene, lycopene or selenium, or coconut oil – check compatibility with any other treatments

- Don't let your German Shepherd get overweight

- Give pure, filtered or bottled water (fluoride-free) for drinking

- Give your dog regular daily exercise

- Keep your dog away from chemicals, pesticides, cleaning products, etc. around the garden and home

- Avoid passive smoking

- Consider natural flea remedies (check they are working) and avoid unnecessary vaccinations

- Check your dog regularly for lumps and any other physical or behavioural changes

- If you are buying a puppy, ask whether there is any history of cancer among the ancestors

One of our dogs was diagnosed with T-cell lymphoma - a particularly aggressive form of cancer - when he was four years old. We had noticed a small lump on his anus, which grew to the size of a small grape within a couple of days.

We rushed him down to the vet and he had surgery the following day. He died, aged 13, having lived a further nine very happy and energetic years.

If your dog is diagnosed with cancer, do not despair, there are many options and new, improved treatments are constantly being introduced. Research is being conducted all over the world, and medical advances are producing a steady flow of new tests and treatments to improve survival rates and canine cancer care.

Disclaimer: The author is not a vet. This chapter is intended to give owners an outline of some of the health issues and symptoms that may affect their dog(s). If you have any concerns regarding your dog's health, our advice is always the same: consult a veterinarian.

13. Skin and Allergies

Allergies are a growing concern for owners of many dogs. Visit any busy veterinary clinic these days – especially in spring and summer – and it's likely that one or more of the dogs is there because of some type of sensitivity. There is anecdotal evidence that some German Shepherds, just like other breeds, can develop food intolerances, seasonal or other allergies.

....

Any individual dog can have issues. Skin conditions, allergies and intolerances are on the increase in the canine world as well as the human world.

How many children did you hear of having asthma or a peanut allergy when you were at school? Not too many, I'll bet. Yet allergies and adverse reactions are now relatively common – and it's the same with dogs. The reasons are not clear; it could be connected to breeding, feeding, over-vaccination – or a combination, but as yet, there is no clear scientific evidence to back this up.

FACT ❯ White or light-coloured dogs of all breeds may have a statistically higher chance of allergies, which may be related to them having less pigment in their skin.

The skin is a complicated topic and a whole book could be written on this subject alone. While many dogs have no problems at all, some suffer from sensitive, itchy, dry or oily skin, hot spots, yeast infections or other skin disorders, causing them to scratch, bite or lick themselves excessively. Symptoms may vary from mild itchiness to a chronic reaction.

Canine Skin

The skin is the dog's largest organ. It acts as the protective barrier between your dog's internal organs and the outside world; it also regulates temperature and provides the sense of touch. Surprisingly, a dog's skin is actually thinner than ours, and it is made up of three layers:

1. **Epidermis** or outer layer, the one that bears the brunt of your dog's contact with the outside world.

2. **Dermis** is the extremely tough layer mostly made up of collagen, a strong and fibrous protein. This where blood vessels deliver nutrients and oxygen to the skin, and it also acts as your dog's thermostat by allowing her body to release or keep in heat, depending on the outside temperature and your dog's activity level.

3. **Subcutis** is a dense layer of fatty tissue that allows your dog's skin to move independently from the muscle layers below it, as well as providing insulation and support for the skin.

FACT ❯ Human allergies often trigger a reaction within the respiratory system, causing us to wheeze or sneeze, whereas allergies or hypersensitivities in a dog often cause a reaction in her SKIN.

- ❖ Skin can be affected from the **INSIDE** by things that your dog eats or drinks
- ❖ Skin can be affected from the **OUTSIDE** by fleas, parasites, or inhaled and contact allergies triggered by grass, pollen, man-made chemicals, dust, mould, etc.

Like all dogs, German Shepherds can suffer from food intolerances as well as environmental allergies. Canine skin disorders are complicated. Some dogs can run through fields, digging holes and rolling around in the grass with no after-effects at all.

Others may spend more time indoors and have an excellent diet, but still experience severe itching and/or bald spots. Some dogs can eat almost anything and everything with no issues at all, while owners of others spend much of their time trying to find the magic bullet – the ideal food for their dog's sensitive stomach.

It's by no means possible to cover all of the issues and causes in this chapter. The aim here is to give a broad outline of some of the ailments most likely to affect your German Shepherd and how to deal with them. We have also included remedies tried with some success by ourselves (we had a dog with skin issues) and other owners of affected dogs, as well as advice from a holistic specialist.

This information is not intended to take the place of professional help; always contact your vet if your dog appears physically unwell or uncomfortable. This is particularly true with skin conditions:

 SEEK TREATMENT AS SOON AS POSSIBLE. If you can find the source(s) of the allergy early, you reduce the chances of it taking hold and causing secondary issues and infections.

Whatever the cause, before a vet can make a diagnosis, you'll have to give details of your dog's diet, exercise regime, habits, medical history and local environment. The vet will then carry out a physical examination, possibly followed by further (expensive) tests, before a course of treatment can be prescribed. You'll have to decide whether these tests are worth it and whether they are likely to discover the exact root of the problem.

One of the difficulties with skin ailments is that the exact cause is often difficult to diagnose, as the symptoms are similar to other issues.

If environmental allergies are involved, specific and expensive tests are available. You'll have to take your vet's advice on this, as the tests are not always conclusive. And if the answer is dust or pollen, it can be difficult – if not downright impossible - to keep your dog away from the triggers while still having a normal life.

German Shepherds are not dogs that can spend their entire lives indoors, so if the cause IS related to the outdoor environment, it is often a question of managing - rather than curing - the condition.

There are many things you as an owner can do to reduce the allergen load – and many natural remedies and supplements that can help as well as veterinary medications.

One issue reported by some GSD owners is food allergy or intolerance - there IS a difference. See **Chapter 7. Feeding a German Shepherd** for more information on food allergies.

Types of Allergies

"Canine dermatitis" means inflammation of a dog's skin and it can be triggered by numerous things, but the most common by far is allergies. Vets estimate that as many as one in four dogs they see has some kind of allergy. Symptoms are:

* Chewing her feet
* Rubbing her face on the floor
* Scratching
* Scratching or biting the anus
* Itchy ears, head shaking
* Hair loss
* Mutilated skin with sore or discoloured patches or hot spots

A German Shepherd who is allergic to something will show it through skin problems and itching; your vet may call this *"pruritus."* It may seem logical that if a dog is allergic to something inhaled, like certain pollen grains, her nose will run; if she's allergic to something she eats, she may vomit, or if allergic to an insect bite, she may develop a swelling. But in practice this is seldom the case.

FACT > In dogs, the skin is the organ most affected by allergies, often resulting in a mild to severe itching sensation over the body and possibly a recurring ear infection. Reddish coloured tear stains can also be a sign of a yeast infection.

Dogs with allergies often chew their feet until they are sore and red. You may see yours rubbing her face on the carpet or couch, or scratching her belly and flanks. Because the ear glands produce too much wax in response to the allergy, ear infections can occur - with bacteria and yeast (which is a fungus) often thriving in the excessive wax and debris.

Digestive health can play an important role. Holistic vet Dr Jodie Gruenstern says: "It's estimated that up to 80% of the immune system resides within the gastrointestinal system; building a healthy gut supports a more appropriate immune response. The importance of choosing fresh proteins and healthy fats over processed, starchy diets (such as kibble) can't be overemphasized. Grains and other starches have a negative impact on gut health, creating insulin resistance and inflammation."

An allergic dog may cause skin lesions or **hot spots** by constant chewing and scratching. Sometimes she will lose hair, which can be patchy, leaving a mottled appearance. The skin itself may be dry and crusty, reddened, swollen or oily, depending on the dog. It is very common to get secondary bacterial skin infections due to these self-inflicted wounds.

An allergic dog's body is reacting to certain molecules called **allergens.** These may come from:

* Trees
* Grass
* Pollens
* Flea bites

-  Specific food or food additives, such as a type of meat, grains, colourings or preservatives
- Milk products
- Fabrics, such as wool or nylon
- Rubber and plastics
- House dust and dust mites
- Mould
- Chemical products used around the home or garden

FACT > These allergens may be INHALED as the dog breathes, INGESTED as the dog eats, or caused by CONTACT with the dog's body when she walks or rolls.

Regardless of how they arrive, they all cause the immune system to produce a protein called IgE that releases irritating chemicals like histamine inside the skin, hence the scratching.

Managing allergies is all about *REDUCING THE ALLERGEN LOAD.*

Inhalant Allergies (Atopy)

The most common allergies in dogs are inhalant and seasonal - at least at first; some allergies may develop and worsen. Substances that can cause an allergic reaction in dogs are similar to those causing problems for humans, and dogs of all breeds can suffer from them.

A clue to diagnosing these allergies is to look at the timing of the reaction. Does it happen all year round? If so, this may be mould, dust or some other trigger that is permanently in the environment. If the reaction is seasonal, then pollens may well be the culprit. A diagnosis can be made by one of three methods of *allergy testing.*

The most common is a blood test for antibodies caused by antigens in the dog's blood, and there are two standard tests: a RAST test and an ELISA test. Many vets feel that the ELISA test gives more accurate results.

The other type of testing is intradermal skin testing where a small amount of antigen is injected into the skin of the animal and after a short period of time, the area around the injection site is inspected to see if the dog has had an allergic reaction. This method has been more widely used in the US than the UK to date.

Our photo shows a Golden Retriever that has undergone intradermal skin testing.

In this particular case, the dog has been tested for more than 70 different allergens, which is a lot. In all likelihood, your vet would test for fewer.

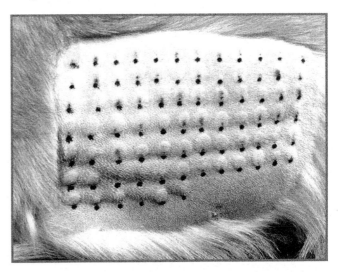

The injections are in kits. If you consider this option, ask the vet or specialist how many allergens are in the kit.

Intradermal skin testing is regarded as *"the gold standard"* of allergy testing for atopy. The dog is sedated and an area on the flank is shaved down to the skin.

A small amount of antigen is injected into the skin on this shaved area. This is done in a specific pattern and order. After a short time, the shaved area is examined to detect which antigens, if any, have created a reaction. It may look pretty drastic, but reactions – the visible round bumps - are only temporary and the hair grows back.

Allergy testing is not particularly expensive, but your dog has to be sedated, and the resulting immunotherapy treatment, or *"hyposensitisation,"* IS expensive. It is a series of injections made specifically for your dog and administered over months (or even years) to make her more tolerant of specific allergens. Vets in the US claim that success rates can be as high as 75%.

Before you get to the stage of considering allergy testing, a vet has to rule out other potential causes, such as fleas or mites, fungal, yeast or bacterial infections and hypothyroidism.

FACT As skin testing is expensive and time-consuming, in practice, vets often treat mild cases of allergies with a combination of avoidance, fatty acids, tablets, and steroid injections for flare-ups.

Many owners of dogs with allergies also consider changing to an unprocessed diet (raw or cooked) and natural alternatives to long-term use of steroids, which can cause other health issues.

Environmental or Contact Irritations

These are a direct reaction to something the dog physically comes into contact with, and the triggers are similar to inhalant allergies. If grass or pollen is the issue, the allergies are often seasonal.

An affected dog may be given treatments such as tablets, shampoo or localised cortisone spray for spring and summer – with a steroid injection to control a flare-up - but be perfectly fine the rest of the year. This was the case with our dog with allergies.

 If you suspect your German Shepherd has outdoor contact allergies, hose her down after walks. Washing her feet and belly will get rid of some of the pollen and other allergens, which then reduces scratching and biting.

The problem may be localised - such as the paws or belly. Symptoms are a general skin irritation or specific hotspots - itching (pruritus) and sometimes hair loss. Readers of our website sometimes report that their dog will incessantly lick one part of the body, often the paws, anus, belly or back.

Flea Bite Allergies

These are a common canine allergy affecting lots of German Shepherds. Flea bite allergy is typically seasonal, worse during summer and autumn - peak time for fleas - and in warmer climates where fleas are prevalent. Unfortunately, some dogs with flea allergies also have inhalant allergies.

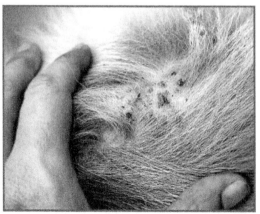

This allergy is not to the flea itself, but to proteins in flea saliva left under the dog's skin when the insect feeds. Just one bite to an allergic dog will cause red, crusty bumps *(pictured)* and intense itching.

If affected, the dog will try to bite at the base of her tail and scratch a lot. Much of the skin damage is done by the dog's scratching, rather than the flea bite, and can result in hair falling out or skin abrasions.

Some German Shepherds also develop hot spots, often along the base of the tail and back.

Flea bite allergies can only be totally prevented by keeping all fleas away from the dog. Various flea prevention treatments are available – see the section on **Parasites**. A vet can make a diagnosis with a simple blood test. If fleas are the cause, you'll also have to make sure her bedding and your home or kennel are flea-free zones – this is particularly difficult if your German Shepherd lives outdoors.

Acute Moist Dermatitis (Hot Spots)

Acute moist dermatitis or **hot spots** are not uncommon. A hot spot can appear suddenly and is a raw, inflamed and often bleeding area of skin. The area becomes moist and painful and begins spreading due to continual licking and chewing.

They can become large, red, irritated lesions in a short pace of time. The cause is often a local reaction to an insect bite - fleas, ticks, biting flies or mosquitoes. Other causes of hot spots include:

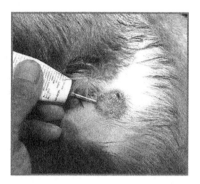

- ❧ Allergies – inhalant, contact and food allergies
- ❧ Mites
- ❧ Ear infections
- ❧ Poor grooming
- ❧ Burs or plant awns
- ❧ Anal gland disease
- ❧ Hip dysplasia or other types of arthritis and degenerative joint disease

Once diagnosed and with the right treatment for the underlying cause, hot spots often disappear as soon as they appeared. Treatments may come in the form of injections, tablets or creams – or a combination of all three. The affected area is clipped and cleaned by the vet to help the effectiveness of any spray or ointment. The dog might also have to wear an E-collar until the condition subsides, but usually not for long.

Some owners have reported good results after dabbing hot spots, interdigital cysts and other skin irritations with an equal mixture of Listerine (the amber-coloured Original, pictured, below), baby oil and water. US owners have also reported success with Gold Bond Powder.

Interdigital Cysts

If your German Shepherd gets a fleshy red lump between the toes that looks like an ulcerated sore or a hairless bump, then it's probably an interdigital cyst - or *interdigital furuncle* to give the condition its correct medical term. These can be very difficult to get rid of, since they are often not the main problem, but a symptom of some other ailment.

Actually, they are not cysts, but the result of *furunculosis*, a skin condition that clogs hair follicles and creates chronic infection. They can be caused by a number of factors, including allergies, poor foot conformation, mites, yeast infections, ingrown hairs or other foreign bodies, and obesity. Bulldogs are most susceptible, but any dog can suffer from them - and often it's dogs that suffer from other allergies as well.

These nasty-looking bumps are painful for your dog, will probably cause a limp and can be a nightmare to get rid of. Vets might recommend a whole range of treatments

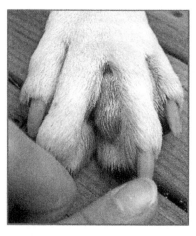

to get to the root cause of the problem. It can be extremely expensive if your dog is having a barrage of tests or biopsies, and even then you are not guaranteed to find the underlying cause.

Your dog may have to wear an E-collar, which is stressful for everybody, as you watch your German Shepherd bumping into door frames and furniture. Some dogs can be resistant to the *"Cone of Shame"* - they may slump down like you've hung a 10-ton weight on their neck or sink into a depression. Fortunately, they don't usually have to wear them for more than a few days.

Consider putting socks on the affected foot or feet instead. This works well while your dog sleeps, but you have to watch her like a hawk when she's awake to stop her licking the affected areas. Here are some remedies your vet may suggest:

- ❧ Antibiotics and/or steroids and/or mite killers
- ❧ Soaking the feet in Epsom salts twice daily to unclog the hair follicles
- ❧ Testing for allergies or thyroid problems
- ❧ Starting a food trial if food allergies are suspected
- ❧ Shampooing the feet
- ❧ Cleaning between the toes with medicated (benzoyl peroxide) wipes
- ❧ A referral to a veterinary dermatologist
- ❧ Surgery (this is a last-resort option)

If you suspect your German Shepherd has an interdigital cyst, get to the vet for a correct diagnosis and then discuss the various options. A course of antibiotics may be suggested initially, along with switching to a hypoallergenic diet if a food allergy is suspected. If the condition persists, many owners get discouraged, especially when treatment may go on for many weeks.

 Be wary of agreeing to a series of steroid injections or repeated courses of antibiotics, as this means that the underlying cause of the furuncle has not been diagnosed. In such cases, it is worth exploring natural diets and remedies – and trying to lower the overall allergen load on your dog.

Before you resort to any drastic action, first try soaking your German Shepherd's affected paw in Epsom salts for five or 10 minutes twice a day. After the soaking, clean the area with medicated wipes, which are antiseptic and control inflammation. In the US these are sold under the brand name Stridex pads.

Surgery is a drastic option. Although it can be effective in solving the immediate problem, it doesn't deal with the underlying ailment. Post-surgery healing is a slow and difficult process, and the dog does not have the same foot as before.

Future orthopaedic issues and more interdigital cysts are a couple of problems that can occur afterwards. All that said, your vet will understand that interdigital cysts are not simple to deal with, but they are always treatable.

Get the right diagnosis as soon as possible.

Bacterial infection (Pyoderma)

Pyoderma literally means **pus in the skin** (yuk)! Early signs of this bacterial infection are itchy red spots filled with yellow pus, similar to pimples or spots in humans. They can sometimes develop into red, ulcerated skin with dry and crusty patches. Fortunately, the condition is not contagious.

Pyoderma **(pictured)** is caused by several things: a broken skin surface, a skin wound due to chronic exposure to moisture, altered skin bacteria, or poor blood flow to the skin.

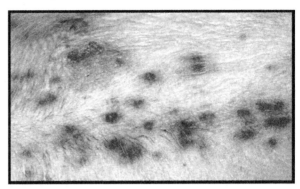

Allergies to fleas, food or parasites, yeast or fungal skin infections, thyroid disease, hormonal imbalances, hypothyroidism, heredity and some medications can all increase the risk. Puppies can develop **puppy pyoderma** in thinly-haired areas, such as the groin and underarms.

If you notice symptoms, get to the vet quickly before the condition develops from **superficial pyoderma** into **severe pyoderma**, which is very unpleasant and takes a lot longer to treat.

Superficial and puppy pyoderma is usually treated with a two to six-week course of antibiotic tablets or ointment. Severe or recurring pyoderma looks awful, causes your dog some distress and can take months to completely cure. Medicated shampoos and regular bathing, as instructed by your vet, are also part of the treatment. It's also important to ensure your dog has clean, dry, padded bedding.

Bacterial infection, no matter how bad it may look, usually responds well to medical treatment, which is generally done on an outpatient basis.

A particularly nasty form of the condition is **German Shepherd Pyoderma,** which results in severe, weeping sores over a dog's back and rear legs. It is often difficult to treat and, the most extreme cases, a German Shepherd may have to be put to sleep.

Seborrhoea

There are two common types of seborrhoea: oily (oleosa) and dry (sicca). German Shepherds usually get the dry type, which causes flaky dandruff and greasy skin and hair.

With seborrhoea, the dog's skin gives off a smelly, waxy substance that clumps in the ears, under the belly and armpits, elbows, and ankles. Dogs may scratch at the affected areas, causing bleeding, crusting, hair loss and secondary infections.

Primary seborrhoea is genetic-based, while secondary seborrhoea results from injury to the skin caused by things such as parasites, allergies, food disorders and hormonal issues like hypothyroidism.

Normally, the condition cannot be completely cured. Treatment involving anti-seborrheic or tar-based shampoos, may last a lifetime and focusses on managing the symptoms. If there is an underlying cause - such as allergies, then this also has to be tackled, along with any yeast or bacterial infections.

Omega-3 fatty acid supplement, such as fish oils, can help. This may seem odd as the dog often already has a greasy coat, but fatty acids are essential for normal skin cell function.

Canine Acne

This is not that common and - just as with humans - generally affects teenagers, often between five and eight months of age with dogs. Acne occurs when oil glands become blocked causing bacterial infection, and these glands are most active in teenagers.

Acne is not a major health problem as most of it will clear up once the dog becomes an adult, but it can recur. Typical signs are pimples, blackheads or whiteheads around the muzzle, chest or groin. If the area is irritated, then there may be some bleeding or pus.

Hormonal Imbalances

These occur in dogs of all breeds, including German Shepherds. They are often difficult to diagnose and occur when a dog is producing either too much (hyper) or too little (hypo) of a particular hormone. One visual sign is often hair loss on both sides of the dog's body, which is not usually itchy. Hormone imbalances can be serious as they are often indicators that glands that affect the dog internally are not working properly. However, some types can be diagnosed by special blood tests and treated effectively.

Hypothyroidism occurs when the dog does not produce enough thyroid hormone, causing her metabolism to slow. Diagnosis is by blood test and symptoms include:

- ❧ Lethargy
- ❧ Intolerance to cold or exercise
- ❧ Dullness, lack of interest
- ❧ Thickening of the skin
- ❧ Increased shedding and hair becoming thin and brittle
- ❧ Unexplained weight gain

Hypothyroidism is treatable with a lifelong daily dose of thyroxine, a hormone replacement, which is not particularly expensive. The dog may have to be retested once or twice a year and the dose adjusted accordingly.

Hyperthyroidism occurs when a dog produces **too much** thyroid hormone, increasing metabolic rate to dangerous levels. This disease is rarely found in dogs; it is much more common in cats.

Parasites

Demodectic Mange

Demodectic Mange is also known as *Demodex, red mange, follicular mange* or *puppy mange.* It is caused by the tiny mite Demodex canis – *pictured -* which can only be seen through a microscope.

The mites actually live inside the hair follicles on the bodies of virtually every adult dog, and most humans, without causing any harm or irritation. In humans, the mites are found in the skin, eyelids and the creases of the nose...try not to think about that!

The Demodex mite spends its entire life on the host dog. Eggs hatch and mature from larvae to nymphs to adults in 20 to 35 days and the mites are transferred directly from the mother to the puppies within the first week of life by direct physical contact.

FACT ⟩ Dogs with healthy immune systems rarely get full-blown Demodex. However, a small number with weak immune systems can't combat the mites, and the disease spreads to the face and forelimbs or across the dog's whole body. Affected skin turns blue-grey due to the presence of thousands of blackheads or "comedones."

Vets currently believe that virtually every mother carries and transfers mites to her puppies, but most are immune to its effects. It is most likely to develop in puppies with parents that have mange, and most lesions develop between three and six months of age. "*Puppy Mange*" is not usually serious and most cases disappear when the pup's immune system kicks in at about 12 months old.

It can also occur when females have their first season, which may be due to a slight dip in their immune systems.

Symptoms – Bald patches, usually accompanied by crusty, red skin that sometimes appears greasy or wet. Hair loss usually begins around the muzzle, eyes and other areas on the head. The lesions may or may not itch.

In *localised mange*, a few circular crusty areas appear, most frequently on the head and front legs of puppies. With *generalised mange* there are bald patches over the entire coat. The skin on the head, side and back is crusty, inflamed and oozes a clear fluid. The skin will often be oily to touch and there is usually a secondary bacterial infection.

Tip Some puppies can become quite ill and can develop a fever, lose their appetites and become lethargic. If you suspect your puppy has generalised demodectic mange, (as opposed to local, which only affects the face and front legs), get her to a vet ASAP.

There is also a condition called *pododermatitis,* when the mange affects a puppy's paws. It can cause bacterial infections and be very uncomfortable, even painful. Symptoms include hair loss on the paws, swelling of the paws (especially around the nail beds) and red, hot or inflamed areas that are often infected. Treatment is always recommended, and it can take several rounds to clear it up.

Diagnosis and Treatment – The vet will normally diagnose demodectic mange after taking a skin scraping. Treatment usually involves topical (on the skin) medication and sometimes tablets. In 90% of cases localised demodectic mange resolves itself as the puppy grows. If the dog has just one or two lesions, these can usually be successfully treated using specific creams and spot treatments. There are also non-chemical treatments, such as the one pictured, to relieve symptoms.

With the more serious generalised demodectic mange, treatment can be lengthy and expensive. The vet might prescribe an anti-parasitic dip every two weeks. Owners should always wear rubber gloves when treating their dog, and it should be applied in an area with adequate ventilation.

Most dogs with a severe issue need six to 14 dips every two weeks. After the first three or four dips, the vet takes another skin scraping to check the mites have gone. Dips continue for one month after the mites have disappeared, but dogs are not considered cured until a year after their last treatment.

FACT ⟩ Some dogs can have a bad reaction to anti-parasitic dips. Before proceeding, check with your vet as to whether an anti-parasitic dip is suitable for your dog.

Other options include the heartworm treatment Ivermectin. This isn't approved by the FDA for treating mange, but is often used to do so. It is usually given orally every one to two days, or by injection, and can be very effective. **Again, some dogs react badly to it.** Another drug is Interceptor (Milbemycin oxime), which can be expensive as it has to be given daily. However, it is effective on up to 80% of the dogs who did not respond to dips – but should be given with caution to pups under 21 weeks of age.

Dogs that have the generalised condition may have underlying skin infections, so antibiotics are often given for the first several weeks of treatment. Because the mite flourishes on dogs with suppressed immune systems, you should try to get to the root cause of immune system disease, especially if your German Shepherd is an adult when she first develops demodectic mange.

....

Harvest Mite

Another parasitic mite that can affect dogs and other animals in late summer and autumn is the harvest mite, particularly if you walk your dog through long, grassy fields. The orange, six-legged

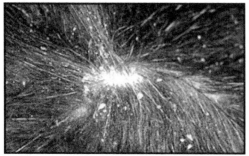

mite is so small, it is barely visible to the human eye. It attacks animals and humans. The larvae feed on tissue fluid and can cause considerable discomfort.

The larvae congregate on small clods of earth or vegetation and are particularly active in dry, sunny weather. They attach to the skin of a passing warm-blooded animal and inject a fluid that breaks down skin cells. The mite then sucks on the same spot for two or three days before dropping off the host, leaving a red swelling that can itch severely for several weeks.

Harvest mite larvae are only active during the day, so if your regular walk is through long, grassy fields, consider going very early in the morning in warm weather, before the mites become active. And if you do have a problem, wash all clothes you were wearing when you think the mites first attacked.

There are sprays from your vet that can help, but it is more important to thoroughly wash your dog with a good insecticidal shampoo. *Thornit* is a remedy used for ear mites that can also be used for harvest mites. Thornit is a powder based on Iodoform that can be lightly dusted on to the itchy areas, or in to itchy ears, bringing relief within two to five days. *Yumega Plus* for dogs can also help to relieve itching.

Cheyletiella (Rabbit Fur Mite)

"My dog appears to have dandruff, there's lots of white scurf in her coat," is a commonly-heard claim. Occasionally, scurf can be caused by a very dry skin or even by shampoo not being thoroughly rinsed out of the coat after a bath, but often, the parasitic Cheyletiella mite is to blame.

There are few symptoms, but a heavy infestation can cause itching, skin scaling and hair loss. The mites, their eggs and the scurf they produce have been called *"walking dandruff,"* which is most

frequently seen on the back and sides of the dog. Skin scales are carried through the hair coat by the mites, so *the dandruff appears to be moving along the back of the animal,* hence the nickname!

The mite spends its entire life cycle on the dog. Eggs are laid glued to the hair shafts and go on to form larvae, then nymph and then adult mites. They are spread by direct contact with an infected individual or infested bedding. These mites are non-burrowing and feed on the keratin layer or epidermis. The mite's life cycle lasts around 21 days on the host, which gives it plenty of time to spread to other areas - and other animals or humans.

Most affected dogs respond quite well to treatment, although it can sometimes take a while to completely cure the infestation. Your vet may prescribe a pyrethrin-based shampoo. Frontline spray has also been proved to be effective. Your dog's bedding area should be treated and you should also be aware that these mites can temporarily infest humans, causing a mild skin irritation and some itching

Sarcoptic Mange (Scabies)

Also known as canine scabies, this is caused by the parasite *Sarcoptes scabiei.* This microscopic mite can cause a range of skin problems, the most common of which is hair loss and severe itching. The mites can infect other animals such as foxes, cats and even humans, but prefer to live their short lives on dogs. Fortunately, there are several good treatments and it can be easily controlled.

In cool, moist environments, the mites live for up to 22 days. At normal room temperature they live from two to six days, preferring to live on parts of the dog with less hair. Diagnosing canine scabies can be somewhat difficult, and it is often mistaken for inhalant allergies.

Once diagnosed, there are a number of effective treatments, including selamectin (Revolution – again, some dogs can have a bad reaction to this), an on-the-skin solution applied once a month that also provides heartworm prevention, flea control and some tick protection. Various Frontline products are also effective – check with your vet for the correct ones.

There is, however, one product recommended by many breeders and gets excellent reviews, both in terms of effectiveness and also the fact that very few dogs have any reaction to it. It is the *Seresto Flea Collar, pictured,* which provides full body protection against all fleas, ticks, sarcoptic mange, lice and other bloodsucking critters!

The Seresto collar lasts up to eight months and is waterproof – although if your German Shepherd goes swimming regularly, it might need replacing more often. Provided your German Shepherd will keep the collar on, I'd recommend it - but it's not cheap, at around £33 in the UK and $50 in the US.

There are also holistic remedies for many skin conditions. Because your dog does not have to come into direct contact with an infected dog to catch scabies, it is difficult to completely protect her. Foxes and their environment can also transmit the mite.

Fleas

When you see your dog scratching and biting, your first thought is probably: *"She's got fleas!"* and you may well be right. Fleas don't fly, but they do have very strong back legs and they will take any opportunity to jump from the ground or another animal into your German Shepherd's lovely, warm, luxuriant coat. You can sometimes see the fleas if you part your dog's hair.

And for every flea that you see on your dog, there is the stomach-churning prospect of hundreds of eggs and larvae in your home.... So, if your dog gets fleas, you'll have to treat your environment as well as the dog in order to completely get rid of them.

The best form of cure is prevention. Vets recommend giving dogs a preventative flea treatment every four to eight weeks – although the Seresto Flea Collar lasts for eight months. If you do give a regular skin treatment, the frequency depends on your climate, the season - fleas do not breed as quickly in the cold - and how much time your dog spends outdoors.

To apply topical insecticides like Frontline and Advantix, part the skin and apply drops of the liquid on to a small area on your dog's back, usually near the neck. Some kill fleas and ticks, and others just kill fleas - check the details. It is worth spending the money on a quality treatment, as cheaper brands may not rid your German Shepherd completely of fleas, ticks and other parasites.

One UK breeder said that many breeders are opposed to chemical flea treatments, such as Spot On or those from the vet, as the cause a reaction in some dogs - in extreme cases some have been known to have seizures. She added that when she found a flea, she simply washed all of her dogs, one after the other, and then washed every last piece of bedding.

There are also holistic and natural remedies to chemical flea treatments, discussed later in this chapter.

NOTE: There is also anecdotal evidence from owners of various breeds that the US flea and worm tablet *Trifexis* may cause severe side effects in some dogs. You can read some owners' comments at: www.max-the-schnauzer.com/trifexis-side-effects-in-schnauzers.html

Ticks

A tick is not an insect, but a member of the arachnid family, like the spider. There are over 850 types, some have a hard shell and some a soft one. Ticks don't have wings - they can't fly, they crawl.

They have a sensor called Haller's organ that detects smell, heat and humidity to help them locate food, which in some cases is a German Shepherd. A tick's diet consists of one thing and one thing only – blood! They climb up onto tall grass and when they sense an animal is close, crawl on.

Ticks can pass on a number of diseases to animals and humans, the most well-known of which is *Lyme Disease*, a serious condition that causes lameness and other problems. Dogs that spend a lot of time outdoors in high risk areas, such as woods, can have a vaccination against Lime Disease.

(**Tip**) One breeder said: "We get ticks from sand dunes sometimes and, if removed quickly, they're not harmful. We use a tick tool which has instructions in the packet. You put the forked end either side of the tick and twist it till it comes out."

If you do find a tick on your German Shepherd's coat and are not sure how to get it out, have it removed by a vet or other expert. Inexpertly pulling it out yourself and leaving a bit of the tick behind can be detrimental to your dog's health.

Tick prevention treatments are similar to those for fleas. If your German Shepherd has sensitive skin or allergies, she might do better with a natural flea or tick remedy.

Heartworm

Heartworm is a serious and potentially fatal disease affecting pets in North America and many other parts of the world, but not the UK. These foot-long worms live in the heart, lungs and associated blood vessels of affected animals, causing severe lung disease, heart failure and damage to organs.

The dog is a natural host for heartworms, enabling the worms living inside a dog to mature into adults, mate and produce offspring. If untreated, their numbers can increase; dogs have been known to harbour several hundred worms in their bodies.

Heartworm disease causes lasting damage to the heart, lungs and arteries, and can affect the dog's health and quality of life long after the parasites are gone. For this reason, **prevention is by far the best option** and treatment - when needed - should be administered as early as possible.

The mosquito **(pictured)** plays an essential role in the heartworm life cycle. When a mosquito bites and takes a blood meal from an infected animal, it picks up baby worms that develop and mature into *"infective stage"* larvae over a period of 10 to 14 days.

Then, when it bites another dog, the infective larvae are deposited onto the surface of the animal's skin and enter the new host through the mosquito's bite wound. Once inside the dog, it takes approximately six months for the larvae to develop into adult heartworms. Heartworms can live for five to seven years in a dog. In the early stages of the disease, many dogs show few or no symptoms. The longer the infection persists, the more likely symptoms will develop. These include:

- A mild persistent cough
- Reluctance to exercise
- Tiredness after moderate activity
- Decreased appetite
- Weight loss

As the disease progresses, dogs may develop heart failure and a swollen belly due to excess fluid in the abdomen. Dogs with large numbers of heartworms can develop sudden blockages of blood flow within the heart leading to the life-threatening caval syndrome. This is marked by a sudden onset of laboured breathing, pale gums and dark, bloody or coffee-coloured urine. Without prompt surgical removal of the heartworm blockage, few dogs survive.

Although more common in the south eastern US, heartworm disease has been diagnosed in all 50 states. The American Heartworm Society recommends that you get your dog tested every year and give your dog heartworm preventive treatment for all 12 months of the year.

If you live in a risk area, check that your tick and flea medication also prevents heartworm. In the UK, heartworm has only been found in imported dogs.

Thanks to the American Heartworm Society for assistance with the section.

....

Ringworm

This is not actually a worm, but a fungus and is most commonly seen in puppies and young dogs. It is highly infectious and often found on the face, ears, paws or tail.

The ringworm fungus is most prevalent in hot, humid climates but, surprisingly, most cases occur in autumn and winter. But it is not that common; in one study of dogs with active skin problems, less than 3% had ringworm.

Ringworm is transmitted by spores in the soil and by contact with the infected hair of dogs and cats, typically found on carpets, brushes, combs, toys and furniture. Spores from infected animals can be shed into the environment and live for over 18 months, but most healthy adult dogs have some resistance and never develop symptoms.

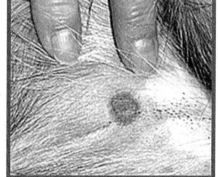

The fungi live in dead skin, hairs and nails - and the head and legs are the most common areas affected. Tell-tale signs are bald patches with a roughly circular shape *(pictured)*. Ringworm is relatively easy to treat with fungicidal shampoos or antibiotics from a vet.

FACT ⟩ Humans can catch ringworm from pets, and vice versa. Children are especially susceptible, as are adults with suppressed immune systems and those undergoing chemotherapy. Hygiene is extremely important.

If your dog has ringworm, wear gloves when handling her and wash your hands well afterwards. And if a member of your family catches ringworm, make sure they use separate towels from everyone else or the fungus may spread.

As a teenager, I caught ringworm from horses at the local stables where I worked at weekends - much to my mother's horror - and was treated like a leper by the rest of the family until it cleared up!

Ear Infections

Adult German Shepherds have pricked-up ears, which allows air to circulate inside, and makes them *less susceptible* to ear infections than Spaniels and other breeds with long, floppy ears.

However, any dog can get an ear infection - often is it a sign of a separate underlying health problem. Or it may be that there's moisture in the dog's ear canal, which has created the warm, damp environment much loved by home-hunting bacteria.

FACT ⟩ The fact that a dog has recurring ear infections does NOT necessarily mean that the ears are the source of the problem – although they might be. They may also be due to inhalant or food allergies, low thyroid function (hypothyroidism) or allergies.

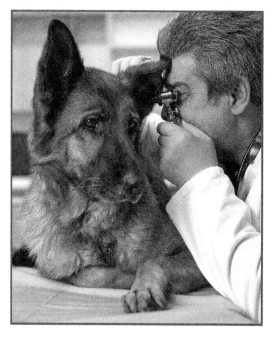

The underlying problem must be treated or the dog will continue to have long-term ear problems. Tell-tale signs include your dog shaking her head, scratching or rubbing her ears a lot, or an unpleasant smell from the ears.

If you look inside, you may notice a reddy brown or yellow discharge, it may also be red and inflamed with a lot of wax. Sometimes a dog may appear depressed or irritable; ear infections are painful. In chronic cases, the inside of her ears may become crusty or thickened. Treatment depends on the cause and what – if any - other conditions your dog may have.

Antibiotics are used for bacterial infections and antifungals for yeast infections. Glucocorticoids, such as dexamethasone, are often included in these medications to reduce the inflammation in the ear. Your vet may also flush out and clean the ear with special drops, something you may have to do daily at home until the infection clears.

A dog's ear canal is L-shaped, which means it can be difficult to get medication into the lower, or horizontal, part of the ear. The best method is to hold the dog's ear flap with one hand and put the ointment or drops in with the other, if possible tilting the dog's head away from you so the liquid flows downwards *with gravity*.

Hold the ear flap down and massage the medication into the horizontal canal before letting go of your dog, as the first thing she will do is shake her head – and if the ointment or drops aren't massaged in, they will fly out.

Nearly all ear infections can be successfully managed if properly diagnosed and treated. But if an underlying problem remains undiagnosed, the ears will continue to become infected.

 To avoid ear infections, check your German Shepherd's ears when you groom her, dry them after swimming and get the vet to check inside on routine visits.

When cleaning or plucking your dog's ears, be very careful not to put anything too far inside. Visit YouTube to see videos of how to clean ears without damaging them. DO NOT use cotton buds inside the ear, they are too small and can cause injury. Some owners recommend regularly cleaning the inside of ears with cotton wool and a mixture of water and white vinegar.

If your dog appears to be in pain, has smelly ears, or if her ear canals look inflamed, contact your vet straight away. If you can nip the first infection in the bud, there is a chance it will not return. If your dog has a ruptured or weakened eardrum, ear cleansers and medications could do more harm than good. Early treatment is the best way of preventing a recurrence.

FACT ❯ **Many German Shepherd puppies have floppy ears until they are a few months old when the cartilage is strong enough to support pricked-up ears.**

Some Allergy Treatments

Treatments and success rates vary tremendously from dog to dog and from one allergy to another, which is why it is so important to consult a vet at the outset. Earlier diagnosis is more likely to lead to a successful treatment.

Some owners of dogs with recurring skin issues find that a course of antibiotics or steroids works wonders for their dog's sore skin and itching. However, the scratching starts all over again shortly after the treatment stops.

FACT ❯ **While a single steroid injection is often highly effective in calming down symptoms almost immediately, frequent or long-term steroid use is not a good option as it can lead to serious side effects.**

Food allergies require patience, a change or several changes of diet and maybe even a food trial, and the specific trigger is notoriously difficult to isolate – unless you are lucky and hit on the culprit straight away.

With inhalant and contact allergies, blood and skin tests are available, followed by hyposensitisation treatment. However, these are expensive and often the specific trigger for many dogs remains unknown. So, the reality for many owners of German Shepherds with allergies is that they manage the condition, rather than curing it completely.

Our Experience With Max

After corresponding with numerous other dog owners and consulting our vet, Graham, it seems our experiences with allergies are common. This is borne out by the dozens of dog owners who have contacted our website about their pet's allergy or sensitivities. According to Graham, more and more dogs are appearing in his waiting room with various types of allergies. Whether this is connected to how we breed our dogs remains to be seen.

Our dog, Max, was perfectly fine until he was about two years old, when he began to scratch a lot. He scratched more in spring and summer, which meant that his allergies were almost certainly inhalant or contact-based and related to pollens, grasses or other outdoor triggers. We decided not to have a lot of tests, not because of the cost, but because the vet said it was highly likely that he was allergic to pollens.

Max was an active dog and if we had confirmed pollen allergy confirmed, we were not going to stop taking him out for thrice-daily walks.

As already mentioned, it's definitely beneficial to have a hose or bath outside to rinse the dog's paws and underbelly after a walk. Regarding medications, Max was at first put on to a tiny dose of Piriton *(pictured)*, an antihistamine for hay fever sufferers (human and canine) and for the first few springs and summers, this worked well.

Allergies can change and a dog can build up a tolerance to a treatment, which is why they can be so difficult to treat. Max's symptoms changed from season to season, although the main ones were: general scratching, paw biting and ear infections.

One year he bit the skin under his tail a lot – he would jump around like he had been stung by a bee and bite frenetically. This was treated effectively with a single steroid injection, followed by spraying the area with cortisone once a day at home for a period. This type of spray can be very effective if the itchy area is small, but no good for spraying all over a dog's body.

A few years ago, he started nibbling his paws for the first time - a habit he persisted with - although not to the extent that they become red and raw. Over the years we tried a number of treatments, all of which worked for a while, before he came off the medication in October when pollen levels fell. He managed perfectly fine the rest of the year without any treatment at all.

Not every owner wants to treat his or her dog with chemicals, nor feed a diet that includes preservatives, which is why this book includes alternatives. Also, 15 years ago, when we were starting out on the *"Allergy Trail,"* there were far fewer options than there are now.

We fed Max a high quality hypoallergenic dry food. If we were starting again from scratch, knowing what we know now, I'd look into a raw or home-cooked diet (which is what he was fed towards the end of his life), if necessary in combination with holistic remedies.

One season the vet put him on a short course of steroids. These worked very well for five months, but steroids are not a long-term solution. Another spring, we were prescribed Atopica, a non-steroid daily tablet sold in the UK only through vets. The active ingredient is **cyclosporine**, which suppresses the immune system. Some dogs can get side effects, although ours didn't.

This treatment was expensive, but initially extremely effective – so much so that we thought we had cured the problem completely. However, after a couple of seasons on cyclosporine he developed a tolerance to the drug and started scratching again.

A few years ago, he went back on the antihistamine Piriton, a higher dose than when he was two years old, and this worked very well again. One advantage of this drug is that is it manufactured by the million and is therefore very inexpensive.

Apoquel

In 2013 the FDA approved **Apoquel** (oclacitinib) – *pictured* - to control itching and inflammation in allergic dogs. Like most allergy drugs, it acts by suppressing the immune system, rather than addressing the root cause. It has, however, proved to be highly effective in treating tens of thousands of dogs with allergies. It proved so popular in the UK and North America that in the two years after release there was a shortage, as the manufacturers weren't able to produce it fast enough.

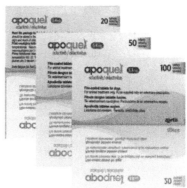

We tried Apoquel with excellent results. There was some initial tweaking to get the daily dose right, but it proved highly effective. The tablets are administered according to body weight – one 16mg tablet per day for a German Shepherd weighing 60lb-90lb. It's not cheap, but Apoquel can be a miracle worker for some dogs.

NOTE: Side effects have been reported in some dogs, and holistic practitioners and Dogs Naturally magazine believe that it is harmful to the dog.

Allergies are often complex and difficult to treat; you should weigh up the pros and cons in the best interests of your own dog. Max's allergies were manageable; he loved his food, was full of energy and otherwise healthy, and lived a happy life to the age of 13.

Other Options

Vets often recommend adding fish oils, which contain Omega-3 fatty acids, to a daily feed to keep your dog's skin and coat healthy all year round – whether or not she has problems.

We added a liquid supplement called Yumega Plus, which contains Omegas 3 and 6, to one of the two daily feeds all year round. When the scratching got particularly bad, we bathed our dog in an antiseborrheic shampoo called Malaseb, *pictured,* twice a week for a limited time. This also helped, although was not necessary once on Apoquel.

Most allergies are manageable, although they may change throughout the life of the dog and you may have to alter the treatment. Here are some suggestions:

Bathing - bathing your dog using shampoos that break down the oils that plug the hair follicles. These shampoos contain antiseborrheic ingredients such as benzoyl peroxide, salicylic acid, sulphur or tar. One example is Sulfoxydex shampoo, which can be followed by a cream rinse such as Episoothe Rinse afterwards to prevent the skin from drying out.

Dabbing – Using an astringent such as witch hazel or alcohol on affected areas. We have heard of zinc oxide cream being used to some effect. In the human world, this is rubbed on to mild skin abrasions and acts as a protective coating. It can help the healing of chapped skin and nappy rash in babies. Zinc oxide works as a mild astringent and has some antiseptic properties and is safe to use on dogs, *as long as you do not allow the dog to lick it off*.

Daily supplements - Vitamin E, vitamin A, zinc and omega oils all help to make a dog's skin healthy. Feed a daily supplement that contains some of these, such as fish oil, which provides omega.

Many owners have tried coconut oil *(pictured)* with some success. Here is a link to an article on the benefits of coconut oils and fish oils, check with your vet first: www.dogsnaturallymagazine.com/the-health-benefits-of-coconut-oil

If you suspect your dog has a skin problem, ear infection or allergy, get her to the vet straight away. You can hopefully nip it in the bud before secondary infections develop – and save a lot of heartache and money in the long run.

The Holistic Approach

As canine allergies become increasingly common, more and more owners of dogs with allergies and sensitivities are looking towards natural foods and remedies to help deal with the issues.

Others are finding that their dog does well for a time with injections or medication, but then the symptoms slowly start to reappear. A holistic practitioner looks at finding the root cause of the problem and treating that, rather than just treating the symptoms.

Dr Sara Skiwski is a holistic vet working in California. She writes here about canine environmental allergies: "Here in California, with our mild weather and no hard freeze in Winter, environmental allergens can build up and cause nearly year-round issues for our beloved pets. Also, seasonal allergies, when left unaddressed, can lead to year-round allergies. Unlike humans, whose allergy symptoms seem to affect mostly the respiratory tract, seasonal allergies in dogs often take the form of skin irritation/inflammation.

"Allergic reactions are produced by the immune system. The way the immune system functions is a result of both genetics and the environment: Nature versus Nurture. Let's look at a typical case. A puppy starts showing mild seasonal allergy symptoms, for instance a red tummy and mild itching in Spring. Off to the vet!

"The treatment prescribed is symptomatic to provide relief, such as a topical spray. The next year when the weather warms up, the patient is back again - same symptoms but more severe this time. This time the dog has very itchy skin. Again, the treatment is symptomatic - antibiotics, topical spray (hopefully no steroids), until the symptoms resolve with the season change. Fast forward to another Spring...on the third year, the patient is back again but this time the symptoms last longer, (not just Spring but also through most of Summer and into Fall).

"By Year Five, all the symptoms are significantly worse and are occurring year-round. This is what happens with seasonal environmental allergies. The more your pet is exposed to the allergens they are sensitive to, the more the immune system over-reacts and the more intense and long-lasting the allergic response becomes. What to do?

"In my practice, I like to address the potential root cause at the very first sign of an allergic response, which is normally seen between the ages of six to nine months old. I do this to circumvent the
 escalating response year after year. Since the allergen load your environmentally-sensitive dog is most susceptible to is much heavier outdoors, I recommend two essential steps in managing the condition. They are vigilance in foot care as well as hair care.

"What does this mean? A wipe down of feet and hair, especially the tummy, to remove any pollens or allergens is key. This can be done with a damp cloth, but my favorite method is to get a spray bottle filled with Witch Hazel *(pictured)* and spray these areas. First, spray the feet then wipe them off with a cloth, and then spray and wipe down the tummy and sides. This is best done right after the pup has been outside playing or walking. This will help keep your pet from tracking the environmental allergens into the home and into their beds. If the feet end up still being itchy, I suggest adding foot soaks in Epsom salts."

Dr Sara also stresses the importance of keeping the immune system healthy by avoiding unnecessary vaccinations or drugs: "The vaccine stimulates the immune system, which is the last thing your pet with seasonal environmental allergies needs.

"I also will move the pet to an anti-inflammatory diet. Foods that create or worsen inflammation are high in carbohydrates. An allergic pet's diet should be very low in carbohydrates, especially grains. Research has shown that 'leaky gut,' or dysbiosis, is a root cause of immune system overreactions in both dog and cats (and some humans). Feed a diet that is not processed, or minimally processed; one that doesn't have grain and takes a little longer to get absorbed and assimilated through the gut. Slowing the assimilation assures that there are not large spikes of nutrients and proteins that come into the body all at once and overtax the pancreas and liver, creating inflammation.

"A lot of commercial diets are too high in grains and carbohydrates. These foods create inflammation that overtaxes the body and leads not just to skin inflammation, but also to other inflammatory conditions, such as colitis, pancreatitis, arthritis, inflammatory bowel disease and ear infections. Also, these diets are too low in protein, which is needed to make blood. This causes a decreased blood reserve in the body and in some of these animals this can lead to the skin not being properly nourished, starting a cycle of chronic skin infections which produce more itching."

After looking at diet, check that your dog is free from fleas and then these are some of Dr Sara's suggested supplements:

✓ **Raw (Unpasteurised) Local Honey** - an alkaline-forming food containing natural vitamins, enzymes, powerful antioxidants and other important natural nutrients, which are destroyed during the heating and pasteurisation processes. Raw honey has anti-viral, anti-bacterial and anti-fungal properties. It promotes body and digestive health, is a powerful antioxidant, strengthens the immune system, eliminates allergies, and is an excellent remedy for skin wounds and all types of infections. Bees collect pollen from local plants and their honey often acts as an immune booster for dogs living in the locality.

Dr Sara says: "It may seem odd that straight exposure to pollen often triggers allergies, but that exposure to pollen in the honey usually has the opposite effect. But this is typically what we see. In honey, the allergens are delivered in small, manageable doses and the effect over time is very much like that from undergoing a whole series of allergy immunology injections."

✓ **Mushrooms** - make sure you choose the non-poisonous ones! Dogs don't like the taste, so may have to mask it with another food. Medicinal mushrooms are used to treat and prevent a wide array of illnesses through their use as immune stimulants and modulators, and antioxidants. The most well-known and researched are reishi, maitake, cordyceps, blazei, split-gill, turkey tail and shiitake. Histamine is what causes much of the inflammation, redness and irritation in allergies. By helping to control histamine production, the mushrooms can moderate the effects of inflammation and even help prevent allergies in the first place.

WARNING! Mushrooms can interact with some over-the-counter and prescription drugs, so do your research as well as checking with your vet first.

✓ **Stinging Nettles** - contain biologically active compounds that reduce inflammation. Nettles can reduce the amount of histamine the body produces in response to an allergen. Nettle tea or extract can help with itching. Nettles not only help directly to decrease the itch, but also work overtime to desensitise the body to allergens.

✓ **Quercetin** – is an over-the-counter supplement with anti-inflammatory properties. It is a strong antioxidant and reduces the body's production of histamines.

✓ **Omega-3 Fatty Acids -** these help decrease inflammation throughout the body. Adding them into the diet of all pets - particularly those struggling with seasonal environmental allergies – is very beneficial. If your dog has more itching along the top of their back and on their sides, add in a fish oil supplement. Fish oil helps to decrease the itch and heal skin lesions. The best sources of Omega 3s are krill oil, salmon oil, tuna oil, anchovy oil and other fish body oils, as well as raw organic egg yolks. If using an oil alone, it is important to give a vitamin B complex supplement.

✓ **Coconut Oil -** contains lauric acid, which helps decrease the production of yeast, a common opportunistic infection. Using a fish body oil combined with coconut oil before inflammation flares up can help moderate or even suppress your dog's inflammatory response.

Dr Sara adds: "Above are but a few of the over-the-counter remedies I like. In non-responsive cases, Chinese herbs can be used to work with the body to help to decrease the allergy threshold even more than with diet and supplements alone. Most of the animals I work with are on a program of Chinese herbs, diet change and acupuncture.

"So, the next time Fido is showing symptoms of seasonal allergies, consider rethinking your strategy to treat the root cause instead of the symptom."

With thanks to Dr Sara Skiwski, of the Western Dragon Integrated Veterinary Services, San Jose, California, for her kind permission to use her writings as the basis for *The Holistic Approach.*

FACT Massage can stimulate your dog's immune system and help to prevent or reduce allergies. It's also good for improving your dog's circulation and flexibility, reducing muscle and arthritis pain and other age-related problems.

Anybody can do it – we do – and your German Shepherd will love the attention! There is a How To Massage article on the All About Shepherds and many other websites.

Holistic practitioners also believe that *acupressure* can specifically help dogs with allergies. Type *"Acupressure for Dogs"* into Google to learn about the theory behind it and how to apply pressure at specific points on your dog's body. Acupressure can also help nervous and elderly dogs.

If your German Shepherd has a skin issue, seek a professional diagnosis as soon as possible before attempting to treat it yourself and it becomes entrenched:

Early diagnosis and treatment give the best chance of a full recovery.

Even if a skin condition cannot be completely cured, most can be successfully managed, allowing your dog to live a happy, pain-free life.

★ Remember that a high-quality diet, attention to cleanliness, and regular grooming and check-overs go a long way in preventing and managing skin problems in German Shepherds.

---

14. Grooming

German Shepherds have many advantages over other breeds: they are the most versatile of all dogs, they are highly intelligent and willing to please, and their loyalty and courage are legendary.

However, some have also earned the nickname "German Shedder" - particularly those with long coats! The length of hair and amount of shedding varies from one German Shepherd to the next, but it's fair to say that most German Shepherds are definitely NOT low-maintenance when it comes to grooming.

Types of Coat

Most German Shepherds, have a double coat consisting of an outer coat with straight, hard, close-lying and dense hair, with a thick undercoat. (A single coat is regarded as a fault by the Kennel Clubs). The hair may be short, medium or long. The UK Breed Standard accepts all coat lengths, describing the long coat as:

"Outer coat longer, not always straight and frequently not lying close and flat to the body. Thick undercoat. Coat distinctly longer inside and behind the ears, forming moderate tufts. Longer hair on the back of the forelegs, through to the loins, and dense feathering on the hindlegs. Tail bushy with light feathering underneath."

Photo, top to bottom: medium, short and long coat. Middle photo courtesy of Marie Donahue.

Although the gene for long hair is recessive, long-haired German Shepherds are extremely popular in the US. However, they are not accepted in the show ring, as the AKC Breed Standard states:

"The ideal dog has a double coat of medium length. The outer coat should be as dense as possible, hair straight, harsh and lying close to the body. A slightly wavy outer coat, often of wiry texture, is permissible. The head, including the inner ear and foreface, and the legs and paws are covered with short hair, and the neck with longer and thicker hair.

"The rear of the forelegs and hind legs has somewhat longer hair extending to the pastern and hock, respectively. Faults in coat include soft, silky, too long outer coat, woolly, curly, and open coat."

Of course, none of this matters if you have no intention of entering your German Shepherd in an AKC conformation show! All types of GSD coats and colours are accepted in all other canine competitions.

FACT There is no getting away from the fact that many German Shepherds do shed a lot. But exactly how much and when depends on a number of factors. Show line German Shepherds usually have thicker, longer coats than working line German Shepherds.

Other factors affecting the amount of coat include: bloodlines, skin condition, diet, gender, age, whether your dog has been neutered or spayed, and temperature of the environment - a dog kept in a centrally-heated house will shed for longer than a working dog kept in an outdoor kennel, where the seasons are more evident.

When choosing grooming tools, find out whether your dog has a double coat. Most German Shepherds do, but some have a single coat. Generally, long-haired GSDs have long, feathery tufts on their ears, tail and back of their legs. Single-coated long-haired German Shepherds still have this feathering, but the outer coat is soft, not coarse, and requires less, more gentle grooming to protect the single coat.

....

Blowing Coat

This is not a breed for the super house-proud! Not only is the German Shepherd a big, athletic dog that loves running and swimming outdoors, but many double-coated dogs *"blow"* or shed their dense undercoat twice a year, usually in spring and autumn (fall). During this time, you'll remove unbelievable amounts of hair during grooming.

It's a big downside to GSDs - unless you happen to be in the pillow-stuffing business! And this twice-yearly shed is in addition to general shedding that goes on throughout the entire year.

When the coat is blowing, your dog will need daily grooming. A rake, *pictured, top,* is a good tool for getting the dense undercoat out. And unless you want to disappear inside a giant fluff ball, we recommend using it outdoors! Breeder **Cheryl Spurr** recommends finishing off after raking with a Kong Grooming Brush, *pictured, below.*

If your dog develops bare patches or dislikes the rake, it may be because he has sensitive skin or a finer coat, so use a gentler brush. Other grooming tools include a pin brush or bristle brush and comb.

If German Shepherds with long or medium coats are not regularly groomed, i.e. a couple of times a week or more and every day when the coat is blowing, they will eventually become matted. In the worst cases, the matts are impossible to get rid of and the dog has to be shaved, which is not good, as it removes the water-repellent outer guard hairs from the coat.

Tip A German Shepherd should never be shaved, except on veterinary advice, or when the coat has become so matted and tangled that it is impossible to brush. Far better to keep up with the grooming.

German Shepherds should not be bathed too often as they can lose their natural coat oils. Most GSD breeders recommend only bathing your dog when he is particularly smelly or dirty, e.g. after he has rolled, paddled or swum in something unmentionable, *pictured.*

If yours regularly returns from walks covered in mud, hose him down before

allowing him back into the house or kennel; a German Shepherd's coat is designed to cope with water.

Do not regularly use shampoos or other products (unless advised to do so by a vet), as a dog needs to keep his coat naturally oily, and general shampoos rid the coat of its natural oils. Never use human shampoos as these will irritate his skin. A dog's skin has a different pH to that of a human. If you do occasionally use a shampoo, use one specially medicated for dogs - such as Malaseb or similar. It is expensive, but lasts a long time. There are also many organic shampoos for dogs.

 **Leaving a German Shepherd in a dirty condition can lead to irritation, skin issues or excessive shedding.**

It's all a question of getting the balance right, and this depends to some extent on whether your GSD lives indoors or in an outdoor kennel, how much outdoor exercise he gets, what sort of areas he's running in, how often he swims and what his natural coat and skin condition is like.

Importance of Regular Grooming

Time spent grooming is also time spent bonding; this physical and emotional inter-reliance brings us closer to our dogs.

Grooming doesn't just mean giving your German Shepherd a quick tickle with a brush a couple of times a week. There are other facets to grooming that play a part in keeping your dog clean and skin-related issues at bay. Routine grooming sessions also allow you to examine your dog's coat, skin, ears, teeth, eyes, paws and nails for signs of problems.

Although puppies require fairly minimal brushing, it's important to get yours used to being handled and groomed from an early age; an adult German Shepherd will not take too kindly to being handled if he is not used to it. Other benefits of regular brushing are that it:

- ✤ Removes dead hair and skin
- ✤ Stimulates blood circulation
- ✤ Spreads natural oils throughout the coat, helping to keep it in good condition

If your young German Shepherd is resisting your grooming efforts, place him on a table or bench. Once he is out of his normal environment - i.e. floor level - and at your level, he may be more compliant.

A few things to look out for are:

Dry skin - A dog's skin can dry out, especially with artificial heat in the winter months. If you spot any dry patches, for example on the inner thighs or armpits, or a cracked nose, massage a little petroleum jelly or baby oil on to the dry patch.

Eyes - These should be clean and clear. Cloudy eyes, particularly in an older dog, could be early signs of cataracts. Red or swollen tissue in the corner(s) could be a symptom of cherry eye, which can affect dogs of all breeds. Ingrowing eyelashes is another issue that causes red, watery eyes.

If your dog has an issue, gently bathe the eye(s) with warm water and cotton wool - never use anything sharp; your dog can suddenly jump forwards or backwards, causing injury. If the eye is red or watering for a few days or more, get it checked out by a vet.

Acne - Little red pimples on a dog's face and chin means he has got acne. A dog can get acne at any age, not just as an adolescent. Plastic bowls can also trigger the condition, which is why stainless steel ones are often better. Daily washing followed by an application of an antibiotic cream is usually enough to get rid of the problem; if it persists it will mean a visit to your vet.

GSD Colours and Markings

The German Shepherd developed as a working breed, and so the ability to do a job and temperament were considered much more important than appearance. Because of this, colours vary from black to white with several in between, although in the show ring, rich, dark colours are preferred.

In his book *"The German Shepherd Dog, A Genetic History of the Breed,"* Malcolm B. Willis stated: "The colour of the GSD is in itself not important and has no effect on the character of the dog or on its fitness for work and should be a secondary consideration for that reason."

Today, German Shepherd colours include:

- ❧ **Black and tan** - the most common, usually with a black saddle and mask
- ❧ **Black and cream** – a lighter variation of black and tan
- ❧ **Black and silver** – similar to black and cream
- ❧ **Black and red** – the colour of most show line GSDs; the red is more intense than tan
- ❧ **Silver -** like a black and tan with silver replacing the tan
- ❧ **Bi-color** – mostly black, the dog may have tan or gold markings on the head, chest, legs and feet
- ❧ **Black** – a recessive trait; both parents must carry the black gene for a puppy to be solid black
- ❧ **Sable** – this is actually a hair pattern caused by the dominant *"agouti"* gene. Each individual hair has coloured bands and is tipped with various amounts of black. There are black, tan, silver and red sables. GSDs from Eastern European lines are often dark sable, and GSDs that look like wolves are sable
- ❧ **Grey -** similar colouring to wolves
- ❧ **White** – a solid white colour and, despite being very popular, they are disqualified from the show ring under Kennel Club and AKC rules

The following colours are considered faults by the Kennel Clubs:

- ❧ **Liver** – a brown dog with a brown nose, described as "Other" on AKC Registration Papers
- ❧ **Blue** – often with blue or light eyes, described as "Other" on AKC Registration Papers
- ❧ **Grey** – a diluted form of a dark colour, described as "Other" on AKC Registration Papers
- ❧ **Dilute** - washed-out varieties of colours, e.g. livers, greys and blues
- ❧ **Panda** – a GSD with white spotting

Here are some of the words used to describe German Shepherd coat markings:

- 🐾 **Saddle** – common black marking on the GSDs back, which sits like a saddle on a horse, common with black and tans and black and reds

- 🐾 **Blanket** – larger black marking covering the back from the ears to the tail

- 🐾 **Mask** – dark colour around a dog's face, often the muzzle

- 🐾 **Reverse mask** – or maskless; lack of a black muzzle

 Tip If you have set your heart on a favourite colour or marking, remember to check that the health-testing and temperament boxes have been ticked as well.

Nail Trimming

If your German Shepherd is regularly exercised on grass or other soft surfaces, his nails may not be getting worn down sufficiently, so they may require clipping or filing.

FACT ❯ Nails should be kept short for the paws to remain healthy. Overly-long nails interfere with a dog's gait, making walking awkward or painful and they can break easily, usually at the base of the nail where blood vessels and nerves are located.

Be prepared: many German Shepherds dislike having their nails trimmed — especially if they are not used to it - so it requires patience and persistence on your part.

Get your dog used to having his paws inspected from puppyhood; it's also a good opportunity to check for other problems, such as cracked pads or interdigital cysts. (These are swellings between the toes, often due to a bacterial infection).

To trim your dog's nails, use a specially designed clipper. Most have safety guards to prevent you cutting the nails too short. Do it before they get too long.

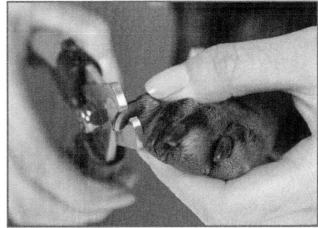

Tip If you can hear the nails clicking on a hard surface, they're too long.

You want to trim only the ends, before *"the quick,"* which is a blood vessel inside the nail. You can see where the quick ends on a white nail, but not on a dark nail.

Clip only the hook-like part of the nail that turns down. Start trimming gently, a nail or two at a time, and your dog will learn that you're not going to hurt him. If you accidentally cut the quick, stop the bleeding with some styptic powder.

Another option is to file your dog's nails with a nail grinder tool. Some Shepherds have tough nails that are harder to trim and this may be a less stressful method for your dog, with less chance of pain or bleeding.

The grinder is like an electric nail file and only removes a small amount of nail at a time. Some owners prefer to use one as there is less chance of cutting the quick, and many dogs prefer them to a clipper. Introduce your dog to the grinder gradually - the noise and vibration take some getting used to.

If you find it impossible to clip your dog's nails, or you are at all worried about doing it, take him to a vet or a groomer - and get your Shepherd's anal sacs squeezed, or "expressed," while he's there!

Anal Glands

While we're discussing the less appealing end of your German Shepherd, let's dive straight in and talk about anal sacs. Sometimes called scent glands, these are a pair of glands located inside your dog's anus that give off a scent when he has a bowel movement. You won't want to hear this, but problems with impacted anal glands are not uncommon in German Shepherds!

When a dog passes firm stools, the glands normally empty themselves, but soft poop or diarrhoea can mean that not enough pressure is exerted to empty the glands, causing discomfort to the dog. If they get infected, they become swollen and painful. In extreme cases, one or both anal glands can be removed – we had a dog that lived happily for many years with one anal gland.

If your dog drags himself along on his rear end – *"scooting"* - or tries to lick or scratch his anus, he could well have impacted anal glands that need squeezing, either by you if you know how to do it, your vet or a groomer. (Scooting is also a sign of worms). Either way, it pays to keep an eye on both ends of your dog!

German Shepherds are prone to an unpleasant disorder called Perianal Fistulas – see **Chapter 12. German Shepherd Health** for full details. If you do notice an unpleasant smell - in addition to any normal gassy emissions and he hasn't been rolling in anything horrible – he could have Perianal Fistulas. Other symptoms are redness, inflammation or discharge around the anus and under the tail, and if you suspect this may be the case, get your dog to a vet straight away.

Ear Cleaning

Ear infections affect dogs of all breeds - German Shepherds suffer fewer infections than many breeds, as they have pricked-up ears that allow air to circulate. Droopy, floppy ears create a warm, moist haven for bacteria and infection. However, any dog can get an ear infection, particularly if they suffer from allergies, or have dense hair inside the ear.

Also, some German Shepherd puppies have floppy ears, *pictured,* until the ears prick up, usually before six months of age.

Ear infections are notorious for recurring once they have taken hold, and cause deafness in very severe cases. So, it pays to check your dog's ears regularly while grooming. Many German Shepherds love swimming, which can also cause ear infections if the area inside the ear remains wet for long periods. A good habit to get into is to towel dry the ears after swimming.

Keep an eye out for redness or inflammation at the inner base of the ear, or a build-up of dark wax, and if your German Shepherd has a particularly long coat with hairy ears, the hair inside the ear should be regularly plucked to allow air to circulate more freely.

 Never put anything sharp or narrow - like a cotton bud – inside your dog's ears, as you can cause damage.

Typical signs of an ear infection are the dog:

❧ Shaking his head a lot

❧ Scratching his ears

❧ Rubbing his ears on the floor

❧ An unpleasant smell coming from the ears, which is a sign of a yeast infection

If your dog exhibits any of these signs, consult your vet ASAP, as simple routine cleaning won't solve the problem, and ear infections are notoriously difficult to get rid of once your dog's had one. Keep your dog's ears clean, dry and free from too much hair right from puppyhood and hope he never gets one.

Teeth Cleaning

Veterinary studies show that by the age of age of three, 80% of dogs show signs of gum or dental disease. Symptoms include yellow and brown build-up of tartar along the gum line, red inflamed gums and persistent bad breath.

Many German Shepherd owners keep their dogs' teeth clean by giving them an occasional bone, or regularly feeding bully sticks or other natural treats. Another option is to brush your dog's teeth. Take things slowly in the beginning and give lots of praise. Once used to the process, dogs love the attention - especially if they like the flavour of the toothpaste!

Use a pet toothpaste, as the human variety can upset a canine's stomach. The real benefit comes from the actual action of the brush on the teeth, and various brushes, sponges and pads are available - the choice depends on factors such as the health of your dog's gums, the size of his mouth and how good you are at teeth cleaning.

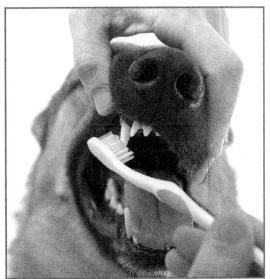

Get him used to the toothpaste by letting him lick some off your finger when he is young. If he doesn't like the flavour, try a different one. Continue this until he enjoys licking the paste - it might be instant or take days.

Put a small amount on your finger and gently rub it on one of the big canine teeth at the front of his mouth. Then get him used to the toothbrush or dental sponge - praise him when he licks it - for several days. The next step is to actually start brushing.

Lift his upper lip gently and place the brush at a 45° angle to the gum line. Gently move the brush backwards and forwards. Start just with his front teeth and then gradually do a few more. You don't need to brush the inside of his teeth as his tongue keeps them relatively free of plaque.

Breeders on Grooming

The level of grooming depends on whether the dogs are working line or show line and how much coat they have, and this is reflected in the breeders' comments, starting in the UK:

Stefanie Millington: "The GSD is a hairy monster who likes to shed a lot, as many double-coated breeds do. If you don't like a lot of dog hairs in your house, then you will need to religiously brush and rake your GSD on a daily basis, and that goes for the short as well as the long coat GSD. I find that metal rakes are the easiest bit of kit to use to get loose hair out of my dogs' coats. I personally only bath about twice a year, but my dogs love the paddling pool as well as swimming in rivers, lakes or the sea."

Cheryl Spurr: "I'm afraid mine don't get bathed very often. They love being brushed and, as I call them German Shedders, that's a good thing! I groom weekly, but I groom daily when they are shedding."

Carolyn Day: "I normally groom every day as my German Shepherd is long-coated. Bathing is up to four times a year, dependent on weather and coat condition."

Wendy Sharp: "Grooming is a good bonding opportunity for owners and dogs. Long hair can get knotted, especially under the ears and neck. Bathing is not necessary frequently."

Teresa Mapp: "I believe that GSDs shed more than most dogs, mainly due to their double coat - the soft, fluffy undercoat sheds in clumps at least twice a year, and their thick coarse overcoat continually sheds all year round. I always emphasise how much Shepherds do shed, although most of our owners are previous owners anyway.

"Bathing is a personal thing for the owners. We have lived in this house for five years and only bathed one girl, once after she rolled in fox mess! We personally feel bathing strips them of their natural oils that gives their coats a good shine. A good, regular brushing is much better for their coats. Weekly during non-moult season, but when moulting, it can be several times a day! This is something I would never mislead people about; it is probably the only negative about GSDs. It can be a bind with six dogs, but it is also a great bonding time for dog and owner."

And here's the US breeders, starting with **Jacqueline Levy,** who breeds working line GSDs: "We don't recommend shaving German Shepherds in the summer. Baths are recommended as needed, and nails are clipped regularly - sometimes easily and sometimes not so easily!"

Marie Donahue: "My dogs' nails are clipped weekly. They are only bathed when needed, as bathing strips the natural oils from their coats."

Bobbi King, RVT: "Brushing daily is so awesome. Do not over-brush the same area at the same time and press too hard against the skin; move the brush around. Sudsy bathes are nice but RINSE well!"

Tammey Tilton: "Grooming your German Shepherd needs to be done on a regular basis. We usually groom them once a week or more when they are blowing their coat. But we only bath our German Shepherds when they are really dirty, as bathing them often will strip their coat of natural oils that protect their skin and your German Shepherd's coat will lose some of its shine and luster.

"While I'm grooming my dogs, I check them over to make sure they have no ticks, cuts, scrapes, lumps or anything that might need to be addressed. I also check their ears to make sure they are clean and that they do not have any signs of an ear infection."

Looking very pleased with herself and her Canine Good Citizen rosette is the beautifully-groomed Annie vom Ursi CGC Spot-On, aged five months, courtesy of Tammey.

She added: "While our German Shepherd puppies are in our care, we make sure we get them used to having their whole bodies touched, including their paws, nails, ears and teeth. Continue this practice starting from the first day you take your new puppy home. Play with his toes and get him used to holding his paw still while you are holding it in your hand. Also, teach him to hold still while you open his mouth, brushing him, and look in his ears, using treats as rewards."

15. The Birds and the Bees

Judging by the number of questions our website receives from owners, there is a lot of confusion about the canine facts of life. Some want to know whether they should breed their dog, while others ask if, and at what age, they should have their dog spayed or neutered.

Owners of females ask when and how often she will come on heat and how long this will last. Sometimes they want to know how you can tell if a female is pregnant or how long a pregnancy lasts. So here, in a nutshell, is a chapter on The Facts of Life as far as German Shepherds are concerned.

....

Females and Heat

Just like all other female mammals, including humans, a female German Shepherd has a menstrual cycle - or to be more accurate, an oestrus cycle *(estrus* in the US). This is the period of time when she is ready (and willing!) for mating and is more commonly called *heat*, being *in heat*, *on heat* or *in season*.

Large breeds tend to have their first heat cycle later than small breeds. A German Shepherd female usually has her first cycle at six to 12 months old, although there are no hard and fast rules. Some may be as old as 18 months to two years before their first heat.

Females may follow the pattern of their mother, so if you are getting a female puppy, it may be worth asking your breeder at what age the dam (mother) first came on heat.

She will then come in heat about every six months. There is no season of the year that corresponds to a breeding season, so it could be winter and summer or spring and autumn (fall), etc.

When a young female comes on heat, it is normal for her cycles to be somewhat irregular, and can take up to two years for regular cycles to develop. The timescale also becomes more erratic with old, unspayed females.

There are no hard and fast rules. **Larry Yates** has bred Lornstone German Shepherds since the 1960s and says: "I have looked back over our last 10 females to find their ages at their first season. I have found that the average age is 12.3 months; the youngest was six months, and the oldest 17 months. Six of the 10 came in heat before 12 months, and of the remaining four, two came in at 14 months, and the other two at 16 and 17 months.

"We always work on a six-monthly calendar for heats. But, rarely do they work to the date. We find that it can happen anytime between four and eight months, and false seasons are not uncommon."

Veterinary technician and breeder **Bobbi King, RVT,** adds: "The German Shepherd can come in heat as early as six months or even as late as 16 months, but those are both very unusual. The average is nine to 11 months for the first cycle and it can last two to four weeks."

Unlike women, female dogs do not stop menstruating when they reach middle age, although the heat becomes shorter and lighter. However, a litter takes a heavy toll on many older females (over seven years old).

Stages and Signs of Heat

One difference between humans and dogs is that women cannot get pregnant during their period, while female dogs can ONLY get pregnant during their heat. The stages of a heat cycle are:

Proestrus – this is the first stage and lasts around nine days. Male dogs are attracted to her, but she is not yet interested, so she may hold her tail close to her body.

You will notice that her vulva (external sex organ, or pink bit under her tail) becomes swollen, which she will lick to clean herself. If you're not sure, hold a tissue against her vulva – does it turn pink or red? The blood is usually light red or brown, turning more watery after a week or so. She may also urinate more frequently.

Oestrus - this is when eggs are released from ovaries and the optimum time for breeding. Males are interested in her - and the feelings are very much reciprocated! She may "flag" - hold her tail up or move it off to the side, "presenting herself" to show she is willing to be mated. Oestrus also lasts around nine days.

Dioestrus - her body produces hormones whether or not she is pregnant. All the hormones are present; only the puppies are missing, if she hasn't been mated. This can sometimes lead to what is known as a "false pregnancy." During this stage she is no longer interested in males.

The canine heat cycle is a complex mix of hormonal, behavioural, and physical changes. Each dog is different. Some show behavioural changes, such as becoming more clingy or short-tempered, going off their food, shedding hair or sulking in their beds.

German Shepherds are big dogs and some can be quite messy on heat, leaving bloody trails around the house. One option is to keep her crated more often. Another is to buy doggie diapers, or nappies **(pictured)**. However, if you leave her unattended with one on, she may chew it to bits or rip it off.

When a female is on heat, she produces pheromones that attract male dogs. Because dogs have a sense of smell several hundred times stronger than ours, your girl on heat is a magnet for all the neighbourhood males. It is believed that they can detect the scent of a female on heat up to two miles away!

They may congregate around your house or follow you around the park - if you are brave or foolish enough to venture out there while she is in season - waiting for their chance to prove their manhood (or mutthood in their case).

Bobbi adds: "Breeders say a week coming in and a week standing for the male (nine to 14 days) and the week going out and, of course, confine from the boys another week just to be safe! I have had females conceive when there is absolutely no sign of heat - even as early as the third day of bleeding - and ovulate as late as the 28th day after the first sign of spotting!"

To avoid an unwanted pregnancy, you must keep a close eye on her throughout her heat and not allow her to freely wander where she may come into contact with other dogs - and that includes the garden or yard, unless it is 100% dog proof. Definitely don't let her run free anywhere where you might come across other dogs. You can compensate for the restrictions by playing more games to keep her mentally and physically active.

The instinct to mate may trump all of her training. Her hormones are raging and, during *her most fertile days, which are Day 9 to 10 of heat for five or more days,* she is ready, able and ... VERY willing!

It is amazing the lengths some intact males will go to impregnate a female on heat. Travelling great distances to follow her scent, jumping over barriers, digging under fences, chewing through doors or walls and sneaking through hedges are just some of the tactics employed by canine Casanovas on the loose. Love is a powerful thing - and canine lust even more so...A dog living in the same house as a female in heat has even been known to mate with her through the bars of a crate!

If you do have an intact male, you need to physically keep him in a separate place or kennel. The desire to mate is all-consuming and can be accompanied by howling or "marking" (urinating) indoors from a frustrated Romeo.

Bobbi adds: "Female scan be just as persistent to get to the males, having been known to tear through chain-link fencing, chew out of crates or even break glass windows!"

You can also buy a spray that masks the natural oestrus scent. Marketed under such attractive names as *"Bitch Spray,"* these lessen, but don't eliminate, the scent. They may reduce the amount of unwanted attention, but are not a complete deterrent. There is no canine contraceptive and the only sure-fire way of preventing your female from becoming pregnant is spaying.

There is a *"morning after pill"* – actually a series of oestrogen tablets or an injection - which some vets may administer after an unwanted coupling, but side effects can be severe, including Pyometra (a potentially life-threatening infection of the womb), bone marrow suppression and infertility.

Breeding Restrictions

A German Shepherd should not be bred before two years old. There are a couple of reasons for this. Firstly, the testing for hip dysplasia, called *hip scoring,* cannot be carried out before 24 months. Secondly, pregnancy draws on calcium and other reserves needed for a young female's own growing body. If bred too soon, she could break down structurally and have health issues in later life.

Good breeders also limit the number of litters from each dog, as litters can take a lot out of a female. To discourage over-breeding, the UK Kennel Club has introduced *Breeding Restrictions* and will not register a litter from any female:

1. That has already had four litters.
2. That is less than one year old at the time of mating.
3. That is eight years or older when she whelps (gives birth).
4. If the litter is the result of any mating between father and daughter, mother and son or brother and sister.
5. That has already had two C-Sections (Caesarean Sections).
6. That is not resident at a UK address at the date of whelping – to try and discourage people buying from foreign puppy farms.

Neutering - Pros and Cons

Once a straightforward subject, this is currently a hot potato in the dog world. Dogs that are kept purely as pets – i.e. not for showing, breeding or working – are often spayed or neutered. There is also the life-threatening risk of **Pyometra** in unspayed middle-aged females. A major argument for neutering of both sexes is that there is already too much indiscriminate breeding of dogs in the world.

As you will read in **Chapter 16. German Shepherd Rescue**, it is estimated that 1,000 dogs are put to sleep every hour in the US alone. It is for this reason that rescue organisations in North America, the UK and Australia neuter all dogs that they rehome.

Some areas in the United States, e.g. LA, have even adopted a compulsory sterilisation policy, aimed at: *"reducing and eventually eliminating the thousands of euthanizations conducted in Los Angeles' animal shelters every year."* The RSPCA, along with most UK vets, also promotes the benefits of neutering. It is estimated that more than half of all dogs in the UK are spayed or castrated.

Another point is that you may not have a choice. Some breeders' Puppy Contracts may stipulate that, except in special circumstances, you agree to neuter your German Shepherd as a Condition of Sale. Others may state that you need the breeder's permission to breed your dog.

The Science

While early spay/neuter has been traditionally recommended, there is scientific evidence that for some breeds, including the German Shepherd, it may be better to wait until the dog is through puberty. Armed with the facts, it is for each individual owner to decide what is best for their dog – unless there was a Spay/Neuter clause in your Puppy Contract.

A 2016 UC Davis School of Veterinary Medicine study involving veterinary records for 1,170 German Shepherds over 14.5 years found that spaying or neutering GSDs before the age of one increased the risk of joint disorders and urinary incontinence.

It stated: "Neutering, however, especially in the first year, can come with its costs with regard to debilitating joint disorders, namely, hip dysplasia (HD), cranial cruciate ligament tear or rupture (CCL) and elbow dysplasia (ED).

"In intact males, 7% were diagnosed with one or more joint disorders, while in males neutered prior to a year of age, a significantly higher 21% were diagnosed with one or more joint disorders.

"In intact females, 5% were diagnosed with one or more joint disorders, while in females neutered prior to a year of age, this measure was significantly increased to 16%. The increased joint disorder incidence mostly associated with early neutering was CCL.

"Urinary incontinence, not diagnosed in intact females, was diagnosed in 7% of females neutered before 1 year, a significant difference."

The one area where early neutering was beneficial, was mammary cancer, the equivalent of breast cancer in women: "MC was diagnosed in 4% of intact females compared with less than 1% in females neutered before one year."

The study concluded: "These findings, profiling the increase in joint disorders associated with early neutering, should help guide the timing of neutering for this breed." To read the study, online, go to https://onlinelibrary.wiley.com and type "**Neutering of German Shepherd Dogs**" in the search box. A 2018 article, published in The IAABC Journal (International Association of Animal Behavior Consultants), highlights the pros and cons of neutering. Written by a vet, it's a bit technical, but worth a read: https://fall2018.iaabcjournal.org/2018/10/31/spay-and-neuter-surgery-effects-on-dogs or Google "*IAABC early neuter in dogs.*" The table at the end of the article summarises the pros and cons.

....

Spaying

Spaying is the term traditionally used to describe the sterilisation of a female dog so that she cannot become pregnant. This is normally done by a procedure called an *"ovariohysterectomy"* and involves the removal of the ovaries and uterus, or womb. Although this is a routine operation, it is major abdominal surgery and she has to be anaesthetised.

One less invasive option offered by some vets is an *"ovariectomy",* which removes the ovaries, but leaves the womb intact. It requires only a small incision and can even be carried out by laparoscopy, or keyhole surgery. The dog is anaesthetised for a shorter time and there is less risk of infection or excess bleeding during surgery.

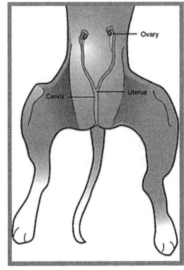

One major reason often given for not opting for an ovariectomy is that the female still runs the risk of Pyometra later in life. However, there is currently little or no scientific evidence of females that have undergone an ovariectomy contracting Pyometra afterwards.

If a female is spayed before her first heat cycle, she will have an almost zero risk of mammary cancer. Even after the first heat, spaying reduces the risk of this cancer considerably. Some vets claim that the risk of mammary cancer in unspayed female dogs can be as high as one in four.

Spaying is much more serious for females than neutering is for males. It involves an internal abdominal operation, whereas the neutering procedure is carried out on the male's testicles, which are outside his abdomen. As with any major procedure, there are pros and cons.

For:

❖ Spaying prevents infections, cancer and other diseases of the uterus and ovaries. A spayed female will have a greatly reduced risk of mammary cancer

❖ Spaying eliminates the risk of Pyometra, which results from hormonal changes in the female's reproductive tract. It also reduces hormonal changes that can interfere with the treatment of diseases like diabetes or epilepsy

❖ You no longer have to cope with any potential mess caused by bleeding inside the house during heat cycles

❖ You don't have to guard your female against unwanted attention from males as she will no longer have heat cycles

❖ Spaying can reduce behaviour problems, such as roaming, aggression towards other dogs, anxiety or fear (not all canine experts agree)

❖ A spayed dog does not contribute to the pet overpopulation problem

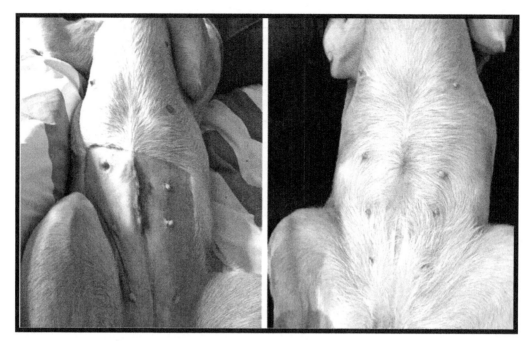

These photographs are reproduced courtesy of Guy Bunce and Chloe Spencer, of Dizzywaltz Labrador Retrievers, Berkshire, England. The left image shows four-year-old Disney shortly after a full spay (ovariohysterectomy). The right one shows Disney several weeks later.

Against:

- Complications can occur, including an abnormal reaction to the anaesthetic, bleeding, stitches breaking and infections; *these are not common*

- Occasionally there can be long-term effects connected to hormonal changes. These include weight gain or less stamina, which can occur years after spaying

- Some females may suffer urinary incontinence

- Cost. This can range from £100 to £250 in the UK, more for keyhole spaying, and approximately $150-$500 at a vet's clinic in the USA, or from around $50 at a low-cost clinic, for those that qualify

- There is evidence that spaying some German Shepherds before one year of age can increase the likelihood of joint problems later

Neutering

Neutering male dogs involves castration (the removal of the testicles). This can be a difficult decision for some owners, as it causes a drop in the pet's testosterone levels, which some humans – men in particular! - feel affects the quality of their dog's life. Fortunately, dogs do not think like people, and male dogs do not miss their testicles or the loss of sex.

 Dogs working in service or for charities are often neutered and this does not impair their ability to perform any of their duties.

There are countless unwanted puppies, many of which are destroyed. There is also the huge problem of a lack of knowledge from the owners of some dogs, resulting in the production of poor puppies with congenital health or temperament problems.

Technically, neutering can be carried out at any age over eight weeks, provided both testicles have descended. However, recent scientific studies, such as the ones already outlined, are coming down on the side of waiting until the dog is one year or older.

Dogs neutered before puberty tend to grow a little larger than dogs done later. This is because testosterone is involved in the process that stops growth, so the bones grow for longer without testosterone.

Surgery is relatively straightforward, and complications are less common and less severe than with spaying. Although he will feel tender afterwards, your dog should return to his normal self within a couple of days.

When a dog comes out of surgery, his scrotum, or sacs that held the testicles, will be swollen and it may look like nothing has been done. It is normal for these to shrink slowly in the days following surgery. Here are the main pros and cons:

For:

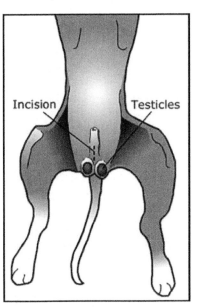

❧ Castration is a simple procedure, and dogs usually make a swift recovery afterwards

❧ Behaviour problems such as aggression and roaming can be reduced

❧ Unwanted sexual behaviour, such as mounting people or objects, is usually reduced or eliminated

❧ Testicular problems such as infections, cancer and torsion (painful rotation of the testicle) are eradicated

❧ Prostate disease, common in older male dogs, is less likely to occur

❧ A submissive un-neutered male dog may be targeted by other dogs. After he has been neutered, he will no longer produce testosterone and so will not be regarded as much of a threat by the other males, so he is less likely to be bullied

❧ A neutered dog is not fathering unwanted puppies

Against:

❧ Recent studies seem to show that some German Shepherds neutered before one year old are more likely to have joint problems

❧ As with any surgery, there can be bleeding afterwards; you should keep an eye on after the procedure. Infections can also occur, generally caused by the dog licking the wound, so try and prevent him doing this. If he persists, use an E-collar. In the **vast majority** of cases, these problems do not occur

❧ Some dogs' coats may be affected (this also applies to spaying); supplementing the diet with fish oil can compensate for this

❧ Cost - this starts at around £80 in the UK. In the US this might cost upwards from $100 at a private veterinary clinic, or from $50 at a low cost or Humane Society clinic

New Techniques

Two other phrases you may hear are *"tubal ligation"* or *"vasectomy." Tubal ligation* is the tying of a female's Fallopian tubes and a ***vasectomy*** is the clamping shut of the sperm ducts from the male's testicles. Many veterinary papers have been written on these topics, but as yet, not many vets offer them as options, possibly because they have not been trained to carry out these procedures.

In both cases, unlike with spaying and neutering, the dog continues to produce hormones, but is unable to get pregnant or father puppies. With further evidence of the positive effects of hormones, these operations could become more common in the future – although more vets will first have to be trained.

There's a new non-surgical procedure to sterilise male dogs called **"Zeutering."** It involves injecting zinc gluconate into the dog's testicles. Dogs are lightly sedated, but not anaesthetised. It's inexpensive, there's little recovery time and no stitches. However, studies show that Zeutering is only 99% effective, and its long-term effects are still being researched. A downside is that, while it makes dogs sterile, they still retain some of their testosterone.

Therefore, habits that usually disappear with traditional castration, such as marking, roaming, following females on heat and aggression towards other males, remain. Zeutering isn't for every dog, but worth discussing with your vet.

Urban Myths

Neutering or spaying will spoil the dog's character - There is no evidence that any of the positive characteristics of your dog will be altered. He or she will be just as obedient, playful and loyal as before. Neutering may reduce aggression or roaming in male dogs, because they are no longer competing to mate with a female.

A female needs to have at least one litter - There is no proven physical or mental benefit to a female having a litter.

Mating is natural and necessary - We tend to ascribe human emotions to our dogs, but they do not think emotionally about sex or having and raising a family. Unlike humans, their desire to mate or breed is entirely physical, triggered by the chemicals called hormones within their body. Without these hormones – i.e. after neutering or spaying – the desire disappears or is greatly reduced.

Male dogs will behave better if they can mate - This is simply not true; sex does not make a dog behave better. In fact, it can have the opposite effect. Having mated once, a male may show an increased interest in females. He may also consider his status elevated, which may make him harder to control or call back.

 If you are considering having your dog spayed or neutered, discuss the optimum age for the procedure with your breeder and vet – and do your research. Many vets still promote early spay and neuter.

Pregnancy

Regardless of how big or small the dog is, a canine pregnancy lasts for 58 to 65 days; 63 days is average. This is true of all breeds of dog from the Chihuahua to the Great Dane. Sometimes pregnancy is referred to as *"the gestation period."*

A female should have a pre-natal check-up after mating. The vet should answer any questions about type of food, supplements and extra care needed, as well as informing the owner about any physical changes likely to occur in your female.

There is a blood test available that measures levels of *relaxin*. This is a hormone produced by the ovary and the developing placenta, and pregnancy can be detected by monitoring relaxin levels as early as 22 to 27 days after mating. The levels are high throughout pregnancy and then decline rapidly after the female has given birth.

A vet can usually see the puppies (but not how many) using Ultrasound from around the same time. X-rays carried out 45 days into the pregnancy show the puppies' skeletons and give the breeder a good idea of the number of puppies.

They can also help to give the vet more information, which is particularly useful if the female has had previous whelping problems.

Signs of Pregnancy

* After mating, many females become more affectionate. However, a few may become uncharacteristically irritable and maybe even a little aggressive!

* She may produce a slight clear discharge from her vagina one month after mating

* Three or four weeks after mating, some females experience morning sickness – if this is the case, feed little and often. She may seem more tired than usual

* She may seem slightly depressed or show a drop in appetite. These signs can also mean there are other problems, so you should consult your vet

* Her teats will become more prominent, pink and erect 25 to 30 days into the pregnancy. Later on, you may notice a fluid coming from them

* Her body weight will noticeably increase about 35 days after mating

* Her abdomen will become noticeably larger from around Day 40, although first-time mums and females carrying few puppies may not show as much

* Many pregnant females' appetite will increase in the second half of pregnancy

* Her nesting instincts will kick in as the delivery date approaches. She may seem restless or scratch her bed or the floor - she may even rip and shred items like your comforter, curtains or carpeting!

* During the last week of pregnancy, females often start to look for a safe place for whelping. Some seem to become confused, wanting to be with their owners and at the same time wanting to prepare their nest. Even if the female is having a C-section, she should still be allowed to nest in a whelping box with layers of newspaper, which she will scratch and dig as the time approaches

If your female becomes pregnant – either by design or accident - your first step should be to consult a vet.

In terms of litter size: generally, the larger the dog, the bigger the litter. Many professional GSD breeders do ovulation timing testing, due to the increased litter sizes and increased chance of conception. Typical German Shepherd litters range from around five to eight pups. But in reality, the number could be anything from one to 15, depending on bloodlines, the age of the dam and sire (young and older dogs have smaller litters), health and diet of the dam, and size of the gene pool – the higher the COI (Coefficient of Inbreeding), the smaller the litter.

False Pregnancies

Occasionally, unspayed females may display signs of a false pregnancy. In the wild it was common for female dogs to have false pregnancies and to lactate (produce milk). This female would then nourish puppies if their own mother died.

False pregnancies occur 60 to 80 days after the female was in heat - about the time she would have given birth – and are generally nothing to worry about for an owner. The exact cause is unknown; however, hormonal imbalances are thought to play an important role. Some dogs have shown symptoms within three to four days of spaying; these include:

- ❧ Making a nest
- ❧ Mothering or adopting toys and other objects
- ❧ Producing milk (lactating)
- ❧ Appetite fluctuations
- ❧ Barking or whining a lot
- ❧ Restlessness, depression or anxiety
- ❧ Swollen abdomen
- ❧ She might even appear to go into labour

FACT ❯ Under no circumstances should you restrict your German Shepherd's water supply to try and prevent her from producing milk. This is dangerous as she can become dehydrated.

Some unspayed females may have a false pregnancy with each heat cycle. Spaying during a false pregnancy may actually prolong the condition, so better to wait until it is over to have her spayed.

False pregnancy is not a disease, but an exaggerated response to normal hormonal changes. Even if left untreated, it almost always resolves itself.

However, if your dog appears physically ill or the behavioural changes are severe enough to worry about, visit your vet. He or she may prescribe *Galastop*, which stops milk production and quickly returns the hormones to normal. In rare cases, hormone treatment may be necessary.

Generally, dogs experiencing false pregnancies do not have serious long-term problems, as the behaviour disappears when the hormones return to their normal levels in two to three weeks.

Pyometra

One exception is **Pyometra,** a serious and potentially deadly infection of the womb, caused by a hormonal abnormality. It normally follows a heat cycle in which fertilisation did not occur and the dog typically starts showing symptoms within two to four months.

Commonly referred to as *"pyo"*, there are **open** and **closed** forms of the disease. Open pyo is usually easy to identify with a smelly discharge, so prompt treatment is easy. Closed pyo is often harder to identify and you may not even notice anything until your girl becomes feverish and lethargic. When this happens, it is very serious and time is of the essence. Typically, vets will recommend immediate spaying in an effort to save her life.

Signs of Pyometra are excessive drinking and urination, with the female trying to lick a white discharge from her vagina. She may also have a slight temperature. If the condition becomes severe, her back legs will become weak, possibly to the point where she can no longer get up without help.

Pyometra can be fatal. It needs to be dealt with promptly by a vet, who will give the dog intravenous fluids and antibiotics for several days. In most cases this is followed by spaying.

Should I Breed From My German Shepherd?

The short and simple answer is: NO, leave it to the experts! The rising cost of puppies and increasing dog ownership are tempting more people to consider breeding their dogs. Producing healthy, happy German Shepherds with good temperaments doesn't just happen; it is a learned skill.

Due to a number of inherited diseases that affect the German Shepherds, anyone who is planning on breeding German Shepherds responsibly should have detailed knowledge of the genetic disorders affecting the breed and the relevant health tests prior to mating. The suitability of a mate with regards to health and temperament then has to be fully researched.

A good breeder also has to be prepared to part with a four-figure sum before a single pup is born. Good care, health screening and stud fees come at a cost. Don't enter into this thinking you will make a lot of money. If you do it properly, you won't.

You can't just put any two dogs together and expect perfect, healthy puppies. Ethical and successful breeding is much more scientific and time-consuming than that. Inexperience can result in tragic health consequences, poor specimens of the breed, the loss of pups - or even the mother.

Sometimes a C-section (Caesarean section) may be necessary. These are carried out when the mother is unable to birth the pups naturally – and timing is critical. Too early and the pups may be underdeveloped or the mother can bleed to death; too late and the pups can die.

Breeding Costs

Breeding healthy German Shepherds to type is a complex, expensive and time-consuming business when all the fees, DNA and health tests, care, nutrition and medical expenses have been taken into account. Here's a list of considerations to do it properly:

- ❧ Hip Scoring
- ❧ Eye tests
- ❧ Other DNA health tests
- ❧ Stud fees
- ❧ Pregnancy – ultrasound scan, worming, extra food and supplements for the mother
- ❧ Equipment – whelping box, vet bed, thermometer, feeding bottles, heat mat, hibiscrub, etc.
- ❧ Birth – vet's fees
- ❧ Puppies – vaccinations and worming, puppy food, coloured collars

And these are just the basics! These four-figure costs are considerable and swallow up a large chunk of any profit you thought you might make. And if there is a problem with the mother, birth or puppies and you rack up vet's bills, you can actually make a loss on a litter.

Ask Yourself This...

1. **Did you get your German Shepherd from a good, ethical breeder?** Dogs sold in pet stores and on general sales websites are seldom good specimens and can be unhealthy.

2. **Is your dog, and her close relatives, free from other health issues?** Hip and Elbow Dysplasia, Degenerative Myelopathy, Haemophilia, and eye and thyroid problems, are just some of the illnesses that German Shepherd puppies can inherit. Have you had your breeding dog and the stud dog DNA-tested for them? Also, an unhealthy female is more likely to have trouble with pregnancy and whelping.

3. **Does your German Shepherd have a good temperament? Does he or she socialise well with people and other animals?** If you can't tell, take your dog to training classes where the instructor can help you evaluate the dog's temperament. Dogs with poor temperaments should not be bred from, regardless of their other attributes.

4. **Does your dog conform to the Breed Standard?** Do not breed from a German Shepherd that is not a good specimen, hoping that somehow the puppies will turn out better. They won't. Talk with experienced breeders and ask them for an honest assessment of your dog.

5. **Is your female two years old or older and at least in her second heat cycle?** Female German Shepherds should not be bred until they are physically mature, have had their hips scored, and are robust enough to whelp and care for a litter. Even then, not all females are suitable. Some are simply poor mothers who don't care for their puppies - which means you have to do it – others may not be able to produce enough milk.

6. **Do you understand COI and its implications?** COI stands for Coefficient of Inbreeding. It measures the common ancestors of a dam and sire and indicates the probability of how genetically similar they are. In the UK, the COI is 3.1%.

7. **Are you financially able to provide good veterinary care for the mother and puppies, particularly if complications occur?** Health can be expensive, and that's in addition to routine veterinary care and the added costs of pre-natal care and immunisations for puppies. What if your female needs a C-section, or the puppies need emergency treatment, can you afford the bills?

8. **Do you have the time to provide full-time care for the mother and puppies if necessary?** Caring for the mother and new-borns is a 24/7 job for the first few weeks. You can't simply go out and leave mother and pups unattended.

9. **Can you offer a health guarantee against genetic defects or other health issues with each puppy?**

10. **Will you be able to find good homes for all the puppies and are you prepared to take one or more back if necessary?** Good breeders do not let their precious puppies go to just any home. They want to be sure that the new owners will take good care of their dogs for their lifetime.

Having said all of this, good breeders are made, not born. Like any expert, they learn over time. If you're serious, spend time researching German Shepherds and their genetics, find a mentor and make sure you are going into it for the right reasons and not just for the money. Ask yourself how you intend to improve the German Shepherd.

Bobbi King gives a personal account of breeding: "Becoming a breeder was the natural progression of a girl that loved all animals. I witnessed the birth of a mating that went well, and that sparked the dream to breed. To be fair, it comes with a ton of work, but has been a labor of love.

"Self-educated in the field of animals from a time when breeders did not want to share their "secrets," I am a firm believer in mentorship. I highly encourage everyone to find someone doing well and follow their example. Finding a good mentor is more than helpful, it is imperative. Ask questions continually and strive always to do your very best."

Bobbi is pictured with her stud ALADIN vom Bergmannsland.

"Quality will always sell. People will seek out your product and services and referrals will happen. With that said, you have a responsibility to check back with your buyers, stay in touch, and on occasion, take that last final goodbye with, or even for, them. Responsible breeders must make difficult decisions on where to place puppies. I have politely and firmly told a client: "I am so sorry, but I just received a deposit for that last puppy," and then given that puppy away to the absolutely right home. Be willing to say, "No!".

"All puppies are cute. I feel it irresponsible to sell someone a cute puppy based on their emotions. If everything else is correctly in place, then yes, by all means review their application and move forward. Sometimes what they write is not what you experience when they arrive - and I am sure many potential buyers have found that with breeders with really cool websites as well. That is why references are so important!"

Bobbi, along with other responsible breeders, only allows health-tested females to breed with her dogs and send this - and a lot of other information - to people with potential mates: "For Aladin to sire your next litter, here are some helpful hints:

"Have your dog fully examined by a vet prior to mating. You will need a current Rabies and DA2PP+CVK+Bordetella, worming for Round and Tapeworms, and health certificate should you need to ship your dog. We also require Brucellosis negative. Have your vet X-ray the hips and elbows and forward the films to OFA for a certificate. There are many other certification tests."

She asks: "My males are far more than just registered. I would love to hear more about your female and what she can add to the gene pool. Is she gentle or out of control? Have you done any testing on her genetically? Have you ever experienced puppies before? What are you seeking to produce in terms of color, style, personality?"

If you are determined to breed from your German Shepherd - and breed properly - do your research. Read as much as you can; one useful resource is *"Book of the Bitch" by J. M. Evans and Kay White.* Visit competitions and shows where German Shepherds are taking part, and talk to breeders.

To find a good breeder: In the USA, visit the AKC website and ideally look for a Bred with H.E.A.R.T. breeder, or one who has attained Platinum, Gold or Silver status as a Breeder of Merit. Visit the German Shepherd Dog Club of America for a list of events involving GSDs, and ask for details of members near you.

In the UK, go to the *Find a Dog Club* page for German Shepherds on the Kennel Club website. You can also find KC Approved Breeders on a county by county basis on the website.

You may have the most wonderful German Shepherd in the world, but don't enter the world of canine breeding without knowledge and ethics. Don't do it for the money or the cute factor – or to show the kids "The Miracle of Birth!" Breeding poor examples only brings heartache in the long run when health or temperament issues develop.

With thanks to Bobbi King, RVT, of Redwood Runs Pet Resort, Northern California, for her assistance with this chapter.

16. German Shepherd Rescue

Not everyone who wants a German Shepherd gets one as a puppy from a breeder. Some people prefer to give a second chance at a happy life to a rescue dog.

What could be kinder and more rewarding than giving a poor, abandoned dog a loving home for the rest of his life?

Not much really; adoption saves lives and gives unfortunate dogs a second chance of happiness. The problem of homeless dogs is truly depressing. It's a big issue in Britain, but even worse in the US, where the sheer numbers in kill shelters are hard to comprehend. In *"Don't Dump The Dog,"* Randy Grim states that 1,000 dogs are being put to sleep every hour in the States.

A German Shepherd is an athletic, demanding breed with a high drive.

That fluffy little puppy with the floppy ear looked so cute. But later down the line, owners who don't put enough time and effort into the dog find they have a challenging 75lb on their hands.

Behaviour is the main reason most German Shepherds end up in rescue. They may have become too vocal, anxious or aggressive, which is almost always due to lack of socialisation, training or both.

Other reasons for German Shepherds being put into rescue include:

- A change in work patterns, so the dog is left alone for long periods

- A change in family circumstance, such as divorce or a new baby

- The dog develops health issues

- Moving into smaller or rented accommodation

- She is growling or biting

- She chews things she shouldn't

- She makes a mess in the house (housetraining requires time and patience from the owner)

- The dog has way too much energy and needs a lot more exercise and attention than the owner is able or prepared to give

- She costs too much to keep

There is, however, a ray of sunshine for some of these dogs. Every year many thousands of people in the UK, North America and countries all around the world adopt a rescue dog and the story often has a happy ending.

The Dog's Point of View...

If you are serious about adopting a German Shepherd, do so with the right motives and with your eyes wide open. If you're expecting a perfect dog, you could be in for a shock. Rescue dogs can and do become wonderful companions, but a lot of it depends on you.

Many German Shepherds do not do well in noisy, busy, crowded rescue centres. If you can, look for a rescue organisation that specialises in Shepherds – and preferably one where the dog has been fostered out. The foster parents may well have started to undo some of the bad habits the dog has developed.

German Shepherds are extremely loyal to their owners. Often those that end up in rescue centres are traumatised. Some may have health problems. They don't understand why they have been abandoned, neglected or badly treated by their beloved owners and may arrive at your home with "baggage" of their own until they adjust to being part of a loving family again. This may take time. Patience is the key to help the dog to adjust to her new surroundings and family and to learn to love and trust again.

Ask yourself a few questions before you take the plunge and fill in the adoption forms:

- Are you prepared to accept and deal with any problems - such as bad behaviour, aggression, timidity, chewing, jumping up or eliminating in the house - which a rescue dog may display when initially arriving in your home?
- Just how much time do you have to spend with your new dog to help her integrate back into normal family life?
- Can you take time off work to be at home and help the dog settle in at the beginning?
- Are you prepared to take on a new addition to your family that may live for another decade?
- Will you guarantee that dog a home for life - even if she develops health issues later?

What could be worse for the unlucky dog than to be abandoned again if things don't work out between you?

Other Considerations

Adopting a rescue dog is a big commitment for all involved. It is not a cheap way of getting a German Shepherd. It could cost you several hundred dollars - or pounds.

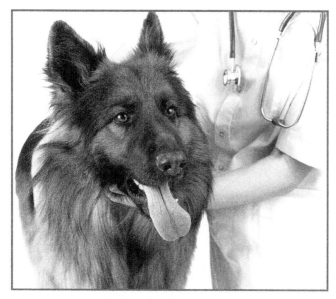

You'll have to pay adoption fees, vaccination and veterinary bills, as well as worm and flea medication and spaying or neutering. Make sure you're aware of the full cost before committing.

You may even have to wait a while until a suitable dog comes up. One way of finding out if you, your family and home are suitable is to become a foster home for one of the rescue centres. Fosters offer temporary homes until a forever home comes along. It's shorter-term, but still requires commitment and patience.

And it's not just the dogs that are screened! Rescue groups and shelters make sure that prospective adopters are suitable and they have fully considered everything before making such a big decision.

They also want to make the right match - placing a boisterous young German Shepherd with a less active couple, or an anxious dog in a noisy household – would be storing up trouble. It would be a tragedy for the dog if things did not work out.

Most rescue groups ask a raft of personal questions - some of which may seem intrusive. If you are serious about adopting a German Shepherd, you will have to answer them. Here are some on a typical adoption form:

- Name, address, age
- Details, including ages, of all people living in your home
- Type of property you live in
- Size of your garden or yard and height of the fence around it
- Extensive details of any other pets
- Your work hours and amount of time spent away from the home each day
- Whether you have any previous experience with German Shepherds
- Your reasons for wanting to adopt a German Shepherd
- Whether you have any experience dealing with canine behaviour or health issues
- Details of your vet
- If you are prepared for aggression/destructive behaviour/chewing/fear and timidity/soiling inside the house/medical issues

- Whether you are willing to housetrain and obedience train the dog
- Your views on dog training methods
- Whether you are prepared for the financial costs of dog ownership
- Where your dog will sleep at night
- Whether you are prepared to accept a German Shepherd cross
- Two personal referees

If you go out to work, it is useful to know that UK rescue organisations will not place dogs in homes where they will be left alone for more than four or five hours at a stretch.

After you've filled in the adoption form, a chat with a representative from the charity usually follows. There will also be a home inspection visit - and even your vet may be vetted! If all goes well, you will be approved to adopt and when the right match comes along, a meeting will be arranged with the dog for all family members. You then pay the adoption fee and become the proud new owner of a German Shepherd.

It might seem like a lot of red tape, but the rescue groups have to be as sure as they can that you will provide a loving, forever home for the dog. It would be terrible if things didn't work out and the dog had to be placed back in rescue again.

All rescue organisations will neuter the dog or, if he or she is too young, specify in the adoption contract that the dog must be neutered and may not be used for breeding. Some German Shepherd rescue organisations have a lifetime rescue back-up policy, which means that if things don't work out, the dog must be returned to them.

<hr />

Training A Rescue German Shepherd

Many German Shepherds are in rescue because of behavioural problems, which usually developed due to lack of attention and training from the previous owner – or rough treatment.

As one rescue group put it: "**Rescue dogs are not damaged dogs; they have just been let down by humans, so take a little while to unpack their bags and get familiar with their new owners and surroundings before they settle in.**"

According to German Shepherd Dog Rescue UK, some groups are finding German Shepherds harder to rehome, due to the *"snowflake"* mentality. They say:

"Clearly, society has changed, and this has been very noticeable this last year, not least

because of the expectations of our adopters who require dogs to be perfect from Day 1. Like people, dogs are never perfect, but we domesticate then reject them when they behave like dogs."

German Shepherd Rescue Elite agrees: "Unfortunately, nowadays, too many people look to adopt a rescue dog and expect the perfect pooch. They think because they are rescuing a dog instead of buying a puppy, they are doing their bit.

"They are, but they do not take into account how many of these dogs have been tainted by another human being and just need understanding and a helping hand to get them on the right road."

If you approach rescue with your eyes wide open, if you're prepared to be patient and devote plenty of time to your new arrival, then rescuing a German Shepherd is incredibly rewarding. You'll have a friend for life.

If you can, adopt from an organisation with experience of GSDs, they are more likely to be able to assess the dog and give you an idea of what you might be letting yourself in for. Often, lack of socialisation and training is the root cause of any issues – but how this manifests itself varies from one dog to another.

 Ask as many questions as you can about the background of the dog, her natural temperament and any issues likely to arise. You are better having an honest appraisal than simply being told that the dog is wonderful and in need of a home.

Training methods for a rescue Shepherd are similar to those for any adult Shepherd, but it may take longer as the dog first has to unlearn any bad habits and behaviour. See **Chapter 9. Training a German Shepherd** for more information.

Tips

❖ Start training the day you arrive home, not once she has settled in

❖ She needs your attention, but, importantly, she also needs her own space where she can chill out. Put her crate or bed in a quiet place; you want your dog to learn to relax. The more relaxed she is, the fewer hang-ups she will have

❖ Show her her sleeping and feeding areas, but allow her to explore these and the rest of her space in her own time

❖ If you have children (or animals), introduce them quietly and NEVER leave them unsupervised with the dog – you do not know what her triggers are

❖ Maintain a calm environment at home

❖ Never shout at the dog – even if she has made a mess in the house - it will only stress her and make things worse

❖ Some GSDs – particularly those that have been roughly treated - may be stressed by touch, so use treats for training rewards until she is more used to you

❖ Don't give treats because you feel sorry for the dog. Only give her a treat when she has carried out a command. This will help her to learn quicker and you to establish leadership

❖ Set her up to SUCCEED and build confidence – don't ask her to do things that she can't

❖ Socialisation is extremely important – introduce her to new places and situations gradually and don't overface her. You want her to grow in confidence, not be frightened by new things. Talk reassuringly throughout any new experience

❖ Mental stimulation is as important as physical exercise for German Shepherds, so have games, toys or challenges to keep your new dog's mind occupied

❖ Don't introduce her to other dogs until you are confident she will behave well – and then not while she is on a leash, when the *"fight or flight"* instinct might kick in

❖ Getting an understanding of your dog will help to train her quicker – is she by nature submissive or dominant, anxious or outgoing, fearful or bold, aggressive or timid? If she shows aggressive tendencies, such as barking, growling or even biting, she is not necessarily bold. Her aggression may be rooted in fear, anxiety or lack of confidence

 The aim of training a rescue German Shepherd is to have a relaxed dog, comfortable in her surroundings, who respects your authority and responds well to your positive training methods.

Rescue Organisations

Rescue organisations are usually run by volunteers who give up their time to help dogs in distress. They often have a network of foster homes, where a German Shepherd is placed until a permanent new home can be found.

There are also online German Shepherd forums where people sometimes post information about a dog that needs a new home. Even if you can't or don't want to offer a permanent home to a German Shepherd, there are other ways in which you can help, such as short-term fostering or helping to fundraise.

UK

Type *"Kennel Club German Shepherd Dog Breed Rescue"* into a search engine to get a list of 23 regional GSD rescue contacts. Other organisations include:

German Shepherd Rescue Elite http://gsrelite.co.uk

German Shepherd Dog Rescue www.germanshepherdrescue.co.uk

UK German Shepherd Rescue www.ukgermanshepherdrescue.co.uk and if you are interested in volunteering, there is more information at: https://reachvolunteering.org.uk/org/uk-german-shepherd-rescue-uk-gsr

German Shepherd Dog Welfare Fund (German Shepherd Rescue) www.gsdwelfarefund.co.uk

German Shepherd Dog Rescue Luosko www.luosko.com

Central German Shepherd Dog Rescue www.cgsr.co.uk, - Lincolnshire, Nottinghamshire, Northamptonshire, Cambridgeshire and Bedfordshire.

GSD 2000 www.gsd2000.com - the South West, Southern Counties, Midlands and South Wales.

German Shepherd Dog Rescue South www.german-shepherd-rescue-hampshire.org.uk

Southern Counties German Shepherd Dog Rescue https://southerncountiesgsdrescue.co.uk

South West GSD Rescue www.southwestgsdrescue.org.uk

German Shepherd Dog Rescue Surrey www.germanshepherdrescuesurrey.com

German Shepherd Rescue West Essex www.germanshepherdwestessex.co.uk

Lancashire German Shepherd Rescue www.lancsgsdrescue.co.uk

German Shepherd Dog Rescue Scotland www.german-shepherd-rescue-scotland.org.uk

Second Chances German Shepherd Rescue https://second-chances.com - Scotland

There's more GSD rescue groups at Animal Rescuers: www.animalrescuers.co.uk/html/gsd.html

USA

The American German Shepherd Rescue Organisation (AGSRA) has a state-by-state list of 73 affiliated GSD rescue organisations at: www.agsra.org/affiliated-rescues

The AKC has a list of 40 German Shepherd rescue organisations and contacts at: www.akc.org/akc-rescue-network then scroll down to German Shepherd Dog.

This is by no means an exhaustive list, there are numerous other GSD rescue groups. You can also type your county or state into an online search engine, followed by *"German Shepherd Rescue."*

If you visit these websites, you cannot presume that all descriptions are 100% accurate. They are given in good faith, but ideas of what constitutes a "lively" or "challenging" dog may vary.

Some dogs advertised may have other breeds in their genetic make-up. It does not mean that these are necessarily worse dogs, but if you are attracted to the German Shepherd for its temperament, intelligence, looks and other assets, make sure you are looking at a German Shepherd.

DON'T get a dog from eBay, Craig's List, Gumtree or any of the other general advertising websites that sell golf clubs, jewellery, old cars, washing machines, etc. You might think you are getting a bargain German Shepherd, but in the long run you will pay the price. If the dog had been well bred and properly cared for, he or she would not be advertised on such websites - or sold in pet shops.

Good breeders do not let their dogs end up in these places. You may be storing up a whole load of trouble for yourselves in terms of health or temperament issues, due to poor breeding and environment.

If you haven't been put off with all of the above... Congratulations, you may be just the family or person that poor homeless German Shepherd is looking for!

If you can't spare the time to adopt - and adoption means forever - you might consider fostering. Or you could help by becoming a home inspector or fundraiser to help keep these very worthy rescue groups providing such a wonderful service.

How ever you decide to get involved, Good Luck!

**Saving one dog will not change the world,
But it will change the world for one dog**

17. Caring for Older Shepherds

If your German Shepherd has been well looked after and had no serious illnesses, she could be expected to live nine to 13 years. UK breeders Larry and Diane Holmes even had a German Shepherd that lived to the ripe old age of 17 years and four months.

Lifespan is influenced by genetics and also by owners; how you feed, exercise and generally look after your dog will all have an impact on her life. German Shepherds can remain fit and active well into old age. But eventually all dogs – even German Shepherds – slow down.

Approaching Old Age

How ever fit your ageing German Shepherd is, at some point, she will start to feel the effects of ageing. After having got up at the crack of dawn as a puppy, you may find that she now likes to have a lie-in in the morning. She may be less keen to go out in the rain and snow.

Physically, joints may become stiffer, and organs, such as heart or liver, may not function quite as effectively. On the mental side - just as with humans - your dog's memory, ability to learn and awareness will all start to dim.

Your faithful companion might become a bit grumpier, stubborn or a little less tolerant of lively dogs and children. You may also notice that she doesn't see or hear as well as she used to. On the other hand, your old friend might not be hard of hearing at all. She might have developed that affliction common to many older dogs of *"selective hearing."*

Our 12-year-old Max had bionic hearing when it came to the word *"Dinnertime"* whispered from 20 paces, yet seemed strangely unable to hear the commands *"Come"* or *"Down"* when we were right in front of him!

Pictured is great-grandmother Missi, left, aged 11, and daughter Boots, aged eight, courtesy of Teresa Mapp.

You can help ease your mature dog into old age gracefully by keeping an eye on her, noticing the changes and taking action to help her as much as possible. This might involve:

❖ A visit to the vet for supplements and/or medications

❖ Modifying your dog's environment

❖ Slowly reducing the amount of daily exercise

❖ A change of diet

Much depends on the individual dog. Just as with humans, a dog of ideal weight that has been active and stimulated all of her life is likely to age slower than an overweight couch potato. Keeping dogs at an optimum weight as they age is important. Their metabolisms slow down, making it easier to put on the pounds unless the daily calories are reduced. Extra weight places additional, unwanted stress on joints and organs, making them have to work harder than they should.

FACT ❯ We normally talk about dogs being old when they reach the last third of their lives. This varies greatly from dog to dog and bloodline to bloodline. A dog is classed as a "Veteran" at seven years old in the show ring. Some German Shepherds may remain active with little sign of ageing until the day they die, others may start to show signs of ageing at seven or eight years old.

Physical and Mental Signs of Ageing

If your German Shepherd is in or approaching the last third of her life, here are some signs that her body is feeling its age – an old dog may have a few or more of these symptoms:

❧ She has generally slowed down and is no longer as keen to go out on her walks, or doesn't want to go as far. She is happy pottering and sniffing - and often takes forever to inspect a single clump of grass! Some are less keen to go outside in bad weather

❧ She gets up from lying down and goes up and down stairs more slowly. She can no longer jump on to the couch or bed; all signs that joints are stiffening, often due to arthritis

❧ Grey hairs are appearing, particularly around the muzzle

❧ She has put on a bit of weight

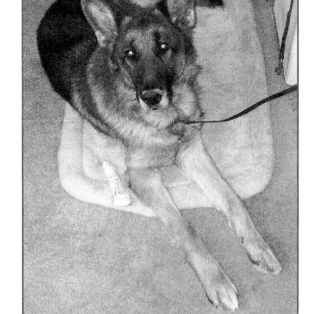

Photo of Whopper, aged 10, looking nice and trim, courtesy of Bobbi King.

❧ She may have the occasional *"accident"* (incontinence) inside the house

❧ She urinates more frequently

❧ She drinks more water

❧ She has bouts of constipation or diarrhoea

❧ She sheds more hair

❧ The foot pads thicken and nails may become more brittle

❧ One or more lumps or fatty deposits (lipomas) develop on the body. Our old dog developed two small bumps on top of his head aged 10 and we took him straight to the vet, who performed minor surgery to remove them. They were benign (harmless), but always get the first one(s) checked out ASAP in case they are an early form of cancer - they can also grow quite rapidly, even if benign

❧ She can't regulate body temperature as she used to and so feels the cold and heat more

❧ Hearing deteriorates

❧ Eyesight may also deteriorate – if her eyes appear cloudy she may be developing cataracts, so see your vet if you notice the signs. Most older dogs live quite well with failing eyesight, particularly as German Shepherds have an extremely well-developed sense of smell

- ❋ Your dog has bad breath (halitosis), which could be a sign of dental or gum disease. If the bad breath persists, get her checked out by a vet

- ❋ If inactive, she may develop callouses on the elbows, especially if she lies on hard surfaces

- ❋ It's not just your dog's body that deteriorates; her mind may too. Your dog may display some, all or none of these signs of *Canine Cognitive Dysfunction:*

- ❋ Sleep patterns change; an older dog may be more restless at night and sleepy during the day. She may start wandering around the house at odd times, causing you sleepless nights

- ❋ She barks more, sometimes at nothing or open spaces

- ❋ She stares at objects, such as walls, hides in a corner, or wanders aimlessly around the house or garden

- ❋ Your dog shows increased anxiety, separation anxiety or aggression

- ❋ She forgets or ignores commands or habits she once knew well, such as the Recall and sometimes toilet training

- ❋ Some dogs may become clingier and more dependent, often resulting in separation anxiety. She may seek reassurance that you are near as faculties fade and she becomes a bit less confident and independent. Others may become a bit disengaged and less interested in human contact

Understanding the changes happening to your dog and acting on them compassionately and effectively will help ease your dog's passage through her senior years. Your dog has given you so much pleasure over the years, now she needs you to give that bit of extra care for a happy, healthy old age. You can help your German Shepherd to stay mentally active by playing gentle games and getting new toys to stimulate interest.

Helping Your Dog Age Gracefully

There are many things you can do to ease your dog's passage into her declining years.

As dogs age they need fewer calories and less protein, so many owners feeding kibble switch to one specially formulated for older dogs. These are labelled *Senior, Ageing* or *Mature.* Check the labelling; some are specifically for dogs aged over eight, others may be for 10 or 12-year-olds.

If you are not sure if a senior diet is necessary for your German Shepherd, talk to your vet on your next visit. Remember, if you do change brand, switch the food gradually over a week or so. Unlike with humans, a dog's digestive system cannot cope with sudden changes of diet.

Years of eating the same food, coupled with less sensitive taste buds can result in some dogs going off their food as they age. If you feed a dry food, try mixing a bit of gravy with it; this works well for us, as has feeding two different feeds: a morning one of kibble with gravy and the second tea-time feed of home-cooked rice and fish or chicken. Rice, white fish and chicken – all cooked – can be particularly good if your old dog has a sensitive stomach.

If you are considering a daily supplement, Omega-3 fatty acids are good for the brain and coat, and glucosamine and various other supplements are available to help joints. We give a squirt of Yumega Omega 3 and half a scoop of Joint Aid in one of the daily feeds.

We had one dog that became very sensitive to loud noises as he got older and the lead up to Bonfire Night was a nightmare. (November 5th in the UK, when the skies are filled with fireworks and loud bangs). Some dogs may also become more stressed by grooming or trips to the vet as they get older.

 There are medications and homeopathic remedies, such as melatonin that has natural sedative properties, to help relieve such anxieties. Check with your vet before introducing any new medicines.

One of the most important things throughout your German Shepherd's life is dental care - either by regular tooth brushing or feeding bones, bully sticks or antlers, etc. to gnaw on. Not only is toothache painful and unpleasant, it can be traumatic for dogs to have teeth removed under anaesthetic after they lose weight due to being unable to eat properly.

If your old friend has started to ignore your verbal commands when out on a walk – either through *"switching off"* or deafness - try a whistle to attract her attention and then use an exaggerated hand signal for the Recall. Once your dog is looking at you, hold your arm out, palm down, at 90 degrees to your body and bring it down, keeping your arm straight, until your fingers point to your toes.

Hand signals worked very effectively with our Max. He looked, understood ......and then decided if he was going to come or not - but at least he knew what he should be doing! More often than not he did come back, especially if the visual signal was repeated while he was still making up his mind.

Weight - no matter how old your German Shepherd is, she still needs a waist! Maintaining a healthy weight with a balanced diet and regular, gentler exercise are two of the most important things you can do for your dog.

Environment - Make sure your dog has a nice soft place to rest her old bones, which may mean adding an extra blanket to her bed. This should be in a place that is not too hot or cold, as she may not be able to regulate her body temperature as well as when she was younger.

She also needs plenty of undisturbed sleep and should not be pestered and/or bullied by younger dogs, other animals or young children. If her eyesight is failing, move obstacles out of her way or use pet barriers to reduce the chance of injuries.

Jumping on and off furniture or in or out of the car is high impact for old joints and bones. She will need a helping hand on and off the couch or your bed - if she's allowed up there - or even a little ramp to get in and out of the car.

We bought an expensive plastic ramp for one old dog as she became hesitant to jump in or out of the car. However, this proved to be a complete waste of money as dogs are tactile and she didn't like the feel of the non-slip surface on her paws. After a couple of tentative attempts, she steadfastly refused to set a paw on it. We ended up helping the dog in and out of the car and donating the ramp to a canine charity!

Exercise - Take the lead from your dog, if she doesn't want to walk as far, then don't. But if your dog doesn't want to go out at all, you will have to coax her out. ALL old dogs need exercise, not only to keep their joints moving, but also to keep their heart, lungs and joints exercised, and their minds engaged with different places, scents, etc.

Ears – Sometimes older dogs – particularly long-coated ones - produce more ear wax, so check inside the ears regularly. If necessary, use clean damp cotton wool to clean out the inner ear and pluck extra ear hair if it's getting waxy.

Time to Get Checked Out

If your dog is showing any of these signs, get her checked out by a vet:

- Excessive increased urination or drinking, which can be a sign of reduced liver or kidney function, Cushing's disease or diabetes

- Constipation or not urinating regularly, a possible symptom of a digestive system or organ disorder

- Incontinence, which could be a sign of a mental or physical problem

- Cloudy eyes, possibly cataracts

- Decreased appetite – often one of the first signs of an underlying problem

- Lumps or bumps on the body - often benign, but can occasionally be malignant (cancerous)

- Excessive sleeping or a lack of interest in you and her surroundings

- Diarrhoea or vomiting

- A darkening and dryness of skin that never seems to get any better, which can be a sign of hypothyroidism

- Any other out-of-the-ordinary behaviour for your dog. A change in patterns or behaviour is often your dog's way of telling you that all is not well

What the Experts Say

Worcestershire breeder Teresa Mapp says: "A German Shepherd becomes a senior at about eight to nine years - although we have a nine-year-old who seems younger than her five-year-old daughters! They still need the love and attention they had when they were full of beans, but they also sleep more, so need some quiet time. Diet depends on the dog, we usually change it at about

10 years old, as ours have had good activity. We add glucosamine, evening primrose oil and green-lipped mussels, which all help joints and activity. EPO (Erythropoietin) is great for skin and coat.

"We have noticed the coat does seem to get thicker and requires more grooming, but we have to be careful as they are more sensitive to being pulled around. Missi, *pictured,* winces a lot more than she used to, but we figure she has earned the right to be a little scruffy!

"There aren't really any health issues particular to older German Shepherds if they are well-bred and cared for. Larger dogs generally have stiff joints as they carry more weight. We have a 13-year-old who still loves her walks and gets up and down stairs at bedtime.

"Of course, they slow down (as do we all). From about nine or 10, they do require less exercise and will let you know when they have had enough, Missi, our great-grandma, just wanders up to the field then lays down watching the others!"

Cheryl Spurr, of Reinglen German Shepherds, West Yorkshire, says: "When I fed kibble, I would change to a senior food at around seven years old, but that would also depend on how active the dog was. I feed raw now.

"Lexi, aged nine, is my oldest dog at the moment, and I have reduced the amount of food and the amount of bone in her food. Next is Kassi at eight years. I haven't changed anything with her food as she is still very active; whereas Lexi has always been very laid back. So, the food stays the same, but amounts change as and when necessary.

"I have found with both the girls that their coat has become drier, but I don't know if that is because they are spayed. I give wheatgerm oil and salmon oil on their food and I find this helps. They are also both shedding their coats more often than they ever used to, pretty much all year round.

"I haven't found any particular ageing issues different to any other breed, I just keep them lean and as active as they are comfortable with. Lexi walks slower now, but still has the same length of walk as the others. I have seen no behavioural changes in the older girls, just slowing down a little. My advice would be to keep them lean and active as long as they are fit and for as long as possible."

Stef Millington, of CunAnnun German Shepherds, Norfolk, adds: "As a raw feeder I do not change a great deal in the diet, apart from adjusting quantities a bit as they become less active. I also give green-lipped mussel supplement, salmon oil and Lintbells Yumove joint supplement.

"As in a lot of older dogs, joint problems start - arthritis etc. - especially in large breeds, hence the supplements. As a raw and bone feeder, we luckily do not have any of the dental problems you often get in ageing dogs.

"My older girls do not have any behavioural changes apart from naturally calming down and mellowing out. Obviously exercise will slow down, but our oldies usually get taken for swims about three times a week during spring, summer and autumn, which is brilliant for muscle- strengthening and suppleness. My advice is not to push your oldies, i.e. over-exercise. Try swimming and give joint supplements."

Larry Yates, of Lornstone German Shepherds, Somerset, has this to say: "I have judged innumerable Veteran classes at shows, and personally, I would prefer to have a parade of Veterans to a class... As far as I'm concerned, at seven years of age, a Shepherd ceases to have any faults!

"Any dog who advances in years should be given the respect they deserve. Each and every one is different. And the dog himself will show his owners. All our dogs remain on the same diet throughout their lives - we also feed oily fish from puppyhood, right the way through to old age."

Pictured, aged two, is Lornstone Veremund, son of the V.A. male Watson vom Thermodos. Veremund's mother was 15 generations of Lornstone breeding.

"Our pensioners, can do whatever they want, amble around the gardens, or sleep whenever they want. We always kennel them with a young puppy overnight and find this is invaluable in giving the youngster some knowledge."

The Last Lap

Huge advances in veterinary science have meant that there are countless procedures and medications that can prolong the life of your dog, and this is a good thing. But there comes a time when you do have to let go.

If your dog is showing all the signs of ageing, has an ongoing medical condition from which she cannot recover, is showing signs of pain, anxiety or distress and there is no hope of improvement, then the dreaded time has come to say goodbye. You owe it to her. There is no point keeping an old dog alive if all the dog has ahead is pain and death. We have their lives in our hands and we can give them the gift of passing away peacefully and humanely at the end when the time is right.

Losing our beloved companion, our best friend, a member of the family, is truly heart-breaking. But one of the things we realise at the back of our minds when we got that gorgeous, lively little puppy that bounded up to meet us like we were the best person in the whole wide world is the pain that comes with it. We know we will live longer than them and that we'll probably have to make this most painful of decisions at some time in the future.

It's the worst thing about being a dog owner.

If your Shepherd has had a long and happy life, then you could not have done any more. You were a great owner and your dog was lucky to have you. Remember all the good times you had together. And try not to rush out and buy another dog straight away; wait a while.

Assess your current life and lifestyle and, if your situation is right, only then consider getting another dog and all that that entails in terms of time, commitment and expense. A dog coming into a happy, stable household will get off to a better start in life than a dog entering a home full of grief.

Whatever you decide to do, put the dog first.

List of Contributors

(in alphabetical order)

Bobbi King, RVT, Redwood Runs Pet Resort, Northern California, USA

Carolyn Day, Carjaylyn German Shepherds, Kent, England

Cheryl Spurr, Reinglen German Shepherds, West Yorkshire, England
www.reinglen.co.uk

Donna Bonney, Hirten Bray Hugel, New York State, USA
www.hirtenbrayhugel.com

Jacqueline Levy, Cross Keys K9 Inc, New Jersey, USA
www.crosskeysk9.com

Larry and Diane Yates, Lornstone German Shepherds, Somerset, England
www.facebook.com/Lornstone-GSDs-710298605745791

Marie Donahue, Rodina Straze German Shepherds, Maryland, USA
https://rodinastraze.com

Stefanie Millington, CunAnnun German Shepherds, Norfolk, England

Tammey Tilton, Tiltonhaus German Shepherds, Deer Park, Washington, USA
www.tiltonhaus.com

Teresa and Tony Mapp, hobby breeders, Worcestershire, England
In memory of Karma "Freya Babylon"

Wendy Sharp, Sharphouse's German Shepherds, Kent, England

and

Dr Sara Skiwski, Western Dragon holistic veterinary practice, San Jose, California, USA
www.thewesterndragon.com

Useful Contacts

German Shepherd Dog Club of America www.gsdca.org

AKC (American Kennel Club) www.akc.org/dog-breeds/german-shepherd-dog

Kennel Club (UK) German Shepherd Assured Breeders
www.thekennelclub.org.uk/services/public/acbr/Default.aspx?breed=German+Shepherd+Dog

Verein für Deutsche Schäferhunde (SV) e.V. www.schaeferhunde.de/en/the-german-shepherd

UK GSD clubs www.thekennelclub.org.uk/services/public/findaclub/breed/list.aspx?id=5106

WUSV has a list of German Shepherd clubs around the world: www.wusv.org/en/countries

German Shepherd lineage at www.pedigreedatabase.com

RSPCA Puppy Contract https://puppycontract.rspca.org.uk/home

AKC Preparing a Puppy Contract www.akc.org/expert-advice/dog-breeding/preparing-a-contract-for-puppy-buyers

AKC Canine Good Citizen www.akc.org/products-services/training-programs/canine-good-citizen

KC Good Citizen Scheme www.thekennelclub.org.uk/training/good-citizen-dog-training-scheme

Association of Pet Dog Trainers UK www.apdt.co.uk

Association of Pet Dog Trainers US www.apdt.com

Canadian Association of Professional Pet Dog Trainers www.cappdt.ca

Useful info on dog foods (US) www.dogfoodadvisor.com (UK) www.allaboutdogfood.co.uk

Helps find lost or stolen dogs in the US, register your dog's microchip www.akcreunite.org

German Shepherd internet forums and Facebook groups are also a good source of information from other owners, including:

German Shepherds Forum www.germanshepherds.com/forums

UK German Shepherd Forum https://gsduk.boards.net

German Shepherd Dog Forum www.forum.breedia.com/dogs/german-shepherd-dog

German Shepherd Home https://germanshepherdhome.net/forum

Pet Forums www.petforums.co.uk/threads/german-shepherd-owners.427207

German Shepherd Owners Club UK www.facebook.com/gsocuk

German Shepherd Owners USA www.facebook.com/groups/1713923952216389

The German Shepherd Dog Community www.facebook.com/TheGSDC

I Love My German Shepherd www.facebook.com/iHeartMyGSD

Disclaimer

This book has been written to provide helpful information on German Shepherds. It is not meant to be used, nor should it be used, to diagnose or treat any medical condition. For diagnosis or treatment of any animal medical problem, consult a qualified veterinarian.

The author is not responsible for any specific health or allergy conditions that may require medical supervision and is not liable for any damages or negative consequences from any treatment, action, application or preparation, to any animal or to any person reading or following the information in this book.

The views expressed by contributors to this book are solely personal and do not necessarily represent those of the author. References are provided for informational purposes only and do not constitute endorsement of any websites or other sources.

Pet Care Tracker

Vet's Name: _ _ _ _ _ _ _ _ _ _ _ _   Groomer's Name: _ _ _ _ _ _ _ _ _ _ _ _

Vet's Phone: _ _ _ _ _ _ _ _ _ _ _   Groomer's Phone: _ _ _ _ _ _ _ _ _ _ _ _

Day Care: _ _ _ _ _ _ _ _ _ _ _ _   Holiday Sitter: _ _ _ _ _ _ _ _ _ _ _ _

Pet's Name	Date	Vet Visit	Groomer	NOTES

Printed in Great Britain
by Amazon